guiding
LIGHTS

Triton Light (Randell Hunt "Doc" Prothro and Gustav F. "Gus" Swainson Jr.)

guiding LIGHTS

United States Naval Academy
Monuments and Memorials

Nancy Prothro Arbuthnot

With historical photographs and site photographs
by Gus Swainson Jr., USNA 1945,
Randell Hunt Prothro, USNA 1945,
and others

This book was made possible through the dedication of the
U.S. Naval Academy Class of 1945 and other generous supporters.

Naval Institute Press
291 Wood Road
Annapolis, MD 21402

Library of Congress Cataloging-in-Publication Data
Arbuthnot, Nancy Prothro.
Guiding lights : United States Naval Academy monuments and memorials /
Nancy Prothro Arbuthnot.
p. cm.
Includes bibliographical references and index.
ISBN 978-1-59114-016-0 (alk. paper)
1. United States Naval Academy—History. 2. United States Naval
Academy—Buildings. 3. United States Naval Academy—Guidebooks.
4. Monuments—Maryland—Annapolis. 5. Memorials—Maryland—
Annapolis. 6. Historic buildings—Maryland—Annapolis. 7. Annapolis
(Md—Buildings, structures, etc. I. Title.
V415.L1A736 2009
359.1'60975256—dc22
2009006325
Printed in the United States of America on acid-free paper

14 13 12 11 10 09   9 8 7 6 5 4 3 2
First printing

To my students, midshipmen at the
U.S. Naval Academy, 1981–2008,
and to my father and his classmates,
Class of 1945.

⟜ঌৎ⟝

The spirit of every great hero of the American Navy from Jones on down to Farragut and Dewey is ground into the soul of the midshipmen at the Academy. This spirit, handed down from class to class, is ever-present in the Fleet today. . . . This tradition [of "perseverance unto victory"], handed down by the naval great of each generation from the incipience of our Navy to the present day, is the trust of the Naval Academy—the trust that makes this institution . . . the guardian of a free and liberty-blessed America.

Lucky Bag, Class of 1945

[Memorials] serve to keep alive the flame of patriotism, and, by honoring the courage of the dead, remind the living that they also will be remembered should their character and services entitle them to the applause of their countrymen.

Adm. David Dixon Porter

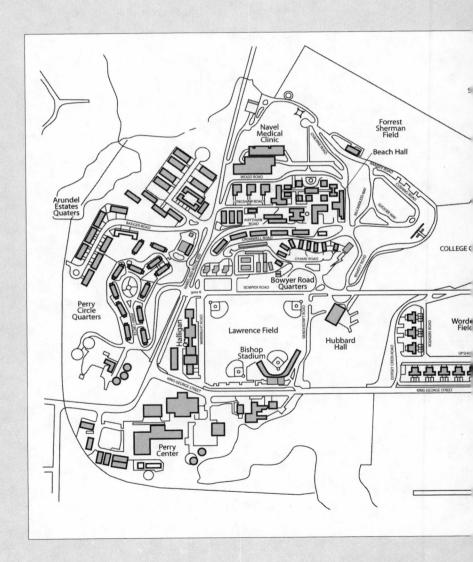

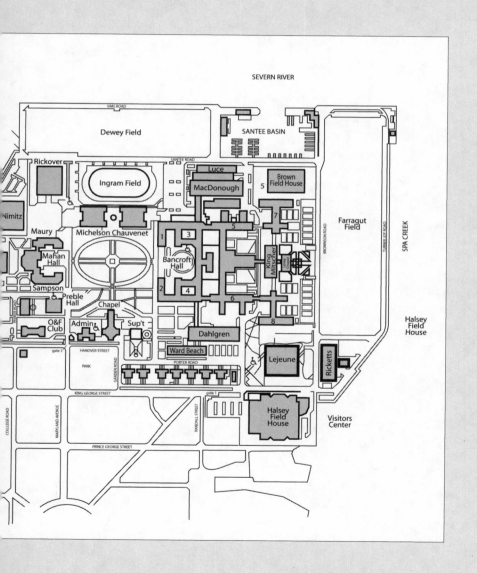

contents

LAWRENCE

Vice Admiral
William Porter Lawrence, USN
"Be first a person of honor"

Test Pilot - First to Fly Mach 2 in Naval Aircraft
Korea: F-14 Pioneer
Vietnam: 208 Missions
Prisoner of War: Vietnam 1967-1973
Superintendent, United States Naval Academy
Commander, U.S. Third Fleet

foreword

As a member of the Naval Academy Class of 1945, I am extremely pleased with this new book published by the Naval Institute Press. Written by USNA English professor Nancy Arbuthnot, *Guiding Lights: United States Naval Academy Monuments and Memorials* presents a fascinating new perspective on many heroic deeds that have helped define our Navy. Reading the stories behind the buildings and monuments memorializing these deeds will offer every man and woman of the Navy outstanding and inspiring examples of leadership, courage, and dedication to country.

The poems and prose reflections by the author and midshipmen on these monuments adds a new dimension to the gallant but often forgotten events in the history of our Navy. The importance of this unique and inspirational approach to the development of future U.S. Navy officers is immeasurable.

The value of *Guiding Lights* will also reach far beyond the Navy to all U.S. citizens and many foreign nationals, who will be motivated to learn more about the incredible history of this great country bathed in the glory and accomplishments of some extraordinary and freedom-loving citizens who lived and died above and beyond the call of duty.

BRIG. GEN. WILLIAM McCULLOCH, USMC (RET.)
USNA 1945

preface

E very step that a midshipman takes around the Yard is a step through history, preserved in part by the naming of each walk, each building, and each monument for a significant figure or event in naval history. *Guiding Lights: United States Naval Academy Monuments and Memorials* is a book that offers stories about some of the people and events memorialized at the Naval Academy as "guiding lights" to inspire new midshipmen as they navigate their ways through the Academy, the Navy, and indeed their whole lives. As a professor of English at the Academy for the past twenty-five years—and before that, as the daughter of an Academy alumnus, then as a high school student attending "tea dances" in Dahlgren Hall—I have grown familiar with these monuments and the stories behind them. Together they compose a history of the Navy, the Naval Academy, and our nation, from our earliest struggles for independence through expansion and the Civil War to the world wars of the first half of the twentieth century and the Cold War and regional wars of more recent times. Throughout these conflicts, naval leaders have offered examples of courage, determination, strength of mind, and concern for the men and women serving beneath them.

Guiding Lights presents a selection of sixty-some memorials—monuments, buildings, athletic fields, and the cemetery, roads, and walks—that figure daily in the midshipmen's routines. For each entry, I have tried to include several items: a photograph of the memorial itself and another of the figure or event memorialized; a brief biographical and historical sketch, including burial site information; historical documents such as *Lucky Bag* entries, ship and ice journals, letters and diary entries, telegrams and official battle reports; and poems and short personal reflections by midshipmen. I have also included my own poems, which are not individually attributed.

In considerations of space, but mostly of the tide that waits for no one, I have left out of the book many memorials honoring important figures. I have included others partly for personal reasons: I often free my mind from teaching and reading and grading plebe papers by looking across the water from a bench in the Class of 1942 Memorial Park or Compass Rose Plaza, or by walking out to Triton Light, on the Yard's northeast corner, where the Severn River joins Spa Creek and the Chesapeake Bay, a navigation light donated by the Class of 1945, my father's class, to which I have felt a lifelong connection. The Naval Academy Museum maintains a list of every identified naval memorial at the Academy and in the surrounding area of Annapolis; I regret that space considerations prevent me from including it here. Blank pages at the end of the book provide opportunities for readers to make notes on other monuments.

Throughout my research for *Guiding Lights*, I have been impressed by the character of leadership I have found in the officers of the U.S. Navy: the dedication to subordinates in leaders such as Adm. Chester W. Nimitz, who noted that "uncommon valor" was a "common virtue" among the men battling for Iwo Jima; the spirit of leaders such as Lt. George De Long, captain of the ill-fated *Jeannette*, trapped for almost two years in the ice of the North Pole, who fought through his own despair to buoy his men's morale through a regular routine of work and exercise and special activities such as hunting and astronomy classes; the selfless determination of his fellow officer, Lt. George Melville, who after his hard-fought return to civilization, turned back around to fight blinding snowstorms, frostbitten feet, and near-starvation to rescue others; and the courage of men such as Adm. William D. Leahy, who stood up for ethical consideration in war by stating that "in being the first to use [the atomic bomb] we had adopted an ethical standard common to the barbarians of the Dark Ages," concluding that "I was not taught to make war in that fashion." Not a warrior myself, but as a teacher of literature whose mission it is to encourage students who are training for war to think deeply about the values of honesty, courage, and commitment, I find myself cheering the fighting spirit of Adm. William F. Halsey Jr., who, when told about the intercepted broadcast from Japan

asking "Where is the American Fleet?" responded, "Send them our latitude and longitude." On a personal note, in part because I had known the
Stockdales in my early years as a "Navy brat," when we lived next door to
each other in Pensacola, Adm. James B. Stockdale has been an enduring
symbol for me of courage and patriotism.

I hope that the brief glimpses provided by *Guiding Lights* into the
lives and actions of the great naval leaders of our past will inspire future
generations of naval leaders. I regret that I was not able to include mention of memorials to female officers or more officers of color—but I hope
that as the Navy recognizes the contributions of these groups, the Academy will also recognize their contributions with appropriate memorials. I
hope, too, that the leadership of the Academy's young graduates will be
tested more often in peace than in war; as Admiral Halsey noted, during
times of peace when subordinates must be encouraged "to pick up the
paintbrush," leaders have an almost harder task of inspiring their people
than in times of war. But no matter the circumstances, the question that
Adm. Hyman G. Rickover demanded that his subordinates ask—"Did I
do my best?"—we must all ask, constantly, consistently, to live our lives
to the fullest. And as Adm. Ernest J. King reminds us, we must learn in
every situation of our lives to "do all that [we] can with what [we] have."

acknowledgments

First, most importantly, I want to thank my students, midshipmen at the Naval Academy, who are the main impetus behind this book and the purpose for it. Throughout my career at the Academy these midshipmen, at the beginning of their own careers, have challenged me to be prepared and inspiring in my teaching. I would like to thank them for enduring with such good nature the challenges that in turn I put to them, to test their own ideals through discussions of meaning in literature and to deepen their awareness of the world around them—including their immediate world of Bancroft Hall and redbrick paths, Tecumseh and the Mexican War Monument. I would like to thank each and every one for the ways that they—honors students as well as those who would rather play lacrosse or baseball or football than write an essay or a poem—contributed to class, in discussion and in writing. Their writings here display both a somber dedication to the ideals of their country and the infectious rebelliousness of youth. For anonymous authors (those whose authorship I could not verify or from whom I was unable to obtain permission), I apologize for not being able to use real names. (I would also like to apologize to my students for not completing other projects I lured some of them into writing for, such as the encyclopedia of personal responses to Academy life. Perhaps some day someone else will put together a "USNA Encyclopedia," or alphabetical collection of stories on such things as chow calls and going over the wall and the Ho Chi Minh Trail and zoomies.) I thank all these students for their enthusiasm to appear in print. Receiving their permission to publish from across the country and the world—from Virginia, California, the Pacific, Iraq—was a special reminder of how much we all have to thank them for as they put themselves in harm's way in service to our country. I want to thank their families, too, who often helped me locate their sons and daughters and who gave these sons and daughters to their country's service.

Second, I want to say how grateful I am to my father and his classmates, the Naval Academy Class of 1945. From my earliest years, my father and his classmates have challenged me to challenge them as I sought to develop my own ideals and inspired me always to "look alive!" (their class motto). For the past two years, they have been crucial in helping me develop *Guiding Lights* into the work that it is today. They not only provided the book's title and the photographs of most of the buildings, but they also offered invaluable editorial and design suggestions; more important, they gave me unstinting encouragement. Without them, I could never have persevered and completed this book.

I would also like to thank the Naval Academy Research Council for a sabbatical during which I conducted research and composed most of my poems for *Guiding Lights*. I owe the staff of the Archives and Special Collections Division of Nimitz Library, especially the director, Jennifer Bryant, and the late Gary LaValley, archivist, my gratitude for their assistance in locating information from their files on the Academy monuments and memorials. Likewise, the staff of the Multimedia Support Center, particularly Cindi Gallagher, the director of the Graphics Lab, deserves my thanks for their always-cheerful assistance with photograph scanning and image development. I owe a special thanks to Jim Cheevers, chief curator at the Naval Academy Museum, who began years ago to introduce my students, and me as well, to the memorial treasures at the Academy. His encyclopedic knowledge and absolute attention to detail have been invaluable to me in polishing my manuscript. I am also grateful for the support of Dean William Miller, Dean Michael Halbig, and my colleagues in the English Department, as well as supporters in the History Department. Finally, I want to thank my family—my husband and children, my parents and siblings, my in-laws—for their support and enthusiasm for this project through the years.

Where I Come From

It's a foreign language but in English.
Unless you are from here you will be lost in translation.
We use words like "chow call," "plebe," and "bilge"
And abbreviations all the time:

"That's UNSAT!"
"Why is there an IP on your uniform?"
"Run in PE gear for the PRT."

LIBERTY never had more meaning.
HERNDON never seemed so sweet.
You ask questions like, "Why did GARCIA have to deliver
    that message?"
"If I pass out during a parade will I really get to meet the
    SILVER BULLET?"
Some YOUNGSTERS really are young, while others are SALTY.
Sleeping in is 0730, and an early night is 2400.
This is the language I speak.
This is where I come from.

Nicholas D. Schwob, USNA 2008

Formation over the Naval Academy, 1938 (U.S. Naval Institute Photo Archive)

The Yard

A Brief Architectural History

Those Quiet Nooks

Gone are dear old skinny steps
And gone the lib'ry arch;
Yes gone is every dear old nook—
Killed by progression's march.

Now, if a fellow wants to go
And sit with some fair maid,
There's not a single seat
That's even in the shade. . . .

Oh, no! the Navy modernized,
Destroying tradition old,
And thinks no more of dear romance
Than of the rovers bold.

And so goodbye to all the spots
So dear to every heart;
Like wooden ships, their day is gone
And sadly must depart;

For in their place new buildings stand,
All stiff and new and white
With not a single quiet nook
That's not out in plain sight.

Lucky Bag, 1908

These verses from the midshipmen yearbook lament the loss of the buildings that composed the Naval Academy at the end of the nineteenth century. Although the Academy has changed greatly over the years since the construction of the "New Naval Academy," built between 1899 (the laying of the cornerstone of the new Armory—later Dahlgren Hall) and 1908 (the dedication of the new Chapel), the heart of the Yard retains the grand Beaux-Arts design of architect Ernest Flagg. Now, as the New Academy nears completion of the first decade of its second hundred years and a new era of growth, it is appropriate to review the Yard's architectural history.

Beginnings of a Naval School, 1800–45

The Naval School, as it was first known, came into existence in 1845. The U.S. Navy was established in 1775 (later disestablished in 1783–84, but then reestablished in 1794), but no formal institution for the training of naval officers was provided for during those periods of the active Navy. As early as 1800, however, President John Adams had suggested to Congress that such a school be started. Decades of attempts followed, including the informal shipboard training offered aboard ships such as the frigate Guerriere in 1821 in New York and the frigate Java in Norfolk, Virginia, in 1822; a training program at the Boston Navy Yard in 1833; and an educational program for midshipmen at the Philadelphia Naval Asylum in 1839. The first successful introduction of steamships into the Navy in 1837 (USS Fulton II, Capt. Matthew C. Perry, commanding) led to increased concern for appropriate training to run the new technology. The Somers incident of 1842—during which three men aboard USS Somers, including Midn. Philip Spencer, son of Secretary of War John Spencer, were hanged for mutiny—renewed interest in the method of appointment of midshipmen and army cadets. In 1844 William Chauvenet, a young professor of mathematics at the Naval Asylum in Philadelphia and before that a shipboard instructor, developed a comprehensive two-year curriculum for naval officer training. A year and a half later, on August 7, 1845, George Bancroft, Secretary of the Navy under President Polk, proposed a plan "to collect the midshipmen who from time to time are on shore, and give them instruction . . . in

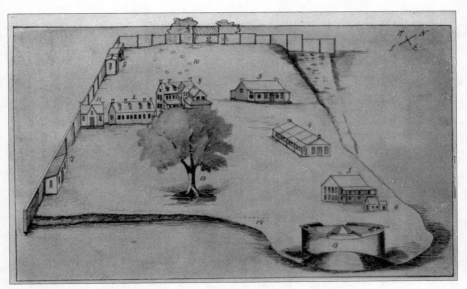

Fort Severn in 1845, from an old map (U.S. Naval Institute Photo Archive)

the study of mathematics, nautical astronomy, theory of morals, international law, gunnery, use of steam, the Spanish and French languages, and other branches essential . . . to the accomplishment of a naval officer."

On August 15, bypassing Congress, Bancroft arranged for the transfer of Fort Severn on the banks of the Severn River in Annapolis, Maryland, to the Department of the Navy, and moved the Naval Asylum to Annapolis. Cdr. Franklin Buchanan was placed in charge, professors were selected (among them William Chauvenet), and midshipmen received orders to report to Annapolis.

At 11:00 AM on Friday, October 10, 1845, Commander Buchanan, the school's first superintendent, declared the Naval School open. He read aloud Secretary Bancroft's August 7 letter of instruction to about fifty midshipmen and seven officers and civilian instructors and charged the midshipmen with new challenges. Reminding them of the "uncalculable benefit" of an education bestowed on them by the government and that "good moral character is essential" to promotion, he closed his remarks by challenging the students to a "strict compliance with all laws, orders and regulations" in the hopes that they "may be benefited by them."

The almost ten-acre grounds of the former Fort Severn on the eastern edge of Annapolis on Windmill Point, a peninsula where the Severn

River joins the Annapolis Harbor, was rapidly adapted to its new use as the Naval School. Within the walls of the old fort were the circular gun battery at the tip of the peninsula, dating from 1808, and other buildings, including the commandant's quarters (a colonial mansion called Dulany House), a row of officers' quarters (later known as Buchanan Row), the quartermaster's office, a barracks, married officers' quarters, a hospital, a bakery, the sutler's shop, the blacksmith shop, and the gatehouse. The barracks was converted into classrooms and mess, and other buildings were converted to midshipmen housing.

The Early Years of the Academy, 1845–61

The late 1840s brought new land to the Academy, and the 1850s and 1860s, a new building program. Land adjacent to the Academy acquired in 1847 added six acres to the grounds. The first monument, the Mexican War Monument, was erected in 1848. An extensive construction program undertaken in 1850–54 provided new dorms, a combined laboratory-armory, a recitation hall, and a chapel. Additional land purchased in 1853 added another eleven acres to the grounds, creating space for a hospital and faculty quarters. By 1859 the population of the Academy had expanded as well to a total of fourteen civilian instructors and about the same number of officers and about eighty midshipmen. The sloop *Plymouth* was brought to the Academy and converted into a lodging and classroom facility for fourth-class midshipmen. Another construction program started in 1859 brought the demolition of several older buildings and the construction of new ones. Three permanent additions to the Yard's landscape were made: the Japanese Bell given to Commodore Perry during his expedition to Japan and donated by Perry's widow; Herndon Monument, erected in June 1860; and the Tripoli Monument, moved from the grounds of the Capitol building in Washington, D.C., to the Academy in November 1860.

The Civil War Years, 1861–65

Soon after the outbreak of civil war, the school buildings and grounds transferred to the War Department. On April 24 Superintendent Blake requested an immediate transfer of the school to Fort Adams, an unused Army post at Newport, Rhode Island, and on April 26 the battalion mustered at the Academy wharf to board *Constitution*. (By this time, a number of Southern midshipmen had resigned to support the Confederacy, which soon established its own naval academy aboard CSS *Patrick Henry*.) On April 27 Secretary of the Navy Gideon Welles approved the transfer of the Academy to Fort Adams. After delivering two companies of soldiers at the New York Navy Yard, *Constitution* departed Brooklyn on May 8 with the midshipmen and reached Newport on May 9. Meanwhile *Baltic*, which had departed Annapolis on May 5, 1861, carrying Academy officers, instructors, and families as well as instructional resources, arrived off Fort Adams on May 9, three and a half hours after *Constitution*'s arrival. Classes convened on May 13, but by July, when the Class of 1865 began reporting (altogether the official register lists two hundred midshipmen, most of whom came in September, October, and November 1861), the deteriorating facilities at Fort Adams had to be abandoned. Although Fort Adams continued to be used for training midshipmen throughout the war, classes were held in Atlantic House, which also housed the faculty and upper class while the fourth class remained quartered on *Constitution*. The Civil War years, requiring the maximum number of midshipmen to be graduated in the minimum time, presented some of the most challenging years the Academy had to face.

During these years, the Academy grounds functioned in a variety of ways: from May 1861 as an Army encampment; from late 1861 to February 1862 as a port of embarkation for a joint Army-Navy operation on the North Carolina coast; and from 1863 to the end of the war as an Army hospital. An eyewitness account published in the *Army and Navy Journal* in 1864 described the hospital conditions on the Academy grounds:

> My eyes were struck by the view of a number of hospital tents occupying the grounds once held sacred from the footprints of anyone. Around these tents were trodden innumerable footpaths, marring the beauty of the grounds. Next came an unsightly board fence dividing the upper from the lower grounds; then came roads and pathways, made on pavements and grass plots, the crossing of which once subjected a student to demerits. . . . The fine buildings I found occupied in various ways. Most of them are

used as hospitals, while other portions are given up as sutler-shops, where lager-beer, etc., is dispensed. The fine old quarters of the Superintendent are used as a billiard saloon. What a transformation from their once legitimate use. . . . Thousands of dollars will be required to restore this valuable institution to its original condition.

The Porter Vision, 1865–69

When classes reconvened at the Academy in October 1865, the grounds had been restored to something of their former state. But size was a pressing concern. Stribling Row, built to house 198 midshipmen, could not accommodate the 566 midshipmen who now enrolled. Rear Adm. David Dixon Porter, appointed on September 9, 1865, as the Academy's sixth superintendent, envisioned a great national institution and embarked on a major expansion and construction campaign. In August 1866 he first purchased the four-acre Maryland Government House and grounds. He turned the former governor's residence into the library and superintendent's office and razed the outbuildings in order to erect a new row of officers' quarters. He also acquired more land for the Academy with purchases of two separate parcels north of Dorsey (now College) Creek: the July 1868 purchase of the sixty-seven-acre Strawberry Hill, where the cemetery was established in 1869, and in May 1869, a forty-six-acre tract known as Prospect Hill (where the huge green water tower is today), where he established the hospital (a decision later known as Porter's folly). Meanwhile, in 1865 he constructed a new armory; in 1866, a hall for the Department of Steam Engineering; in 1868, a new chemistry laboratory and brick chapel (the old chapel was converted into the lyceum); and in 1869, a science building and the midshipmen's New Quarters. (The dormitories along Stribling Row, now known as the Old Quarters, were used as overflow housing.) The USS *Delaware* figurehead, now known as Tecumseh, was brought to the Academy and placed near the Lyceum sometime around 1868. USS *Santee*, first brought to the Academy as quarters for enlisted personnel and a brig for midshipmen, became a gunnery ship for the practice firing of broadsides.

Adm. David Dixon Porter (U.S. Naval Institute Photo Archive)

The Quiet Years, 1868–96

Over the next thirty years, relatively few changes were made to the Academy grounds. The first superintendent's quarters, Dulany House, was demolished in 1883–84, and a second superintendent's house was completed there in 1886. An additional fifteen acres along the College Creek shoreline were purchased, and construction was begun on the red-brick officers' quarters on Upshur Row. Most of the older buildings were in dangerously dilapidated condition.

The Flagg Years, 1895–1908

In 1895 the Board of Visitors condemned the existing facilities and asserted that only reconstruction along modern architectural lines would raise the Academy to the level of a premier institution. The board then commissioned Ernest Flagg to develop a master plan for a new Academy.

Ernest Flagg (1857–1947), an American architect trained at the Ecole des Beaux-Arts in Paris and the architect of the Corcoran Gallery of Art (1892–97) in Washington, D.C., and the Singer Tower (1906–8) in New York City, devised a plan for a "New Naval Academy" of architectural monuments to the Navy's grand traditions. To accomplish his

Flagg design of the Yard (Special Collections and Archives Division, Nimitz Library, U.S. Naval Academy)

vision required almost complete demolition of existing buildings (with the exception of the Gate 3 gatehouses, built in 1876 and now the oldest surviving buildings in the Yard), expansion with sizable landfills along both the river and harbor shores, and buildings in monumental Beaux-Arts style, grouped in functional units: a dormitory flanked by buildings for the professional training of midshipmen in the southern part of the Yard; an "academic group" at the northern end; a chapel to provide spiritual guidance to midshipmen; an administrative building; quarters for the superintendent and faculty; and an officers' club.

The dormitory (now called Bancroft Hall), built between 1902 and 1905 to replace the Old Cadet Quarters, stands on the southeastern part of the central Yard as the centerpiece of Flagg's plan. The building's original design included the rotunda, Memorial and Smoke Halls, today's third and fourth wings—and room for expansion, which has been used to add six more wings over the years. In front of Bancroft, Tecumseh Court (T-Court) provides a wide bricked yard for midshipmen formations.

As planned for in Flagg's design, the dormitory is flanked by professional buildings—the identical facades of one building to house the gymnasium and the Department of Seamanship (now Macdonough Hall), originally abutting the shore, and the Armory (now Dahlgren Hall), housing the Department of Ordnance and Gunnery. At the end of Stribling Walk, two long parallel brick paths running from Bancroft through the central yard, Flagg placed the academic group, a set of three joined structures: Sampson Hall and Maury Hall facing each other across the open, recessed courtyard in front of the middle building with the clock tower, Mahan Hall.

Sampson originally housed the Physics and Chemistry Department and the Mathematics Department, and Maury, the English and Law Department and the Modern Languages Department. In addition to the clock tower, Mahan provided an auditorium and library. In the rear of these of buildings stood Isherwood Hall, housing the Marine Engineering and Naval Construction Department and the Mechanics Department.

Sited on the highest ground in the Yard and almost midway between the dormitory and the academic group, facing east toward the Severn River, is the Chapel. Flagg modeled the Chapel on the dome of the Hôtel des Invalides in Paris, originally designed by Jules Hardouin Mansart (1646–1708) to house disabled veterans, but since 1840 better known as the tomb of Napoleon Bonaparte. The Superintendent's Quarters (now called Buchanan House) sits on one side of the Chapel, and the Administration Building sits on the other.

In 1905, an officers' club was erected on Goldsborough Row, and additional officer housing was planned for Porter and Rodgers roads.

Flagg's grand plan also called for placing monuments and nautical mementos (such as cannons, anchors, ships' bells, and figureheads) around the central grounds to "assist [midshipmen] with the contemplation of the past while observing the present."

> Flag dances below sky
>> Squirrels scurry beneath trees
> Cannon readies, facing east
>
>> *Jeffrey Dubinsky*, USNA 2009

One hundred years later, although a number of new buildings have been added to the Academy grounds, Ernest Flagg's Beaux-Arts design still dominates the central Yard.

New Growth in the Twentieth Century

Increased student population in the twentieth century brought the need for more space. Luce Hall was erected in 1919 as a new building for the Department of Seamanship and Navigation. In the 1930s new buildings included the museum (Preble Hall) and the dispensary or medical clinic (Leahy Hall, called Misery Hall by the midshipmen). One of several class gift benches, the granite and limestone Class of 1897 Bench, donated by the class on their fortieth anniversary, was placed behind Tecumseh.

> the cold wind blowing,
>> leaves scattered everywhere,
> the benches empty
>
>> *Christopher Montgomery*, USNA 2008

Officers' and Faculty Club (Randell Hunt "Doc" Prothro and Gustav F. "Gus" Swainson Jr.)

In the 1950s a need for more space for physical fitness led to construction of a new field house (later named Halsey Field House) in 1956.

In 1961 Adm. Ben Moreell was appointed as head of a commission
to produce a new construction plan for the Academy. After abandoning
the first plan, which suggested annexation of historic buildings outside
the Academy gates in Annapolis, the commission contracted with John
Carl Warneke and Associates (architect of President John F. Kennedy's
gravesite in Arlington National Cemetery) to design a master plan to
accommodate the Academy's growing emphasis on technology. Over the
next few years, a complex of new structures was built: Nimitz Library,
connected by a high plaza to the new engineering facility, Rickover Hall,
and, down the steps from this plaza, the Michelson-Chauvenet math-
science complex. All of these structures were to resonate with the spirit
of Flagg's massive, gray stone structures.

The last three decades of the twentieth century brought additional
changes to the Academy, including the contemporary wooden structure of the Robert Crown Sailing Center, with visible framework and a

Robert Crown Sailing Center (Randell Hunt "Doc" Prothro and Gustav F. "Gus" Swainson Jr.)

sharply angled green copper roof as designed by Ellerbee and Associates of Minnesota, which was built in 1974.

A 1960s plan to replace the engineering facility and build a new auditorium was begun in 1982 with the demolition of Isherwood, Melville, and Griffin halls and the construction of Alumni Hall, a multipurpose space able to seat the entire brigade at one time. Lejeune Hall, built in 1982, added two new pools to the Yard. In 1992 a plan for new building at the Academy reemphasizing water views led to a pedestrian-friendly promenade along the water, with seating provided at the Compass Rose Plaza and other locales. The glass walls of the Armel-Leftwich Visitor Center, built in 1995, provide views of Annapolis Harbor.

The Twenty-first Century Academy

The terrorist attacks of September 11, 2001, at the dawn of the twenty-first century presented the United States, and the Naval Academy, with new security issues. Gate 1 near the Visitor Center was reconfigured as the main gate into the Academy. The Uriah P. Levy Center and Jewish Chapel, dedicated in 2005, provides not only separate worship space for

Jewish midshipmen but also facilities for leadership and ethics training for all midshipmen.

The Glenn Warner Soccer Facility and the Max Bishop (Baseball) Stadium, along with the FitzGerald Clubhouse, provide additional facilities for soccer and baseball training; and the Wesley Brown Field House, opened in 2008, adds a new emphasis on readiness training. The Master Plan for 2014 envisions further buildings as well as new uses for older structures and expansion across the Severn River on government property, where a new ice hockey/indoor tennis facility has opened. But the National Historic Landmark status of the central Yard will ensure that Flagg's Beaux-Arts design will not be lost in "progression's march."

Administration Building

Within the hallowed halls
A sleeping giant dwells.
Oh midshipman, watch your step
Lest your soul he sells.

Jordan P. Bradford, USNA 2009

Administration Building (Randell Hunt "Doc" Prothro and Gustav F. "Gus" Swainson Jr.)

The Administration Building, or Admin, houses the offices of the superintendent, the academic dean, and other Academy administrators. In Ernest Flagg's Academy plan for buildings grouped in functional units, the spiritual center of the Academy, the Chapel, is flanked by administration buildings—the Superintendent's House on one side, and the offices of the administration on the other.

> Outside, an historic building of thick carved stone,
> The tallest flagpole on the Yard proudly in front.
> Inside, walls hung with old paintings of ships of the line.
> Here schedules are written, applications reviewed,
> Futures determine for incoming plebes
> And every new grad in the fleet.

Melanie M. Salinas, USNA 2009

Flagpole at Admin (Randell Hunt "Doc" Prothro and Gustav F. "Gus" Swainson Jr.)

Flanking the walkway to Admin are two large 600-pound cannonballs and two guns. The cannonballs, typical of Turkish cannonballs during the conquest of Constantinople in 1453, were brought to the Academy by Commo. John Rodgers, who had been in Constantinople in 1825 negotiating a treaty with the Ottoman Empire. The cannon on the right is a 12-pounder cast in 1686, and the one on the left, an 18-pounder cast in 1789 and captured from the Mexicans in 1847. Each day when reveille and taps are played, midshipmen and officers in the Yard stop and stand at attention facing the flag on the flagpole in front of Admin.

> As our flag flies high above me, I wonder about my life here at this institution. . . . The first time I saluted her, I was proud to be an American, to be a Marine, and to be free. My heart jumped a beat or two when I snapped to attention and gave the best salute I knew how. My hands started shaking, sweat formed on my brow. . . . I look up into the shadow of the flag and remember. . . . My drill instructor, thumbs along the seams of his trou, right on the vertical dark blood-red stripe, down his side. It is surrounded by that wave of navy blue. That stripe made the uniform even though it was only an inch and a half wide. But from his belt to his shoes, that stripe seemed proud. It shouted out, cried out, "I represent honor, courage and commitment." . . .
>
> I stare at the flag. Tears fill my eyes. Will I live with the honor, the commitment of my drill instructor? Will I die with the courage others before me have?
>
> *Trevor J. Felter*, USNA 2002

Alumni Hall

Brigade Activities Center

Alumni Hall (Randell Hunt "Doc" Prothro and Gustav F. "Gus" Swainson Jr.)

The Brigade Activities Center, designed by John Carl Warneke and Associates with generous funding provided by alumni, opened in 1982 as Alumni Hall. A multipurpose space that can seat the entire brigade of midshipmen for Forrestal Lectures and other briefings, it also provides venues for basketball games, music and dance concerts, and the annual State of the Academy briefing by the superintendent to the faculty. In addition it has classrooms for academic courses and character development seminars and houses the Music Department offices. Perhaps most memorably, Alumni Hall is where civilians get their first taste of military life as they line up for uniforms, vaccines, and general indoctrination on Induction Day, or I-Day.

Induction Day, July 1, 1998

The day began in a never-ending line, streaming outside and around this strange new building. Looking around at all the others in line, I was attempting to see if anyone had that same nervous look that I was sure I had. After waiting patiently outside I finally made it in the doors after about an hour. At the doors, greeting each new plebe as they entered, was a friendly guy with a red name tag. I learned later that these guys with the red name tags were actually not so friendly. Induction turned out to be an all-day event. I was led through the long winding corridors like a pack mule. We would stop at a station to pick up some issued items, then hurry off to the next. At one such station the red name-tag people would give us shots like lab rats. There was even a station to take your money. When I left Alumni Hall I had a bald head, empty wallet, sore shoulder from all the shots, and weird clothes. In all, Induction Day was one of the better days of plebe summer.

Charles Dawson, USNA 2002

Similar in style to other Warneke buildings on the Yard—including Nimitz, Rickover, and Michelson-Chauvenet—the massive stone facade of Alumni Hall is broken by the glass doors of four grand entrances, including three named entrances: Isherwood, Griffin, and Melville. Each of these is adorned with a large bronze crest. Donated by the Class of 1947, these crests contain metallic mementos—class rings, rank insignia, and uniform buttons—contributed by class members. The dedicatory plaque from the Class of 1947 notes, "As the lives of all members of our Class have been inextricably joined since 1943, so our gifts are intimately commingled for all time in our gift of love to the Academy and the young men and women who are our fortunate successors."

The named entrances of Alumni Hall pay tribute to three former Academy structures that stood near the site. Isherwood Hall, built as part of the Flagg plan in 1905, was named for Benjamin Franklin Isherwood (1822–1915), an engineering officer during the early days of steam-powered warships who in the 1860s helped found the Bureau of Steam Engineering in the Department of the Navy.

Alumni Hall, Melville Entrance (Randell Hunt "Doc" Prothro and Gustav F. "Gus" Swainson Jr.)

Named for the pioneer
Of the fast cruiser
And the creator
Of the Bureau of Steam,
After seventy years
This modern ferroconcrete
Engineering structure
Of glazed brick and wrought-iron
With inner courtyard
And central sweeping stair
Had grown outdated.
Some still lament
the cost of progress—
Isherwood demolished.

Griffin Hall, the engineering building, erected in 1918, was named for Robert S. Griffin (1857–1933), USNA 1878, the engineer in chief of the Bureau of Steam during World War I who was best known for his design and construction of machinery for new vessels. Melville Hall, another engineering facility, erected in 1938, was named for George Melville (1841–1912), the engineer in chief of the Navy from 1887 to 1903 who was also known for his participation on the *Jeannette* Arctic expedition and his heroic rescue attempt of Capt. George Washington De Long. (See also the *Jeannette* Monument entry.)

No other place on the Yard holds more meaning for me than Alumni Hall. Located alongside the Severn River and adjacent to Worden Field, Alumni Hall was the site of Induction Day, my first taste of the Naval Academy.

"What is your name, plebe?" a uniform barked loudly at me.

"Forrest, Tyler Forrest," I replied confidently.

"That is now followed by a 'sir,' plebe," he retorted. Suddenly I realized that my college experience wasn't going to be a normal one. For the next five hours, I walked throughout Alumni Hall receiving shots, uniforms, and a new "haircut." Even though I walked for what seemed like eternity, there was always a new hall around the next corner, and more luggage to carry. By the time I finally exited this labyrinth, I was carrying more clothes than I'd ever seen and was getting yelled at with each step. In spite of all this, I gained a certain fondness for this new atmosphere. I actually found myself enjoying the yelling, hauling, and fast-paced environment. It was with this attitude that I was able to make it through Plebe Summer and other hard times at the Academy.

Tyler W. Forrest, USNA 2002

Armel-Leftwich Visitor Center

Mids never really go to the Visitor Center. Over the summer, though, when my fiancee's family headed to Annapolis for a tour, I accompanied them, entering the facility for the first time in my career. Initially, I felt out of place. As I took it in, though, a smile crept across my face. The Naval Academy was actually a cool place to be, and I was a celebrity.

David E. Setyon, USNA 2009

Armel-Leftwich Visitor Center (Randell Hunt "Doc" Prothro and Gustav F. "Gus" Swainson Jr.)

IN MEMORIAM

LYLE OLIVER ARMEL, II
CAPTAIN
UNITED STATES NAVY
1931-1989

U.S. NAVAL ACADEMY - CLASS OF 1953
EXECUTIVE OFFICER USS TURNER JOY (DD951)
COMMANDING OFFICER USS EVANS (DE 1023)
COMMANDING OFFICER USS WADDELL (DDG 24)
COMMANDING OFFICER USS PIEDMONT (AD 17)
SENIOR NAVAL ADVISOR VIETNAM
NAVY DISTINGUISHED SERVICE MEDAL,
LEGION OF MERIT, BRONZE STAR (2), AIR MEDAL (2)

MIDSHIPMAN, NAVAL OFFICER, HUSBAND, FATHER

ONE OF AMERICA'S FINEST SONS

Capt. Lyle Oliver Armel II, Visitor Center plaque (Randell Hunt "Doc" Prothro and Gustav F. "Gus" Swainson Jr.)

The Armel-Leftwich Visitor Center, designed by CSD Architects of Baltimore and built in 1995, was part of the 1992 vision for new Academy buildings, which sought to reemphasize the strong connection to the water that had been a major part of Flagg's plan. Sitting just inside Gate 1 (now the Academy's main gate) and a short walk from downtown Annapolis, the Visitor Center provides an ideal location for orientation to the Yard. Its two floors display exhibits of midshipmen life and Navy lore and memorabilia, such as the original wooden figurehead of the USS *Delaware* and an exhibit about John Paul Jones. The building also houses a gift shop.

The Visitor Center is named for USNA 1953 classmates Lyle Oliver Armel II, USN (1931–89), and William Groom Leftwich Jr., USMC (1931–70), both of whom were advisers in Vietnam.

Capt. Lyle Oliver Armel II

Captain Armel's early assignments were in destroyers and as aide to commander, Destroyers, Atlantic Fleet. After attending Naval Intelligence School, he served in the Office of Naval Intelligence, and then as executive officer of destroyer *Turner Joy*, as commanding officer of destroyer escort *Evans* in Southeast Asia (1963–65), and as commanding officer of guided missile destroyer *Waddel* (1967–69). He also served as senior naval adviser in Vietnam (1972–73) and commanding officer of destroyer tender *Piedmont*. His awards include two Bronze Stars with Combat "V" and two Air Medals.

Quotations about Armel

> Lyle possessed a fine sense of humor, and was good company at all times. His disposition was calm and his manner sincere . . . excellent qualities for a man interested in submarine service. Never one to neglect academics for athletics or social life, Lyle always escaped the clutch of the academic departments by a very comfortable margin. . . . Everyone who knew Lyle liked him, admired him, and looked forward to serving with him in the fleet.
>
> *Lucky Bag,* 1953

One of America's finest sons.

Dedicatory plaque, Visitor Center

Burial Site

Arlington National Cemetery, Arlington, Virginia

Lt. Col. William Groom Leftwich Jr.

As brigade commander at the Academy, Lieutenant Colonel Leftwich was commended for his officerlike qualities, which contributed to "the development of naval spirit and loyalty within the Brigade." From 1957 to 1960, he served as company officer at the Academy. After receiving Vietnamese language training, Leftwich was transferred to Vietnam as senior adviser to the Vietnamese Marines. He spent more than three hundred days in the field and participated in twenty-seven major operations against the Viet Cong in the central highlands. Wounded in the battle of Hoai An on March 9, 1965, he received the Purple Heart and the Navy Cross for extraordinary heroism. In 1970, during his second tour as special assistant and commander of the 1st Reconnaissance Battalion, Lieutenant Colonel Leftwich was killed in a helicopter rescue mission. For his "conspicuous gallantry," he was awarded the Silver Cross posthumously.

A bronze statue of Leftwich by Felix de Welden, sculptor of the Iwo Jima Memorial and the busts of Admiral Nimitz and Admiral Moreell at the Academy, was dedicated at the Basic School at Quantico, Virginia, in 1985. The Leftwich Trophy, endowed in 1979 by USNA classmate Ross Perot and given annually to the outstanding Marine captain serving at the time of nomination with the ground forces of the Fleet Marine Force, is a miniature replica of this statue.

Leftwich Quotation

As a serviceman I can do my duty . . . and do it cheerfully with a common sense seasoning and a serene spirit.

IN MEMORIAM

WILLIAM GROOM LEFTWICH, JR.
LIEUTENANT COLONEL
UNITED STATES MARINE CORPS
1931-1970

U.S. NAVAL ACADEMY-CLASS OF 1953
MIDSHIPMAN BRIGADE COMMANDER
PLATOON COMMANDER
MARINE ADVISOR VIETNAM
MARINE AIDE TO UNDERSECNAV
BATTALION COMMANDER VIETNAM
NAVY CROSS, SILVER STAR, LEGION OF MERIT (3),
AIR MEDAL (2), PURPLE HEART (3)

DEVOTED HUSBAND AND LOVING FATHER
AN INSPIRATIONAL LEADER IN PEACETIME AND IN WAR

Lt. Col. William Groom Leftwich Jr., Visitor Center plaque (Randell Hunt "Doc" Prothro and Gustav F. "Gus" Swainson Jr.)

Quotations about Leftwich

"Lefty," modest almost to the point of denying all accomplishments, participated in varsity football and tennis. . . . As an indication of his well-rounded personality, even temperament and capability, Bill's standing in aptitude put him at the top in '53. His willingness and dependability made him a perfect choice for such activities as Crest and Ring Committee and Sports Editor of *Reef Points*. What a guy! . . . What a personality . . . it just can't be described. . . . You have to meet him for yourself.

Lucky Bag, 1953

[An] inspirational leader in peacetime and in war.

Visitor Center plaque

[Bill] was a great leader, gifted athlete, outstanding scholar, and a man of absolute honor, integrity, and commitment. He was a pillar of strength, but had a warm, kind, gentle nature.

Ross Perot, USNA 1953

For conspicuous gallantry and intrepidity in action . . . in connection with combat operations against the enemy in the Republic of Vietnam. On 4 August 1970, upon learning from intelligence sources that high level enemy commanders were planning to meet at a designated location in Quang Nam Province, Lieutenant Colonel Leftwich conceived a bold plan for an attack on the meeting place. . . . Fully aware of the danger involved, he elected to forego [sic] the normal prelanding reconnaissance activities and landing zone preparatory fires and, to avoid detection by the enemy, moved his men into the area by helicopters maneuvering at treetop level. Following his plan, Lieutenant Colonel Leftwich surreptitiously deployed his unit around the hostile headquarters and launched an aggressive attack which took the enemy commanders completely by surprise. When the now disorganized enemy attempted to escape, he directed his men in vigorous pursuit and disregarded his own safety as he moved to the most forward position to coordinate supporting arms fires. . . . By his tactical skill, bold fighting spirit, and unflagging devotion to duty, Lieutenant Colonel Leftwich upheld the highest traditions of the Marine Corps and of the United States Naval Service.

Silver Star Citation

~e9~

Leftwich lived—and as things turned out, died—by the soldier's principle: "Never send a man where you won't go yourself."

Fellow Marine

Burial Site

Forest Hill Cemetery, Memphis, Tennessee

Bancroft Hall

(Including Memorial Hall)

Bancroft Hall (Randell Hunt "Doc" Prothro and Gustav F. "Gus" Swainson Jr.)

The bizarre, grandiose dream-child . . . the cultural foundation of our Admirals-in-embryo . . . The cradle of navy spirit.

Lucky Bag, 1929

It is often said that home is where you hang your hat or lay your head. Bancroft is that to me, and so much more. The hall is where I come together with my shipmates and classmates after a long and hard marathon of school and exercise. We joke, we laugh, and we talk together about things that happen to us, and then we sleep. The next day we get up and do it again. If Bancroft had eyes or ears on its walls, which I sometimes think it does, it would know every detail of my present life.

Plebe, c. 2002

Portrait of an Officer

Broken and battered—confined in this place,
Tours, duty—prisons—all work and no play.
Bravo; not a compliment. The inspector draws near,
Dust, dirt, possessions adrift—gross negligence,
Dedalus, memories, past, free, flying away,
Air ahead above and under,
Behind me, Bancroft, my Dublin,
Where I forged my conscience,
And achieved everything I treasure today.

Matthew C. Forman, USNA 2009

Bancroft Hall, designed by Ernest Flagg as the midshipman dormitory, is one of the highlights of his Beaux-Arts Academy design. Reminiscent of French military architecture, it boasts a grand and formidable facade: two sweeping curved ramps and a large marble staircase rising to a set of monumental bronze double doors beneath a sculpted naval motif of boats and dolphins.

The exterior doors open to the hall's ceremonial areas—the domed Rotunda and Memorial Hall. Beyond these formal public spaces, Bancroft Hall is out of bounds to visitors. The more extensive, private spaces of

Bancroft make up the major part of the building. Originally built with two wings but now composed of eight, "Mother B" is one of the largest dormitories in the world with about five miles of corridors and about two thousand rooms for approximately four thousand midshipmen. Operating as a small city, with its own zip code, it also supports a post office, barbershop, uniform shop, and other facilities, as well as a mess, King Hall, where the entire brigade can eat together at once (see the King Hall entry). At the Mid Store, midshipmen can purchase snacks, pens, paper, clothes, and cleaning supplies to keep uniforms and rooms polished for inspections.

To My Back Room

Oft in the stilly night,
    Ere slumber's chains have bound me,
I've risen nearly dead with cold
    And pulled my blanket round me.
        My overcoat,
        And raincoat too,
    Upon my bed were thrown,
        To stop the cold,
        By north wind bold,
    In through my window blown.
Thus oft in the stilly night,
    Ere slumber's chain has bound me,
I've cursed out a back room
    And pulled my blanket round me.

Lucky Bag, 1897

Bancroft Hall and the magical mystery of it all—for those not residing there for the next four years. As for plebes, Mother B is as far from a sanctuary as you can get. We are forced to chop everywhere. Let me explain: We plebers are the starving, barking, screaming greyhounds racing, not toward the rabbit, but toward those ridiculous silver deck plates. We race toward them, achieving them, and shouting blindly, "GO NAVY, SIR!" only to see the next plate just within our reach, chop, chop, chop, it's getting closer! "BEAT ARMY, SIR!" Oh, no, there's another,

Bancroft Rotunda (Randell Hunt "Doc" Prothro and Gustav F. "Gus" Swainson Jr.)

and another! Will I be chopping my whole life through the maze that is Bancroft Hall? But—a door, I have spotted a door! Breathless I chop toward it, anxiously greeting those upper class as I pass, chopping quicker and quicker so as not to give them a chance to stop and rate me. A rush of daylight and fresh spring breeze (or cold winter freeze or hot sticky summer air) hits me. Yes! Free until I must return on deck for noon meal formation. My momentary, short-lived, greyhound victory.

Courtney E. Natter, USNA 2008

Rotunda

These columns soaring to heights from marbled floor have oft vibrated to the cheer of victory.

Lucky Bag, 1929

Memorial Hall steps (Randell Hunt "Doc" Prothro and Gustav F. "Gus" Swainson Jr.)

Memorial Hall

Look up at the domed
Memorial sky, consecrated
To those who gave their lives,
At eagles carved on the ceiling,
Wings set to fly.
All you who stand
On this mosaic marble floor,
With all the art you can bring,
With all your heart,
Let dreams soar.

~e9~

A quickened pulse, higher held head, the every-passing effect. Mute, impressive memorials to our country's ultra-valorous heroes; deep-felt lessons on loyalty these, stirring the soul, pervading the mind, with the wealth of a Navy's tradition.

Lucky Bag, 1929

With Memorial Hall, Flagg sought to create a spacious public area that would convey the somber duties and traditions of naval service. The hall is dedicated to all Naval Academy alumni, especially those who have been killed in war and who have died in the line of duty. Marine paintings, busts of naval officers, dedicatory plaques, and other objects in Mem Hall memorialize both naval events and naval figures, including those whose names are well-known and others whose names are almost forgotten.

"Don't Give Up the Ship" Replica Flag

On first climbing the interior marble staircase from the Rotunda, the visitor is greeted by a replica of Commo. Oliver Hazard Perry's famous flag, which he flew in battle with the British on Lake Erie on September 10, 1813. In 1812 Congress had declared war against the British because of their trade restrictions, impressment of American sailors, and support of Native Americans' defense of tribal lands, and Perry was ordered to Lake Erie to build a fleet to oppose the British threat of invasion along the northern U.S. border. The phrase "Don't Give Up the Ship," crudely but memorably embroidered on the flag that flew from Perry's USS *Lawrence*, echoes the last command of Capt. James Lawrence (1781–1813), the courageous commander of the frigate *Chesapeake* who had died of wounds suffered in battle against HMS *Shannon* only a few months before the Battle of Lake Erie. (The battle between *Chesapeake* and *Shannon* was short and bloody, and ended with most of the American crew killed; the remaining crew did in fact surrender.)

The original flag from the USS *Lawrence* has been on almost continuous display in the Naval Academy museum since 1849. Captain Lawrence is further honored at the Academy by Lawrence Field, a complex of varsity baseball fields located across College Creek near Gate 8. (See the Max Bishop Stadium entry for more on Academy baseball.) He is buried in Trinity Churchyard, New York City.

"Don't Give Up the Ship" flag (Randell Hunt "Doc" Prothro and Gustav F. "Gus" Swainson Jr.)

Lawrence Quotation

Tell the men to fire faster and not to give up the ship.

> Commanding USS *Chesapeake* in battle
> with HMS *Shannon*, June 1, 1813

Perry Quotation

Commodore Perry is remembered for the message he sent to Gen. William Henry Harrison after the defeat of the British at Lake Erie: "We have met the enemy and they are ours."

The flag is tattered and old, but the words on it, which are the words of Captain Lawrence when he was mortally wounded during a fight with the HMS *Shannon* in the War of 1812, are words that will live forever: "Don't give up the ship." Almost two hundred years later, these words still serve as an inspiration to me. Whenever times get tough and I'm thinking that things are so bad that I might not be able to make it here, all I have to do is take a trip over to Memorial Hall and look at Captain Lawrence's dying words and I am given strength to know that I can make it through.

Joshua J. Lostetter, USNA 2003

Killed in Action Panel Dedication

Dedicated to the honor of those alumni who have been killed in action defending the ideals of their country.

With immortal valor and the price of their lives these proved their love of country and their loyalty to the high traditions of their alma mater by inscribing with their own blood the narrative of their deeds above, on, and underneath the seven seas. They have set the course. They silently stand watch wherever Navy ships ply the waters of the globe.

The Purpose

We were tired. So were the second class. That's why they left us with Mr. Charles, our platoon commander, and went out for some fun on the town. Mr. Charles took us in the front doors of Bancroft and up the staircase to Memorial Hall. He spoke to us about the true purpose of the Academy and why we were really there, to serve our country and possibly give our lives in defense of freedom. He then said something that nobody had said all summer: "Just walk about and look at everything." Busts of famous admirals sat on pedestals. Plaques were everywhere—one listed all Academy graduates who were awarded the Congressional Medal of Honor; another held the names of all midshipmen who had died before graduating. A model showed an action for which a Marine captain had won a Navy Cross. Everywhere were symbols of the past, men who had fought and died for their country. Mr. Charles called us back to the center of the room and pointed out the flag before us, the "Don't Give

Master Commandant James Lawrence, Gilbert Stuart portrait, 1812 (U.S. Naval Institute Photo Archive)

Up the Ship" flag. Below it was a list of all Academy graduates who had been killed in combat. "Pick out a name," he told us, "and write it down. Whenever you feel sorry for yourself, remember the name of that man who paid the ultimate price for his country." George Wilkins, Class of '56, killed in Vietnam, is forever written in my *Reef Points* and in my mind.

Plebe, c. 2002

Medal of Honor Plaque and Operational Loss Panels

The Medal of Honor Plaque lists the names of USNA alumni who are Medal of Honor recipients. The Operational Loss Panels, donated in 2004 by the Class of 1954, honor "the courage and commitment of Naval Academy graduates who gave their lives in performance of their duties."

Historic Flags and Murals

In addition to Perry's flag, other historic flags from various naval actions are on display around Mem Hall. High on the walls, just under the ceiling, are eight murals of famous Navy ships and battles, painted by Marine artists Charles Patterson (1878–1958) and Howard B. French (1906–87):

> ⊳ "USS *Constellation* and *L'Insurgente*, February 9, 1799," Patterson. (*Constellation*," the last all-sail ship built for the U.S. Navy, served in the Mediterranean and African Squadrons and during the Civil War, then became a training ship for midshipmen (1871–93). In World War II she served as the flagship for the commander in chief, U.S. Atlantic Fleet.)

> ⊳ "Opening Action between USS *Constitution* and HMS *Java*, December 29, 1812," Patterson. (This mural depicts one of the most famous battles of the War of 1812, in which Capt. William Bainbridge, USN, defeated his British counterpart after a grueling three-hour fight.)

- ☞ "USS *Hartford* and USS *America*," French and Patterson. (*Hartford* was Adm. David G. Farragut's flagship; both ships later became Naval Academy training ships.)

- ☞ "First Foreign Salute to the Stars and Stripes, February 14, 1778," French. (The gun salute by French Admiral La Motte Picquet to the *Ranger*, commanded by Capt. John Paul Jones in Quiberon Bay, marked the first time the Stars and Stripes was saluted by a foreign power.)

- ☞ "Battle of Lake Erie, September 10, 1813" Patterson and French. (This mural rests above the Perry flag.)

- ☞ "USS *Delaware*," French. (The original figurehead, which represents Tamanend, chief of the Delawares, but which is now known as Tecumseh, remains on permanent display in the Visitor Center.)

- ☞ "USS *Monangahela*," French. (An academy training ship, 1894–97 and 1899.)

Portraits and Busts

A number of portraits hang on the walls around Mem Hall, including those of Admiral of the Navy George Dewey, Rear Adm. William Sampson, and Fleet Adm. Ernest J. King. Sculpted busts on display include those of Adm. William Sims, commander of U.S. naval forces in Europe in World War I, and Rear Adm. Robley Dungliston "Fighting Bob" Evans (1846–1912), USNA 1864, gallant leader of the 1865 attack on Fort Fisher and commander of the Great White Fleet in its 1907–8 voyage from the Atlantic through the Strait of Magellan to the Pacific.

Individual Plaques

A number of historic marble, wood, and metal plaques presented by family members, classmates, or shipmates honor individuals who dedicated their lives to naval service.

Capt. Charles Gridley (1844–98), USNA 1864 (graduated 1863)

Charles Gridley served with Admiral Farragut in 1863–64 and with Admiral Dewey at the Battle of Manila Bay on May 1, 1898, during which he commanded the flagship *Olympia*. He died in Kobe, Japan, from injuries suffered in performance of duty on *Olympia*. He is buried in Lakeside Cemetery, Erie, Pennsylvania.

Capt. Charles Gridley, Louis Amateis wood bas relief (Randell Hunt "Doc" Prothro and Gustav F. "Gus" Swainson Jr.)

Capt. Herbert George Sparrow (1877–1924), USNA 1899

Concerned not for himself but for the safety of his men and ship he was finally overcome by heavy seas that for hours had swept the decks of the *Tacoma*.

Dedication on the panel erected by classmates

LT. JOHN G. TALBOT, USN, PETER FRANCIS, QUARTERMASTER,
JOHN ANDREWS, COXSWAIN, AND JAMES MUIR, CAPTAIN OF THE HOLD

Talbot, Francis, Andrews, and Muir were crew members on USS *Saginaw* who were drowned while attempting to land on Kauai in the northern Pacific, after a fifteen-hundred-mile voyage seeking aid for their wrecked shipmates.

> To commemorate their adventurous voyage, and in admiration of their heroism, and to keep alive the remembrance of their noble and generous devotion, this tablet is erected by their shipmates and by officers of the U.S. Navy.
>
> Dedication on panel

❦

Piano

The piano at home
    In Memorial Hall
  Fills the room
    With vibrant tones
And thunder,
    Echoes the cannon shot
In painted battles
    Between fighting frigates,
Whose decks were wood,
    Whose men were iron.
A new song begins . . .

That melts an iron man
    Back into a boy
Who stands in Memorial Hall
    To remember.

Christopher George, Labyrinth, 1996

❦

The paintings on the wall have eyes that stare at me and trace my every movement. The men in the pictures are in full military dress, in bold poses. They talk to me and ask, "What are you doing here? Will you ever measure up to any of these great heroes who have made the ultimate sacrifice?"

Ryan C. McDonough, USNA 2009

George Bancroft

Bancroft Hall is named for George Bancroft (1800–1891), who as secretary of the Navy under President James K. Polk established the Academy as the Naval School in 1845. Bancroft's early interest in education led him to establish one of the first serious schools of secondary education, Round Hill School for Boys in Northampton, Massachusetts, in 1823. In 1837 he entered government service with an appointment by President Martin Van Buren as collector of customs of the Port of Boston. He later was appointed U.S. minister to Great Britain (1846–49) and U.S. minister to Prussia and Germany (1867–74). During this period, Bancroft initiated "naturalization treaties" with Prussia and other north German states. The "Bancroft treaties," which offered the first international recognition of rules of expatriation, were important in their time, but American constitutional law eventually made them obsolete and they were officially terminated during President Jimmy Carter's administration. Bancroft was also a popular historian, whose monumental ten-volume *History of the United States* (1834–78) was highly influential in its use of primary sources and promulgation of American expansion. He also published a two-volume *History of the Formation of the Constitution of the United States* (1882).

In spite of support by previous presidents and a number of bills submitted to Congress over the years for the establishment of a naval school, it was not until Bancroft bypassed Congress that a permanent home for midshipmen training to be naval officers was finally established. On October 10, 1845, under the supervision of Superintendent Franklin Buchanan, faculty, staff, and midshipmen were convened at the Academy.

George Bancroft, Brady Studios (U.S. Naval Institute Photo Archive)

Bancroft Quotations

Each generation gathers together the imperishable children of the past, and increases them by new sons of light, alike radiant with immortality.

The exact measure of the progress of civilization is the degree in which the intelligence of the common mind has prevailed over wealth and brute force.

In collecting [the midshipmen] at Annapolis for purposes of instruction, you will begin with the principle that a warrant in the Navy, far from being an excuse for licentious freedom, is to be held a pledge for subordination, industry, and regularity, for sobriety and assiduous attention to duty. Far from consenting that the tone of discipline and morality should be less than at university or colleges of our country, the President expects such supervision and arrangement as shall make of them an exemplary body of which the country may be proud.

Letter to Navy Department, August 7, 1845

The United States of America constitute an essential portion of a great political system, embracing all the civilized nations of the earth. The sovereignty of the people is here a conceded axiom, and the laws, established upon that basis, are cherished with faithful patriotism. . . . Domestic peace is maintained without the aid of a military establishment. . . . A gallant navy protects our commerce. . . . Our national resources are developed by an earnest culture of the arts of peace. . . . Nor is the constitution a dead letter, unalterably fixed: it has the capacity for improvement; adopting whatever changes time and the public will may require, and safe from decay, so long as that will retains its energy.

The History of the United States, Vol. 1

I was trained to look upon life here as a season of labor. Being more than fourscore years old, I know the time for my release will soon come. Conscious of being near the shore of eternity I await without impatience and without dread the beckoning of the hand which will summon me to rest.

Letter, May 30, 1882

Quotations about Bancroft

The nation's historian, and the oldest prominent man of the country.

Washington Post, January 18, 1891

~❧~

Our great Professor of Patriotism . . . an example for the youth of our country.

Eulogy by William A. Bartlett, January 20, 1891

Burial Site

Worcester Rural Cemetery, Worcester, Massachusetts

Beach Hall (Randell Hunt "Doc" Prothro and Gustav F. "Gus" Swanson Jr.)

Beach Hall

The only way to get out of this alive is to make 'em think we're
all dead.

    Lieutenant Bledsoe in *Run Silent, Run Deep*, 1958

Beach Hall (Randell Hunt "Doc" Prothro and Gustav F. "Gus" Swanson Jr.)

Beach Hall, built in 1958 as the last wing of the former U.S. Naval
Academy Hospital, has been home to the Naval Academy Founda-
tion and the U.S. Naval Institute since 1999. It is named for Capt.
Edward Latimer Beach Sr. and his son, Capt. Edward "Ned" Beach Jr., both
Navy captains, USNA graduates, and prolific authors who "superbly ful-
filled the objectives of the Naval Institute." At the dedication ceremony

Capt. Edward L. Beach Sr. (U.S. Naval Institute Photo Archive)

for the hall, the U.S. Naval Institute's publisher and chief executive officer James A. Barber Jr., noting the legendary contributions of father and son, praised them as men of both the pen and the sword who represented the "heart and soul of the Navy" for more than a century.

Edward Latimer Beach Sr. (1867–1943), USNA 1888

Captain Beach served in the Navy for thirty-seven years, participating in action in the Spanish-American War in 1898, the Philippine Insurrection in 1899, and the Veracruz occupation in 1904. He also participated in peacekeeping operations in Haiti in 1914. During World War I, Beach was named commanding officer of the battleship *New York* (BB-34), the flagship of the American battleship squadron attached to the British Home Fleet. In the early 1900s, between tours of duty at sea, Beach taught English at the Naval Academy and wrote a number of young adult novels, in the style of Horatio Alger stories, about life at sea.

Beach Sr. Quotation

Looking back to June 1884 . . . I see myself awaiting dinner formation on the lawn in front of the "New Quarters" (demolished long ago) at the U.S. Naval Academy in Annapolis, Maryland. This to me was an exciting and fearful time. Age seventeen, I had just been admitted as a naval cadet—though in cadet language I was a "plebe," at the bottom of the human, or at least the U.S. naval, scale.

From Annapolis to Scapa Flow:
The Autobiography of Edward L. Beach Sr (1930)

Quotations about Beach Sr.

Early shipmates were Civil War vets; later ones became leaders in World War II. He served in wooden sailing ships, in the cruiser *Baltimore* during the 1898 victory in Manila Bay, commanding cruisers *Washington* and *Memphis* in the Caribbean, and the battleship *New York* during World War I. As Secretary-Treasurer of the Naval Institute, he published the first Bluejackets' Manual. He wrote 13 novels, leading a generation of young men to aspire to naval careers. After he retired in 1921, he became a professor of history at Stanford University.

Commemorative plaque, Beach Hall

Beach Sr. Burial Site

Golden Gate National Cemetery, San Bruno, California

Edward Latimer Beach Jr. (1918–2002), USNA 1939

Edward Beach Jr. was the recipient of the Class of 1897 Midshipman Leadership Award in 1939. The large silver trophy engraved with his name is usually kept in an exhibit case across from the commandant's office in Bancroft Hall. In World War II Beach carried out twelve submarine patrols and received ten decorations for gallantry in combat, including the Navy Cross, two Silver Stars, and two Bronze Stars. Under his command, USS *Trigger* became the Pacific Fleet's top-scoring submarine. When Beach was given orders to depart *Trigger* in May 1944 and report as executive officer of *Tirante*, a newly built submarine, the entire *Trigger* crew came to bid him farewell. "What I didn't realize," Beach said later, "was that we were splitting—those who were going to live from those who were going to die." In March 1945 the Japanese sunk *Trigger*, and all hands were loss.

In 1960, in command of USS *Triton* (SSRN-586), Beach completed the first submerged circumnavigation of the globe, a feat for which *Triton* received the Presidential Unit Citation Legion of Merit from President Dwight D. Eisenhower.

Like his father, Ned Beach was a prolific novelist. His first book, *Run Silent, Run Deep*, was written while he was naval aide to President Eisenhower (he had plenty of time to write, he said, as he did not go to parties). His memoir of his years in submarine service, *Salt and Steel: Reflections of a Submariner*, was published in 1999.

Beach Jr. Quotation

What is there about the Navy? To me, it's always been a tremendous feeling that I am part of an organization that's much bigger than I am. The Navy has done things for me that most people just couldn't comprehend. Of all my school friends, I was the one who had the biggest adventure. . . . During the war, I was driving submarines. The Navy made that possible. Now look at the commanding officer of an aircraft carrier, or a nuclear engineer, a naval aviator or a Sailor in command of his own boat. They all have responsibility—they're part of something much bigger than themselves. They are adventurers. They do wonderful

Capt. Edward L. Beach Sr. (U.S. Naval Institute Photo Archive)

things that other people can't do. This is one of the tremendous things the Navy can do for you.

Dedication ceremony, Beach Hall, 1999

Quotations about Beach Jr.

Ned believes in doing something even if it is wrong; and he has the uncanny knack of seldom being wrong. He barges right into a knot of struggling soccer players, and the ball soon emerges in the direction of the opponent's goal. This same drive characterizes his more professional activities. As a midshipman officer Ned displays both loyalty to the Naval Service and genuine loyalty to his comrades. Knowing Ned "at ease" is quite a pleasure. Association with him reveals numerous mannerisms, expressions, and humorous points of view.

Lucky Bag, 1939

For meritorious achievement from the 16th of February 1960 to the
10th of May 1960. During this period TRITON circumnavigated the
earth submerged, generally following the route of Magellan's historic
voyage. In addition to proving the ability of both crew and nuclear
submarine to accomplish a mission which required almost three months
of submergence, TRITON collected much data of scientific importance.
The performance, determination and devotion to duty of TRITON's
crew were in keeping with the highest traditions of naval service.

Presidential Unit Citation, 1960

[Beach was] one of the most outstanding submariners of all time—he
was absolutely fearless.

Capt. George L. Street III, commanding officer, *Tirante*, c. 2000

Like a lot of us, Captain Beach's heroism and simple but great storytelling
led me to the submarine service. Which helped to change an immature
eighteen year old into a man that learn[ed] to take responsibility and
realized he could do most anything he wanted. . . . Last May when I
thanked Captain Beach for what he had done for me, he said, "Don't
thank me, you did it, and I thank you for your service." I was a little
stunned him thanking me. I never did anything that could remotely
compare to his contribution. But his saying that goes to show what a
fantastic man and leader of men he was.

Mike Hemming, shipmate, c. 2002

No recruiting program roped in adventurous young lads and hauled
them off to Sub School like Beach's books. He got me . . . a gift, I once
had the opportunity to thank him for. . . . Capt. Beach, if you had not
passed this way, a lot of us would have never worn faded dungarees and
hydraulic oil-stained raghats and gone to sea in submersible scrap yard
cheaters . . . missing what for many of us were by far the best times of

our lives. Tell me, how in the hell do you thank a man for that? I hope that wherever he is, he understands. . . . Did anyone pipe . . . TRITON, DEPARTING? They damn well should have.

Robert "DEX" Armstrong, shipmate, c. 2002

Now he's gone. Or is he? It's a custom in the U.S. Navy to name its warships for those who have graced the uniform with their service. So, one can hope, in not too long a time, there will be a USS *Beach* carrying our battle ensign around the world, and Ned will again be at sea, looking after the nation he served so well in life. Fair winds, Skipper.

Tom Clancy, c. 2002

Bill the Goat Statue

The Goat is old & gnarly & he's never been to school,
But He can take the bacon from the worn out Army mule;
He's got no education, but he's brimmin' full o' fight,
And Bill will feed on Army mule tonight!

"The Goat Is Old and Gnarly," Naval Academy fight song

Bill the Goat (Randell Hunt "Doc" Prothro and Gustav F. "Gus" Swainson Jr.)

A fierce bronze "Bill the Goat" lunges forward in "attitude rampant" in front of Lejeune Hall near Gate 1. Created by Clemente Spampinato (1912–93), an Italian-born artist known for his spirited sculptures of dancers, golfers, and other athletes, the sculpture was presented in 1957 by the Class of 1915 as a tribute to the Naval Academy mascot. One legend suggests that the goat was chosen as the Navy mascot owing to the tradition of keeping goats aboard ship as pets (as well as for milk, garbage disposal, and meat). One of the earliest Navy goats to serve as mascot at the Army-Navy game was acquired from an Army enlisted man's yard as the midshipmen marched to the field.

Another early goat that served as mascot was El Cid, the pet goat aboard USS *New York*. El Cid was brought to Annapolis for the game by the ship's crew. Navy won that game—thanks, according to midshipmen lore, to the goat. El Cid, the first named Navy mascot, was pictured in a sketch in the first Academy yearbook, *Lucky Bag*, in 1894. Nowdays the goats are all named "Bill." An early Bill (originally Bill IV) was nicknamed "3 to 0 Jack Dalton" after Midn. John Patrick "Jack" Dalton, who kicked field goals to win the game over Army two years in a row. 3 to 0 Jack Dalton died in 1912 but still resides in Halsey Field House, stuffed and in fighting posture. During most home games and the annual Army-Navy game, a live goat is paraded around the field.

The bronze sculpture of Bill the Goat, which has been displayed at the Naval Academy since 1957, endures riding, polishing, and "annual ritualized graffiti" every year during Army-Navy Week.

The Story of the Goat

On their march from the ferry station at Highland Falls up the steep hill to West Point to play the first Army-Navy football game, the naval cadets (as they were then known) saw a goat outside the noncoms' houses at West Point and promptly commandeered "Billy" for their mascot.

Monument plaque

Dedication

As each team strives for excellence on the field of competition may a higher degree of appreciation and mutual respect evolve between our nation's future leaders.

Monument plaque

～✦～

Golden Goat

Once sailors' companion,
Now Navy's mascot,
Bill the Goat's paraded proudly
In the yearly football rivalry
With Army.

From his pedestal in the Yard,
In attitude charging rampant
And with jewels of polished gold,
He lunges toward attack.
Nothing can get this goat.

Max Bishop Stadium

(With FitzGerald Clubhouse and Terwilliger Brothers Field)

Max Bishop Stadium (Randell Hunt "Doc" Prothro and Gustav F. "Gus" Swainson Jr.)

aseball, one of the first sports at the Academy, was introduced in 1867 under Superintendent Rear Adm. David Dixon Porter. The Academy's Max Bishop Stadium, located in the Lawrence Field baseball complex, is a premier collegiate baseball facility. Built in 1962 and renovated in 2007, it boasts chairback stadium seating and a state-of-the-art FieldTurf playing surface. The newly renovated playing field is named Terwilliger Brothers Field for three brothers—Jackson Ronald "Ron"

(USNA 1963), Bruce (USNA 1964), and George (USNA 1969)—all of whom were baseball players at USNA. The FitzGerald Clubhouse, named for William H. G. FitzGerald (USNA 1931), ambassador to Ireland under President George H. W. Bush, holds locker rooms, a training room, a press box, coaches offices, and a museum-style display area.

Quotation about the Terwilliger Brothers

[The abilities of Ron and Bruce Terwilliger in baseball and basketball] made a brother team that will long be remembered in the annals of USNA athletics.

Lucky Bag, 1964

Quotation about FitzGerald

Here is a man whose idiosyncrasies are as numerous as his talents. To explain: Supposing you forget such a thing as your laundry number, class standing or even Plebe Year multiple. Don't worry, just ask Fitz and if he doesn't come down with it to five places, we miss our guess. Athletically our hero stands up with the best of them. . . . [I]n spring go across to Lawrence Field where you will find him operating on baseballs like a professional.

Lucky Bag, 1931

Max Frederick Bishop (1899–1962)

Bishop stadium is named after USNA coach and Major League second baseman Max Frederick Bishop. Bishop, a superb leadoff hitter, was nicknamed "Camera Eye" and "Eagle Eye" for his keen awareness of the strike zone and his ability to draw walks from pitchers, which in turn enabled the heavy sluggers to drive in runs. In the Major League, Bishop played with Connie Mack, one of baseball's all-time great managers. He helped take the Philadelphia Athletics to three World Series (in 1929, 1930, and 1931), two of which they won (1929 and 1930). Bishop's reputation as a ballplayer continues to rise, even seventy-plus years after his retirement from baseball: recent statistical analysis of his on-base percentage (OBP) has found that he was tied at thirteenth with Shoeless Joe Jackson for number of walks and was second only to Ted Williams, legendary for his "good eye," or knowledge of the strike zone. In his second outstanding career, as coach of the Academy baseball team from 1938 to 1962, Bishop compiled over three hundred wins and achieved a 24-2 record in his last season.

Quotation about Bishop

"Eagle Eye" Max, the unassuming star second baseman and lead-off man of the Athletics, is another of the Baltimore Alumni on the team. Bishop joined Jack Dunn's Orioles direct from Baltimore City College in 1918 and was purchased by Connie Mack in 1924. He is a master on the defense, but his greatest forte is his uncanny ability to judge a pitched ball. He averages over one hundred bases on balls per season and receives more unintentional passes than any player in the game. This year has been Max's greatest and his all-round play has recalled the days of [Eddie] Collins to many of the older fans.

Souvenir Program, 1931 World Series

Burial Site

Woodlawn Memorial Park, Baltimore, Maryland

Wesley Brown Field House

Wesley Brown Field House (Randell Hunt "Doc" Prothro and Gustav F. "Gus" Swainson Jr.)

The Wesley Brown Field House, built by the Hensel Phelps Construction Company, was completed in 2008 to house physical fitness and training facilities for varsity athletes and others. It sits between the seventh wing of Bancroft Hall and Santee Basin and boasts a full-length retractable Astroturf football field. A statue of Adm. William Lawrence stands in a plaza in front of the field house, facing a statue of Adm. James Stockdale across the road, in front of Luce.

The field house is named for Lt. Cdr. Wesley A. Brown (b. 1927), USNA 1949, the first African-American graduate of the Naval Academy and a twenty-year career officer in the Civil Engineering Corps. Brown attended Dunbar High School in the District of Columbia, where he served in the Cadet Corps as battalion commander and held an after-school job as a junior clerk in the Navy Department. He first enrolled at Howard University, but with an appointment in 1944 by New York congressman Adam Clayton Powell Jr. in 1945, Brown was able to pursue his dream of attending the Academy. While in the Navy, he built Navy housing in Hawaii, roads in Liberia, wharves in the Philippines, a nuclear power plant in Antarctica, and a desalinization plant in Guantanamo, Cuba. After his Navy career, Brown joined the staff at Howard as a physical facilities analyst. He is a motivational speaker for D.C.-area high schools and the Black Studies Club at the Academy.

Midn. Wesley A. Brown, 1949 (Special Collections and Archives, Nimitz Library)

Brown Quotation

We had more to do [during plebe year] than there were hours in the day. We ran to formation, learned customs and regulations, memorized "can's" and "can'ts" until our eyes popped. We shot on the rifle range, sailed, rowed, tied knots, practiced semaphore and blinking and soaked up salt from the seamanship chiefs. We drilled, drilled, drilled until the bottoms of our feet had half-inch calluses. . . .

I was no angel, broke my share of regulations. When I got in hot water I kept reminding myself, "Brown, you're in trouble because you're a dumb cluck and have made a mistake. You're getting the same treatment as your classmates, and that's how it should be." . . . All through my years at the Naval Academy my instructors treated me impartially. I never received special attention, either positive or negative. It was a lesson in democracy which many institutions could imitate.

"The First Negro Graduate of the Naval Academy,"
Saturday Evening Post, 1947

Quotations about Brown

The future seems very bright for Wes today, and with determination, courage, and high purpose he will shape a well-deserved career.

Lucky Bag, 1949

❧

Fifty years on, integration in America seems to many Americans to have been inevitable, or to have been the work of giants like Martin Luther King Jr. or Rosa Parks. Yet it was also the work of little-known heroes at individual institutions, people like Wesley Brown who wanted to serve their country alongside their fellow Americans and whose example inspires us in the struggle for freedom to this day.

Editorial in the *New York Sun*, March 27, 2006

Buchanan House

Buchanan House (Randell Hunt "Doc" Prothro and Gustav F. "Gus" Swainson Jr.)

Buchanan House, first known as the Superintendent's House, was designed by Ernest Flagg in the early 1900s as the third official residence of the Naval Academy superintendent. The federal government had purchased the first official residence, Dulany House (c. 1750), from the Dulany family to become part of the newly established Fort

Severn. It functioned as quarters for the commandant until Fort Severn's transfer to the Navy Department in 1845, when Dulany House became the home of the Academy's first superintendent, Cdr. Franklin Buchanan.

These quarters were demolished in 1883–84 to be replaced by the second superintendent quarters, a large redbrick Queen Anne revival, completed in 1886. Within twenty years, this residence was also demolished as part of Flagg's plan for the new Academy.

After it was completed in 1906, the Superintendent's House was at first considered too grand for a residence and was used for other purposes. But since 1909 it has served, as originally intended, as the quarters of the Naval Academy's superintendent. It functions both as a private residence, with the two upper floors reserved as private quarters and guest bedrooms, and as a public meeting area, with its two lower floors offering a formal parlor and dining room, large enclosed porches, and an open porch overlooking the garden. Receptions for graduating students and their families are held in the garden each spring during Commissioning Week. Buchanan House has also hosted presidents, kings, queens, admirals, and distinguished visitors from many countries. Located throughout the thirty-four rooms are historical objects such as the desk of Capt.

Superintendent's Quarters, c. 1876 (U.S. Naval Institute Photo Archive)

Samuel Chester Reid, who drafted the design for the number of stripes on the American flag, and works of marine art such as John C. Schetky's oil painting, *The Battle of Trafalgar, October 21, 1805.* The Franklin D. Roosevelt Head, or bathroom, was built on the main floor especially for President Roosevelt, a frequent visitor, who often boarded ships at Annapolis for travel to distant ports. (Although he had experienced airplane rides from the Naval Aerodrome on Greenbury Point in Annapolis, Roosevelt preferred ocean travel).

Buchanan House was named in 1976 after Cmdr. Franklin Buchanan (1800–1874), the Academy's first superintendent, from 1845–47. At the time of his appointment by Navy Secretary Bancroft to the newly established Naval School, Commander Buchanan had completed thirty years of naval service. His initial midshipman cruise in 1815 aboard the frigate *Java*, commanded by Oliver Hazard Perry, was followed by cruises on every ocean in the world and on every class of ship in the American Navy. Buchanan's technical competence and attention to duty and discipline helped make him a model superintendent.

His U.S. naval career ended early when he resigned in 1861 and transferred his loyalty to the Confederacy, becoming one of its greatest naval officers. The battle of CSS *Virginia*, under Buchanan's command, against a federal fleet of wooden ships in Hampton Roads, Virginia, on March 8, 1862, was the deadliest naval battle in the Civil War. When Buchanan was incapacitated by injuries, Lt. Catesby ap Roger Jones took over command against the ironclad USS *Monitor*—the ship that signaled the end of the era of wooden ships in the Navy. (In that same battle in Hampton Roads, Buchanan's brother, Paymaster McKean Buchanan, was an officer aboard USS *Congress*.)

In the famous Battle of Mobile Bay on August 5, 1864, Buchanan fought aggressively against Adm. David Farragut, surrendering only after being rammed by USS *Monongahela* and then USS *Lackawanna*. Buchanan was taken prisoner and exchanged and returned to Richmond in March 1865. In 1868 Buchanan became president of the Maryland Agricultural College (founded 1856, the precursor to the University of Maryland) but resigned when it was discovered that the college was in debt. He died at his family home near Easton, Maryland, on May 11, 1874.

Franklin Buchanan (Special Collections and Archives Division, Nimitz Library, U.S. Naval Academy)

Buchanan Quotations

The Govt, in affording you the opportunity of acquiring an education, so important to the accomplishment of a naval officer, has bestowed upon you all an incalculable benefit. But few if any now in the service have had the advantages that you are about to receive. The Regulations of the Navy require you to pass through a severe ordeal, before you can be promoted; you must undergo an examination on all the branches taught at the Naval School before you are eligible to a Lieutenancy; your morals and general character are strictly enquired into, it is therefore expected that you will improve every leisure moment in the acquirement of a knowledge of your profession, and you will recollect that a good moral character is essential to your promotion and high standing in the Navy. By carefully avoiding the first step towards intemperance, shunning the Society of the dissolute and idle, and by cherishing the wish to deserve and the hope of receiving the approbation of your country, you can alone render yourself able to öccupy with honor the high standing in the Navy to which many of you are destined.

Opening Address, Naval School, October 10, 1845

Go to your guns!

Order for battle, CSS *Virginia* v. USS *Cumberland*,
Hampton Roads, Virginia, March 8, 1862

Plug hot shot into her and don't leave her until she's afire!

Order to Lt. Catesby ap Roger Jones to fire on USS *Congress*,
Hampton Roads, March 8, 1862

Quotations about Buchanan

The veteran soldier, the beau ideal of a naval officer of the old school, with his tall form, harsh features, and clear piercing eyes, was pacing the deck with a stride I found difficult to match although he was then over sixty and I but twenty-four.

Lt. H. Ashton Ramsey, Chief Engineer, CSS *Virginia*,
February 10, 1912

⟿⟾

Admiral Franklin Buchanan, late of the confederate navy, and for many years a distinguished officer of the United States navy, died on Tuesday at his residence in Talbot county, Maryland.

The Daily Constitution, Talbot, Maryland, May 15, 1874

Burial Site

Wye House Cemetery, Talbot County, Maryland

The Cemetery

A world of peace populated by men of war.

John Sherwood, "Among the Stones of Strawberry Hill,"
c. 1868

Cemetery (Randell Hunt "Doc" Prothro and Gustav F. "Gus" Swainson Jr.)

On grassy knolls where heroes rest,
The sun shines down on patriots.
Rising from the hallowed ground,
Pride and patriotism fill the air,
The souls of heroes enlightening us
And generations still to come.

Jeffrey Lenar, USNA 2010

The Naval Academy Cemetery, on a wooded peninsula overlooking the confluence of College Creek and the Severn River, serves as the final resting place for legendary Navy heroes as well as midshipmen, faculty, unnamed infants, and even a nineteenth-century blacksmith. Those buried there include most of the enlisted ranks, all of the Navy officer ranks, most of the Marine Corps ranks, and even a few Army and Air Force ranks. There are a few Academy faculty members buried there as well. The cemetery also holds monuments that commemorate the lives of those who died for their country but are buried elsewhere, such as the members of the *Jeannette* Arctic Expedition of 1879–81 and the Americans who died in the Battle of Veracruz during the Mexican War. The cemetery's history dates to 1868, when, as part of expansion efforts after the Civil War, Superintendent David Dixon Porter purchased a sixty-seven-acre tract known as Strawberry Hill from the Reese family of Annapolis. Part of the land was immediately designated for the Naval Academy Cemetery and part for a park.

> On a high point of land in this last purchase, has been laid out a Cemetery for the burial of Officers and Seamen and others belonging to the Navy. Beyond the cemetery there is a handsome Park. The park and cemetery consist of alternate wood and lawn, with considerable diversity of level. Winding woods and paths have been laid out in very tasteful manner, making all parts accessible. So attractive are these two places that although the improvements are scarcely yet begun, they have become a very favorite resort for the people in the vicinity, a large number of persons visiting each, every pleasant day.
>
> *Lt. Cdr. Edward P. Lull, Description and History of the U.S. Naval Academy from Its Origin to the Present Time, 1869*

At the foot of the Academy cemetery, nestled between the sacred hills guarding the graves, lies the Naval Academy Columbarium. Row upon row of marble tablets bear the names of our institution's graduates claimed by the ocean deep. While the endless names of these silent lost souls speak volumes about sacrifice and honor, even more striking are the many plaques that hold no names. These heartless scrolls silently await the day that the names of young men and women will be inscribed in them: men and women who walk the very halls that I walk, who know the same world that I know. So many young scholars, eager for the chance to serve their country, unaware that their names will soon adorn those empty walls.

Richard M. Pescatore, USNA 2009

The white marble columbarium, situated on the shore of College Creek, was constructed in 1987 by the Naval Academy Alumni Association, with funding from alumni family and friends, including a major bequest by the George and Carol Olmstead Foundation in memory of Jerauld L. Olmstead, Class of 1922. The columbarium provides a resting

Columbarium (Randell Hunt "Doc" Prothro and Gustav F. "Gus" Swainson Jr.)

place in individual niches for alumni and others who want to be inurned at the Academy. The Class of 1937 Columbarium Dedication Panel honors all U.S. Naval Academy graduates whose burial places are unknown.

> Here we remember our shipmates whose resting places are known only to God. Their bodies have been left in the seas or in remote places but their spirit lives with us always. Let this sacred place serve as the symbolic grave stone of our comrades who, going forth from the U.S. Naval Academy to serve God and country, have given their lives beyond the opportunity for burial in known graves.

Class of 1937 Dedication Panel

❦

Headstones

Beneath tall oaks above the tide
Lion and lamb together lie,

Seasoned warrior, death-defying,
Innocent child, surprised by life.

Midshipmen, on the fields of play
Below these monuments of stone,

Consider all these resting here
Guides for who you might become.

Selected Notable Monuments (in Alphabetical Order)

ADM. ARLEIGH A. BURKE (1901–96), USNA 1923

During his forty-two years in the Navy, Admiral Burke served in World War II and the Korean War and, from 1955 to 1961, as chief of naval operations. As a commander of a destroyer squadron in World War II, he earned the nickname "Thirty-One-Knot Burke," a popular recognition of his hard-charging nature, coined after a boiler accident limited Burke, accustomed to pushing his destroyers to high speed, to a mere thirty-one knots. The monument engraving depicts USS *Arleigh Burke* (DDG-51), the first in a class of guided missile destroyers named for Admiral Burke.

The burial site, across from the two sailors who drowned in 1852 during training on USS *Preble*, is especially appropriate.

Epitaph: *Sailor.*

CDR. WILLIAM BARKER CUSHING (1842–74)

The grave of William Cushing, a naval officer described by Secretary of the Navy Gideon Welles as "the hero of the [Civil] War," is marked by a prominent monument overlooking the Severn River. Cushing, who had attended the Academy from 1857 to 1861, had been forced to resign because of his low grades and poor conduct. However, with the help of his friend Charles W. Flusser, USNA 1853, he managed to secure a commission in the Navy and soon became known as a fearless fighter. When Flusser was killed in battle with CSS *Albemarle*, Cushing destroyed *Albemarle* in one of the war's most daring acts: on the night of October 27–28, 1864, he and his men rammed the spar-torpedo from their steam launch, Picket Boat Number One, into the ironclad, sinking it. The graves of Cdr. Charles W. Flusser and Lt. Samuel W. Preston, USNA 1862, who was killed at Fort Fisher while standing next to Cushing, are located near Cushing's grave, an arrangement that Cushing may have in fact designed.

The Destruction of CSS *Albemarle*

I have the honor to report that the rebel ironclad *Albemarle* is at the bottom of the Roanoke River. On the night of the 27th, having prepared my steam launch, I proceeded up toward Plymouth with 13 officers and men, partly volunteers from the squadron. . . .

Passing her closely, we made a complete circle so as to strike her fairly, and went into her bows on. By this time the enemy's fire was fairly severe, but a dose of canister at short range served to moderate their zeal and disturb their aim. Paymaster Swan, of the *Otsego*, was wounded near me, but how many more I know not. Three bullets struck my clothing, and the air seemed full of them.

In a moment we had struck the logs, just abreast of the quarter port, breasting them in some feet, and our bows resting on them. The torpedo boom was then lowered and by a vigorous pull I succeeded in diving the torpedo under the overhang and exploding it at the same time that the *Albemarle*'s gun was fired. A shot seemed to go crashing through my boat, and a dense mass of water rushed in from the torpedo, filling the launch and completely disabling her.

The enemy then continued his fire at 15 feet range, and demanded our surrender, which I twice refused, ordering the men to save themselves, and removing my own coat and shoes. Springing into the river, I swam, with others, into the middle of the stream, the rebels failing to hit us. . . . Completely exhausted, I managed to reach the shore, but was too weak to crawl out of the water until just at daylight, when I managed to creep into the swamp, close to the fort. While hiding a few feet from the path, two of the *Albemarle*'s officers passed, and I judged from their conversation that the ship was destroyed.

Lieutenant Cushing, October 30, 1864

Rear Adm. John Halligan (1876–1934)

Halligan Hall, originally the Marine barracks, was named for John Halligan, USNA 1898, the first director of the Naval Postgraduate School, established in 1913 at the Academy. After his graduation from the Academy, Halligan participated in the Spanish-American War aboard the *Brooklyn*. During World War I he served as chief of staff to the commander of the U.S. naval forces in France. In 1925 he was appointed chief, Bureau of Engineering, and in 1930, assistant chief of naval operations. He died while serving as commandant of the Thirteenth Naval District, in Washington state. The Naval Postgraduate School was officially moved to Monterey, California, in 1951.

Huron Monument

This is a commemorative stone marker surrounded by smaller gravestones of individual men aboard USS *Huron*, a sloop-rigged steamer, when it was wrecked in a storm off Nag's Head, North Carolina, on November 24, 1877.

Jeannette Arctic Expedition Monument (see also the *Jeannette* Monument entry)

This memorial, modeled on the original grave of Capt. George Washington De Long, USNA 1865, and other crew members of USS *Jeannette*, honors the members of the 1879–81 expedition to the Arctic. Their remains were recovered from the Arctic, brought home, and reburied in Woodlawn Cemetery in the Bronx, New York.

REAR ADM. CHARLES TURNER JOY (1895–1956), USNA 1916

As commander of a cruiser division, C. Turner Joy saw fierce combat against the Japanese in World War II. During the Korean War, he served as commander, Naval Forces, Far East. In 1951 he served as the senior UN delegate to the Korean Armistice talks; in a comment on these talks, Joy described how "the field of combat was a long, narrow, green-beige covered table. The weapons were words." Vice Admiral Joy served as superintendent of the Academy from 1952 to 1954.

> Turner . . . does quite a few things with grace and agility, but never with ennui. . . . Naturally quiet and reserved, Turner is one of those fellows who, to use a time-worn expression of biographers, "is hard to know, but when you know him you cannot help but like him."
>
> *Lucky Bag*, 1916

FLEET ADM. ERNEST J. KING

King, chief of naval operations during World War II, is the only five-star admiral buried in the cemetery. (See also the King Hall entry.)

> I sit atop the hill at the Naval Academy Cemetery. Each stone has its own life, its own story. Even though most of these dead experienced the deafening sounds of battle, the silence in the cemetery is eerily peaceful. Signifying a young infant, an innocent Lamb of God lies atop one of the smaller headstones. Other bold monuments represent the great battlefield commanders now at rest underneath—men such as Fleet Adm. Ernest King, who distinguished himself in World War II as the commander in chief of U.S. naval operations and as the chief of naval operations. . . . I can't help but think about my own death and how I will be remembered. I wonder if I will pass as an elder into the good night, or in battle rage against the dying of the light.
>
> *Russell G. Cude*, USNA 2009

KRISTENSEN MONUMENT

A polished black granite family monument marks the future graves of Rear Adm. Edward Kristian Kristensen (b. 1941), USNA 1965, and his wife Suzanne Samsel Kristensen (b. 1941), and the resting place of their son, Lt. Cdr. Erik Samsel Kristensen (1975–2005), USNA 1995.

> Everything interested him: he was curious about all aspects of people and the world. . . . He was shaped to do something extraordinary with his life.
>
> *Michael P. Parker*, USNA professor

An English major at the Academy, Lieutenant Commander Kristensen returned to the Academy in 1999 to teach in the English Department. Trained as a Navy SEAL, he went on to serve in Afghanistan. Early in 2005 he was selected to participate in a two-year program at the Institute for Policy Studies in Paris beginning in the fall. But while leading a rescue mission with his SEAL unit on June 28, his helicopter was shot down, and he and the fifteen others aboard were killed. The epitaph on his gravestone is from "Chattanooga 1863," a poem by Herman Melville commemorating young Civil War dead:

> Quelled on the wing like eagles struck in air—
> Forever they slumber young and fair.

COMMO. ISAAC MAYO (1791–1861)

Commodore Mayo, one of the few people born in the eighteenth century who is buried in the cemetery, was awarded two congressional medals for his actions on USS *Hornet* and against HMS *Penguin* during the War of 1812. He served in June 1845 on the board of senior officers that recommended the first curriculum and the location of the Naval School in Annapolis (the countyseat of his native Anne Arundel County). Although he resigned from the U.S. Navy in 1861 because of the Civil War, as commander in chief, U.S. Naval Forces, West Coast Africa in 1853, Mayo had been diligent in attempting to stop the illegal slave trade. His widow commissioned the monument that now stands in the cemetery, in 1874, but there are no burial records for Mayo and it is uncertain whether his remains are actually interred here. The Mayo family home still stands in the town, south of Annapolis, bearing his name.

Report on Capture of Suspected Slave Trader H. N. Gambrill

I have the honor to report that on the morning of the 3rd of Novr., while near the African Shore, about Sixty Miles South of the river Congo, I fell in with the American Schooner *H. N. Gambrill*, of New York, and found on board of her the most unquestionable evidence of her being on the eve of receiving a cargo of slaves. I have therefore felt obliged to seize and send her home for trial. . . .

In this connection I beg leave to state my belief that, the Slave trade is reviving on this Southern Coast, and that the American flag is extensively used in its prosecution. Several cargoes of Slaves have been recently carried off in American Vessels, which having regular papers, defy the English cruisers, and hope to elude the vigilance of our Squadron, knowing it consists of only Three Vessels, serving on a coast of great extent, and dependent for provisions upon our depot at Porto Praya, in going to and from which much time is unavoidably consumed.

Information concerning the movements of all vessels of War, is carried along the Coast, by the Slave dealers, with wonderful celerity, and the Masters of the Slave vessels are provided with every expedient to avoid capture, by means of double sets of papers and flags, and every other device that experience and interest can suggest. I have become convinced that the large force concentrated in the *Constitution* might be much more advantageously distributed, at the same expense, in several smaller vessels.

Commodore Mayo, November 10, 1853

CAPT. ALFRED HART MILES (1883–1956), USNA 1907

Midshipman Miles wrote the original lyrics to "Anchors Aweigh." (See the Zimmerman Bandstand entry.)

THOMAS TAYLOR (C. 1829–52) AND JOSEPH WHIPPARD (C. 1829–52)

This stone is erected to the memory of Thomas Taylor by his classmates and shipmates as a token of their regard and friendship. He was drowned

on the night of the 21st of April 1852 from the US Sloop *Preble* in the
23rd year of his age and is buried here.

By the 1850s a summer training cruise had become a part of the regular program of instruction at the Academy. In 1851 USS *Preble*, a third-
class sailing sloop-of-war transferred to the Academy for use as a training
vessel, made its first Academy cruise to foreign ports when it sailed to
the West Indies and Madeira in the summer of 1852. As an officer later
noted, midshipmen "were not well cared for" aboard the training vessel,
an oversight perhaps leading to the 1852 deaths of Midshipmen Taylor
and another midshipman on the *Preble*, Joseph Whippard.

Battle of Veracruz Marker

A la memoria de los americanos que sugumbieron en esta forteleza el
ano de 1847 [To the memory of the Americans who died in this fortress
in the year 1847].

One of the oldest markers in the cemetery, and one of the few in a foreign language, this stone with its hand-carved Spanish inscription commemorates Americans lost in actions in Veracruz during the Mexican
War of 1846–48 (which had begun with an attack by the Mexicans on
American troops in Texas, partly as a response to the U.S. annexation
of Texas in 1845). The landing at Veracruz on March 9, 1847, the first
amphibious landing by joint U.S. forces, was followed by a siege and subsequent surrender of the city on March 29. Although few soldiers and
sailors died in the initial assault, many died after contracting yellow
fever. The marker, originally a memorial placed by Americans in the fort
at Veracruz, was removed by American forces in the Veracruz invasion
of 1914.

Charles A. Zimmerman (1862–1916)

Charles Zimmerman was a popular Academy bandmaster and the composer of "Anchors Aweigh." (See the Zimmerman Bandstand entry.)

ADM. ELMO R. ZUMWALT JR. (1920–2000), USNA 1943 (GRADUATING 1942)

Admiral Zumwalt served in World War II and the Korean War; as commander of U.S. Naval Forces and chief, Naval Advisory Group, in Vietnam from 1968 to 1970; and as chief of naval operations from 1970 to 1974. He initiated wide-ranging reforms of the Navy, ordering the end of racial and sexual discrimination and of demeaning restrictions on sailors. President Bill Clinton, who called Zumwalt "One of the greatest models of integrity, leadership and genuine humanity our nation has ever produced," awarded him the Presidential Medal of Freedom in 1998.

Epitaph: *Reformer.*

From a distance, the water, home to a myriad of fish, crabs, and million dollar boats, beautifully and slowly crashes against the concrete sea wall. In sharp contrast with the living, bustling, and chaotic water, the cemetery looms in the distance. The bodies and ashen remains there are kept neat and orderly. Nothing moves except the water and the passing of time.

1/C, USNA 2007

The Chapel and Crypt

Chapel (U.S. Naval Institute Photo Archive)

A shrine, ivy-covered and gold-domed . . . the glorification of . . .
faith . . . the sepulcher of the famed John Paul Jones.

Lucky Bag, 1929

The Chapel

The Chapel holds a special interest for me. During the day while I am walking to and from class, it is a reminder of the Lord and His glory. I think that it was strategically placed where it is to help midshipmen remember the Lord when their minds may be elsewhere. During the weekend, my main priority is to go to church. It is difficult at times to get up and take an hour out of my busy schedule, but I do my best to go.

Plebe, USNA 2003

The Chapel's green copper dome with gold spire, visible not only across the Yard but from beyond the Academy walls and across the water, is the first sight that midshipmen returning from their youngster cruises have of the Academy. The words above the Chapel's door, *Non Sibi Sed Patriae* (not self but country) are reminders for all who enter of the sacrifices made by the men and women of the naval service.

The Chapel serves as the landmark by which everything is found on the Yard, and it is also distinguished as a place of transition. Seeing the Chapel on Induction Day, a midshipman realizes that he or she will be forever changed; spotting the copper dome when returned from YP cruise signifies the awaited transition from a mere plebe to a finally recognized youngster. . . . A place of both joy and sadness, it serves as a reminder that, although the trials of life at the Naval Academy may seem to be the most important thing at the moment, we are still the people of a greater Being, whose plan for us is bigger than any paper or test that may challenge us now and whose strength can carry us through those difficult times.

Plebe

The present Chapel, a modification of Ernest Flagg's chapel, was dedicated in 1908 and is the third chapel at the Academy. The first chapel, designed in Greek revival style with Ionic columns, was completed in 1854. After the Civil War this building became the Lyceum, or museum, and in 1873 the home of the new U.S. Naval Institute. In 1902, when the Flagg plan for extending and modernizing the Academy was developed, it was torn down. A second structure built as a chapel in 1868, a redbrick Victorian Gothic church with a steeple, was also torn down at that time. Flagg's new Chapel, in the form of a Greek cross with four wings of experimental ferroconcrete material, was modeled on the seventeenth-century dome of the Hôtel des Invalides in Paris, a home for disabled veterans to which Napoleon's tomb was added in 1840. As the "architectural crown" of Flagg's grand Academy design, it was erected on the highest land in the Yard, and Admiral of the Navy George Dewey laid the cornerstone in June 1904. The ornate bronze double doors, designed by sculptor Evelyn Longman, were presented in 1909 by Robert Means Thompson in memory of his class of 1868. In 1939–40 the Chapel was expanded to accommodate a growing brigade, following the design of Paul Philippe Cret (1876–1945), a well-known French-American architect of several major buildings in Washington, D.C. He extended an arm of the Chapel, changing the shape to a Latin cross. When the extension was dedicated in 1940, two massive anchors, one dated 1914, were placed to flank the Chapel steps.

> Not for self alone
> do we exist
> proclaim the doors
> opening to chapelled dark.
>
> Here stone silence
> and high arched spaces
> cleanse mind and soul
> of insignificance.
>
> Symbol of commerce
> between two worlds,
> a model fifteenth-century carrack
> sails off with prayers
>
> for those in peril
> on land or sea or in air.

During daylight hours, the Chapel's interior is suffused with a bluish glow, from light filtered through blue glass windows. Other stained

Chapel interior (Randell Hunt "Doc" Prothro and Gustav F. "Gus" Swainson Jr.)

glass windows, including several large ones, add to the Chapel's grandeur. Frederick Wilson (1858–1932), who worked at both Tiffany Studio and Gorham, designed four windows: the Porter window, presented as a memorial to Adm. David Dixon Porter by the Class of 1869 (see the Porter Road entry); the Sampson window, commemorating Rear Adm. William T. Sampson, most famous for his victory over the Spanish fleet in the Battle of Santiago in 1898 (see the Sampson Hall entry), a 1909 gift of naval officers and enlisted men; the Sir Galahad window of a knight in armor ready to serve his country, a memorial to Lt. Cdr. Theodorus Bailey Myer Mason (1848–99), USNA 1868; and the Farragut window, honoring Adm. David Farragut, with the lower half depicting his dramatic act of lashing himself to the mast of USS *Hartford* during the Battle of Mobile Bay in 1864 and the upper section depicting the four-star blue flag of a U.S. admiral in recognition of Farragut's achievement in being the first naval officer to advance through all the flag ranks (see the Farragut Field entry). The 1928 "Commission Invisible" window of a young graduate in white ensign's uniform, a gift of the Class of 1927, honors graduates who "in war and peace have realized [the] ideals of honor, courage, loyalty, and duty, in the service of God and country."

Suspended from the arch of the nave near the main entrance, a votive ship for carrying prayers, modeled after a fifteenth-century Flemish carrack, reflects the tradition of hanging a ship model in a temple or church frequented by sailors. Downstairs from the main chapel are St. Andrew's Chapel and the Crypt of John Paul Jones.

Votive ship in Chapel (Randell Hunt "Doc" Prothro and Gustav F. "Gus" Swainson Jr.)

The Chapel not only gives rejuvenation but also offers refuge. . . .
Simply sitting in its sacred spaces and looking up at its hallowed arches
allows a complete calm and serenity to settle upon the mind. At that
time nothing else matters; nervousness and anxiety from the hectic life
outside fade away.

Plebe

The Crypt of John Paul Jones

Under the Chapel of the Academy
Protected by roving guards,
He lives in death as he did in life—
Within view, beyond reach, like the stars.

Kyle R. Vandegriff, USNA 2006

Located beneath the Chapel is the crypt of one of the Navy's first heroes,
John Paul Jones (1747–92), who, as the floor plaque at the head of the
sarcophagus states, "gave Our navy its earliest traditions of heroism and
victory." Born in Scotland, John Paul left his home at age thirteen to
follow the sea, signing on as an indentured seaman-apprentice to a ship

bound for the New World. In the tradition of shipboard education, Jones studied navigation, French, naval history, and social etiquette. After killing the ringleader of an attempted mutiny in Tabago in 1773, he fled to Virginia and adopted the New World as his home.

In 1775, with rebellion against England mounting, Jones joined the Continental Navy and was commissioned a first lieutenant. His daring raids along the coast as he circumnavigated the British Isles made him a hero to his men and a celebrity to the French allies. Although Britain possessed the most powerful navy of the time, Jones attacked the British vessels with his single ship, *Ranger*. On February 14, 1778, when Jones entered French waters on *Ranger*, flying the newly adopted U.S. flag, he saluted the French admiral's flagship with a nine-gun salute, to which the French responded in kind, recognizing for the first time that the Stars and Stripes represented an independent nation. Continuing to wage war against English merchant trade and the British Navy, Jones entered the Irish Sea, where no enemy had ventured in over one hundred years. Later, in command of *Bonhomme Richard*, Jones and his squadron captured fifteen merchant ships and defeated HMS *Serapis* in a

Crypt of John Paul Jones (Randell Hunt "Doc" Prothro and Gustav F. "Gus" Swainson Jr.)

John Paul Jones, oil portrait (U.S. Naval Institute Photo Archive)

battle off Flamborough Head. In 1783, when the Treaty of Paris brought the war to an end, the Continental Navy was disbanded, ending Jones' career with the American Navy.

Jones then joined the Russian Imperial Navy, where he was commissioned as a rear admiral. Although he fought brilliantly, his efforts were undercut by political intrigue. In poor health, he moved to Paris where, in June 1792, he was appointed by President Washington to negotiate with the Dey of Algiers. However, Jones died (at age forty-five) before he received this commission and was buried in St. Louis Cemetery for foreign-born Protestants. Four years later, during the French Revolution, the cemetery was sold and almost forgotten, as was John Paul Jones. A century later President Theodore Roosevelt appointed Gen. Horace Porter, the U.S. ambassador in Paris, to begin a search for Jones' remains. In April 1905 they were discovered in the cemetery, and preparations were made for their repatriation to America and the Naval Academy. An elaborate memorial service was held in Paris on July 6, 1905, the 158th anniversary of his birth, and then his casket was transferred to USS *Brooklyn*. Another service was held upon the arrival of the remains in Annapolis on July 24, 1905, after which Jones' casket was placed in a temporary vault across from the new Chapel, which was then under construction.

On April 24, 1906, the anniversary of *Ranger*'s defeat of HMS *Drake* in the Irish Sea, a commemoration was held in the new Armory (now Dahlgren Hall), with speeches by President Theodore Roosevelt, French ambassador J. J. Jusserand, Maryland governor Edwin Warfield, and Ambassador Horace Porter. Following this ceremony, Jones' casket lay in state for seven years in Bancroft Hall while the Chapel and crypt were being completed. An irreverent ditty depicts Jones at this time:

> Everybody works but John Paul Jones!
>   He lies around all day,
> Body pickled in alcohol
>   On a permanent jag, they say.
> Middies stand around him
>   Doing honor to his bones;
> Everybody works in "Crabtown"
>   But John Paul Jones!

On January 26, 1913, Jones' remains were placed in the crypt, in a sarcophagus of black and white Pyrenees marble, a gift from the French government, where they have rested now for nearly one hundred years.

The circular crypt, designed by Whitney Warren (1864–1943), offers a calm, meditative space. The central sarcophagus, sculpted by the French artist Sylvain Salieres (1865–1918), who also sculpted portrait busts of George Washington, Ben Franklin, and Voltaire, is surrounded by eight black and white marble columns that form an octagon around the sunken marble floor. Inscribed in bronze letters on the floor are the names of the ships commanded by Jones during the Revolutionary War: *Serapis, Alliance, Alfred, Bonhomme Richard, Ariel, Providence,* and *Ranger.* Placed between the surrounding columns are replicas of flags used during Jones' time, including the Grand Union flag, the thirteen-star flag, and the flags flown by *Serapis* and *Alliance.* Circling the restricted sunken area is an upper walkway and viewing area displaying memorabilia such as Jones' swords, medals, and commissions and a marble portrait bust by Jean-Antoine Houdon.

He gave our navy its earliest traditions of heroism and victory.
Erected by the Congress, A. D. 1912.

> Bronze floor inscription

❧

The Establishment of the U.S. Navy

The Commanders of all ships and vessels belonging to the THIRTEEN UNITED COLONIES are strictly required to shew in themselves a good example of honor and virtue to their officers and men, and to be very vigilant in inspecting the behaviour of all such as are under them, and to discountenance and suppress all dissolute, immoral and disorderly practices.

> *Rules for the Regulation of the Navy of the United Colonies of North-America,* November 28, 1775

John Paul Jones, Jean-Antoine Houdon bust (Randell Hunt "Doc" Prothro and Gustav F. "Gus" Swainson Jr.)

Jones Quotations

Without a Respectable Navy, Alas America!

Letter to Robert Morris, October 17, 1776

I have not yet begun to fight!

> Response to Capt. Richard Pearson, HMS *Serapis*,
> during battle with *Bonhomme Richard*,
> September 23, 1779, as recalled by Lt. Richard Dale

None other than a Gentleman, as well as a seaman, both in theory and practice is qualified to support the character of a Commissioned Officer in the Navy, nor is any man fit to command a Ship of War who is not also capable of communicating his Ideas on Paper in Language that becomes his Rank.

> Address to Marine Committee, January 21, 1777

I wish to have no Connection with any Ship that does not Sail fast for I intend to go in harm's way.

> Letter to le Ray de Chaumont, November 16, 1778

Leith and its port now Lays at our mercy; and did not the plea of humanity Stay the hand of Just retaliation I Should, Without advertisement, lay it in ashes. Before I proceed to that Stern duty as an officer; my Duty as a Man induces me to propose to you by the means of a reasonable ransome to prevent Such a Scene of horror and distress. For this reason I have authorised Lieutenant-Colonel De Chamillard to Conclude and agree With you on the terms of ransome, allowing you Exactly half an hour's reflection before you finally accept or reject the terms Which he Shall propose.

> Letter to the Provost of Leith, September 14, 1779

I have only time, my dear friends, to inform you, that I have this day anchored here, having take this ship in the night of the 23rd ult. on the coast of England, after a battle of three hours and a half; two hours and a half of that time the *Good Man Richard* and this ship [*Serapis*], being fast along side of one another, both ships being flames, and the *Good Man Richard* making water faster than all the pumps could deliver it. This ship mounts 44 guns, and has two entire batteries, one of them eighteen pounders, so that my situation was severe enough, to have to deal with such an enemy, in such a dreadful situation. Judge then, what it must have been when the *Alliance* came up, towards the close of the Action, and, instead of assisting me, directed her whole fire against the *Good Man Richard*, not once or twice, but repeatedly, after being spoken to, and shewing a private signal of recognition. The *Alliance* killed eleven men, and mortally wounded an officer on the *Good Man Richard*'s forecastle, at one volley. I have lost, in killed and wounded, the best part of my men. The *Good Man Richard* went to the bottom on the morning of the 25th ult. in spite of every effort to bring her into port. No action before was ever, in all respects, so bloody, so severe, and so lasting.

Letter to friends, October 3, 1779

Quotations about Jones

The board . . . find favorable mention is made of his abilities as an officer by the Duke de Vauguyon, M. de Sartine, and Dr. Franklin, and this is also corroborated by that valor and intrepidity with which he engaged his Britannic Majesty's ship, the *Serapis*, of forty-four cannon, twelve and eighteen pounders, which, after a severe contest for several hours, surrendered to his superior valour, thereby acquiring honour to himself and dignity to the American flag.

The board therefore humbly conceives that an honourable testimony should be given to Captain Paul Jones, commander of the *Bon Homme Richard*, his officers and crew, for their many singular services in annoying the enemy on the British coasts, and particularly for their spirited behaviour in an engagement with his Britannic Majesty's ship of war, the *Serapis*, on the 23rd of September, 1779, and obliging her to surrender to the American flag.

Admiralty Office Report, U.S. Congress, June 16, 1781

~e9~

On Monday morning, July 24 [1905], the body of America's greatest naval hero was transferred from the Brooklyn to the Naval Academy on the naval tug Standish amid the booming of guns fired in his honor by the American and French men-of-war. . . .

After the leaden coffin had been placed in a hearse, the cortege proceeded slowly, accompanied by the strains of a funeral dirge played by the Naval Academy band, to the front of the temporary vault, near the new Memorial Chapel, where Chaplain Clark read the burial service and offered prayer.

When the prayer had been concluded the French and American sailors who acted as body-bearers, carried the casket into the vault while the Naval Academy band played Chopin's Funeral March.

The pall-bearers then stepped back and saluted the dead hero, a squad of marines fired a volley over the vault and a bugler sounded taps, the strains of this exquisite tune dying out slowly, listened to by a large crowd of reverent spectators, who witnessed the ceremony in dead silence. It was a most solemn and impressive spectacle.

Professor H. Marian, eyewitness to ceremonies for John Paul Jones

~e9~

Every officer . . . should feel in each fiber of his being an eager desire to emulate the energy, the professional capacity, the indomitable determination and dauntless scorn of death which marked John Paul Jones above all his fellows.

President Theodore Roosevelt, Commemoration Address,
April 24, 1906

~e9~

Darkness surrounds everything, and the only lights are dim incandescent bulbs. Plaques and medals shine out from this light; they signify the greatness of the man who is laid to rest in this sacred area, this area of solemnity and silence. . . . The absence of light allows the mind to concentrate, without the usual bombardment of the senses, [on the man] who is the true exemplification of what it means to be a naval officer: courageous, intelligent, and headstrong.

Plebe

~~~

Here lies John Paul Jones
From olden days and times unknown
Here lies John Paul Jones
Remember the man
More than a man
But "Father of the Navy"
Who forged ahead and helped us win
Our freedom
Here lies John Paul Jones
Encased in stone
The one to never give up
No, not one to go so
Gentle into that good night
But one who would yell
"I have not yet begun to fight!"

<div align="center">Plebe, USNA 2007</div>

Chauvenet Hall

And then there was Naval Academy Mathematics. I say Naval Academy because it seemed all the math we learned could be applied directly or indirectly to some problem having to do with the Navy. . . . We learned algebra and complex numbers only to learn that they applied to electrical circuits; calculus, to Marine Engineering. . . . I was well on my way toward becoming versed in the science of being Navy . . . through and through.

Lucky Bag, 1953

Chauvenet Hall (Randell Hunt "Doc" Prothro and Gustav F. "Gus" Swainson Jr.)

The gray granite structures of the math-science complex, composing Chauvenet Hall (completed 1968) and Michelson Hall (completed 1969), designed by John Carl Warnecke and Associates, sit on the central Yard's eastern side. The two buildings are separated by Radford Terrace, allowing an open view of the Severn River from the Chapel steps.

Radford Fountain

Buzzing through my head are thoughts of running from class to class, screaming out the menu for breakfast, lunch, and dinner, and standing at attention for hours that seemed like days. In order to escape these thoughts, I begin my journey for a peaceful, silent, and relaxing moment. Walking through the hazy air of the young night, I reach deep down into the depths of my soul, reviewing the day's events to ensure I will not make the same mistakes again tomorrow. As I reach the top of the mountainous stairs, I absorb the soothing and gentle sound of flowing water. I know I've reached my journey's end when I feel the tiny particles of mist colliding with my skin. I am cooled by these particles and relaxed by the soothing sound of the fountain. As I stare into the streaming water, I realize there's no need to worry about yesterday, today, or tomorrow. Though the fountain is made of cold stone, I feel a peaceful tranquility. This fountain seems placed here especially for me at the U.S. Naval Academy.

Ryan P. Murtha, USNA 2010

Chauvenet Hall honors William Chauvenet (1820–70), world-renowned mathematician and one of seven original instructors on the faculty at the founding of the Naval School in 1845. In fact, it was largely through Chauvenet's efforts that the Naval Academy was established. First as instructor in math aboard USS *Mississippi* in 1840, when shipboard education was traditional, and then as head of the Philadelphia Naval Asylum in 1842, Chauvenet pushed for more adequate education of midshipmen. With George Bancroft he helped establish the Naval School in 1845, and as head of the Mathematics Department from 1842 to 1859, he strove to make the Academy the greatest institution of its kind in the world. In 1859 he accepted a position teaching mathematics at Washington University, where he became chancellor in 1862. Chauvenet's leadership was crucial in advancing mathematics and astronomy and in raising math instruction to the highest level. His textbooks, *The Treatise on Plane and Spherical Trigonometry* and *The Manual of Spherical and Practical Astronomy*, are internationally recognized classics, written, according to Chauvenet biographer William H. Roeuer, with "a power of expression and purity of language unexcelled in American scientific literature." Chauvenet Hall, named as it is for a faculty member, pays homage to the faculty's contributions to the Academy.

Chauvenet Quotation

The question—What shall we teach, and how shall we teach it?—when proposed in relation to a community, involves the whole question of life. What kind of lives shall we live? What shall be our aims, our occupations? What kind of beings shall we be?

Inaugural address as chancellor of Washington University,
St. Louis, Missouri, June 17, 1863

Quotations about Chauvenet

In his assiduous devotion to scientific studies he did not neglect the more elegant arts, but was a skillful musician, and possessed of great general culture and refinement of taste. In his social and moral relations he was marked by rare elevation and purity of character, and has left to the world a standard of excellence in every relation of life which few can hope to attain.

Thomas Sterry Hunt, Acting President,
American Association for the Advancement of Science

He, too, was one of nature's noblemen. He was not only a man of genius, but had improved his natural gifts by an intellectual and moral culture as rare, in the present day, as it is admirable.

William Greenleaf Eliot, Washington University

Professor William Chauvenet portrait (U.S. Naval Institute Photo Archive)

Burial Site

Bellefontaine Cemetery, St. Louis, Missouri

Robert Crown Sailing Center
(Including Santee Basin)

Helm's A-Lee

The sail whips across the foredeck
as the boat swings into the wind—
The line, ripped from its secure winch
Snakes through leads and blocks, around the shrouds
In a wild clamour of crackling sails . . .

D. L. Blackburn, Labyrinth, 1986

Robert Crown Sailing Center (Randell Hunt "Doc" Prothro and Gustav F. "Gus" Swainson Jr.)

T he Robert Crown Sailing Center on Santee Basin and the Severn River functions as the headquarters of the USNA sailing program. It was named for Capt. Robert Crown (1921–69), who graduated from Northwestern University on an NROTC scholarship in 1942 and was commissioned into service in World War II. After the war, Crown remained in the reserves, rising to the rank of captain. Later, as the president of the Navy League, a private organization that supports the Navy, he won two Navy Distinguished Public Service Awards. Following his death in a car accident, his family donated generously to the construction of a new sailing center for the Academy.

Burial Site

Unable to identify

> The Crown Center and all that it stands for have been my dream for several years now. I have always been a sailor, at home on the water. The boats bobbing peacefully in the basin and the halyards slapping lazily in the wind lift me from my surroundings. This building is not like the others—ominous stone giants that tower around me. It is my refuge. I look out over the green Severn and the Bay beyond and think of my summers spent relaxing on the family sailboat. Turning around, I see the great trophies, signs of the glorious past and promising future. Sailing has been a big part of the Academy's heritage. I am proud to take this place and become a part of its heritage while making it a part of my own.
>
> *Benjamin R. Hawbaker*, USNA 2003

The precursor to the Sailing Team was the Midshipman Boat Club, established in 1936 and headquartered in Santee Basin aboard *Reina Mercedes*, a Spanish naval ship captured during the Spanish-American War of 1898. Santee Basin was named for USS *Santee*, a ship moored at the basin from 1865 to 1912 that was used as a brig for midshipmen caught smoking or committing other infractions and as housing for enlisted personnel. *Reina Mercedes* also previously served as quarters for enlisted personnel assigned to the Academy and for the ship's commanding officer, who was responsible for all waterfront activity. Repair and maintenance of the sailboats was handled by Navy yards and local boat yards up until World War II, when wartime construction placed an overload on these repair facilities, forcing the Naval Academy Sailing Team to become self-supporting. In 1943 the North Severn boat basin and boat repair shop (officially, the U.S. Naval Small Craft Facility) was built to meet the demands of the growing sailing program.

Home Seas

Ships moored in the harbor
Snow-white sails stowed 'way
Ropes coiled and laid upon the decks
At home, at rest
Dauntless challengers easing against the lines
Their halyards whining, sighing
A gentle symphony in the evening light
Against the cleats, the lines creak and grind
As the bows dip and rise in ceaseless gentle rock
It almost seems that these boats dream
Pulling lightly, gently at the moorings as a hound
     would sprint in sleep
Imagining, wishing for, the rush of winds and the dash of waves
Already eager, even in sleep, to be off again; gone once more
Fearless seekers. Vigilant dashers.
Yearning for adventure, full life
Even as the sun sets, leaving their masts as black horns
     against the sky
I still hear them sighing against the lines
Bold spirits. Restless flirts.
At home only when gone to sea
At sea, in cradled sleep, back home

Ernest T. Jaramillo-Hanes, USNA 2006

In 1957 *Reina Mercedes* was decommissioned and sold for scrap, and a small one-story building was constructed on Santee Pier as substitute headquarters. When the bow of a wayward boat punctured and seriously damaged this temporary structure, a more permanent replacement was

Capt. Robert Crown, Crown Center plaque (Randell Hunt "Doc" Prothro and Gustav F. "Gus" Swainson Jr.)

called for, and the Crown Center, with major funding provided by the
Crown family, was the result. The Intercollegiate Sailing Hall of Fame,
headquartered in the Crown Center, displays trophies and other college
regatta memorabilia. A recent refurbishing was accomplished with a new
grant from the Crown family and major funding from the class of 1945.

> Wide to starboard
> the YP swings,
> part of the wind,
> part of the rolling tide.
>
> On Yard patrol
> The heart too
> Swells with pride,
> With the duty
> to protect and defend.

~≈≈~

Pirates on the Severn . . . was one of the highlights of my summer. My
roommate and I were prepared for war as we entered our small vessel
and set sail on the mighty Severn. The weather was perfect with high
temperatures and a strong breeze. Using our expert sailing techniques,
my partner and I navigated into the small armada already afloat. We
spotted our first victim alone on the horizon. "Hard-a-starboard!" I yelled
as we guided our craft toward our right side in order to face our target.
In a matter of minutes we executed a perfect hit-and-run maneuver that
left our victim capsized. However, unbeknown to my shipmate and me,
we were now being hunted by another vessel. As we sailed innocently
among the other boats, one suddenly steered our way. With no time to
counter the assault, we were left at the mercy of our aggressors. Before
we knew what hit us, my partner and I were floating aimlessly in the
Severn. From that point on, we realized that you can never turn your
back, or boat, on the enemy.

Tyler W. Forrest, USNA 2002

Dahlgren Hall

The steel-bright flashes of militant bayonets . . . a glittering
June Ball, flag-bedecked, cannon-dotted, music-laden . . .
Dahlgren Hall.

Lucky Bag, 1929

Dahlgren Hall (Randell Hunt "Doc" Prothro and Gustav F. "Gus" Swainson Jr.)

Dahlgren Doors

Lions roar
Above the doors—
Images of ferocity
The building once prepared
Midshipmen for—
Storehouse of munitions,
Training ground for the ordnance
Of war—

Floating
In the high-arched window,
The green image
Of the Chapel dome
Rises and falls
Like a ship at anchor,
In harbor, home.

The arched exterior windows and the vast open interior make Dahlgren Hall one of the most impressive buildings at the Academy. Construction on Dahlgren, the first building of Flagg's New Academy, began on March 28, 1899, and was completed March 7, 1903. Because it was located close to the Academy's original parade grounds, Dahlgren was ideally suited to be the Armory. On the upper level, midshipmen learned about weapons construction; on the open lower level, they trained in firearms and close-order drill. This spacious lower level could also be used as a ceremonial area, as it was for the commemoration of the return of John Paul Jones' remains in 1906 and other formal occasions such as Farewell Balls. The lower level is also the venue for the Ring Dance, which the 1945 *Lucky Bag* described as "next to graduation, perhaps the most important event in the life of a midshipman," where he receives the ring "that designates him a member of the great fraternity of seafaring men that have graduated from the United States Naval Academy." Graduation exercises were also held in Dahlgren Hall, from 1903 to 1956, with only a few exceptions.

Rear Adm. John A. Dahlgren, oil portrait (U.S. Naval Institute Photo Archive)

In the 1970s Dahlgren underwent a transformation into a student union: the upper level became a reception and informal meeting area, decorated with state flags, a seaplane suspended in the air, and a large replica of an old sailing ship-of-the-line; and the lower level became a cafeteria known as Drydock and a multipurpose space most often used as a basketball court or an ice rink. In 2007 the ice rink was rebuilt across the Severn on the Naval Station grounds in the new Brigade Sports Complex at Greenbury Point.

Ice Rink in Dahlgren

Swiftly striding, sliding, gliding
Beneath the starry lights.
Music playing; swaying, praying
Not to fall from any heights.
People cheering, sneering, fearing
The possibility of fights.
A mixture of feelings
This building bestows,
Not quite an escape,
Not quite repose.

Evan J. Miller, USNA 2006

In 1976 this newly renovated building received an award from the American Institute of Architects for the preservation of the original design of "unimpeded open space while changing the function from an armory to a student activities center." That same year the Department of Defense awarded its Most Outstanding Design award to the renovators of Dahlgren Hall for the "sensitive and outstanding example of adaptive use of an old building to a new contemporary use."

The Drydock is at all possible times filled with midshipmen. Here they find a pleasant escape from their dreary life in Bancroft and the tedious food in King Hall. Mids find themselves waiting in long lines to get a greasy burger, slice of pizza, or some Ben & Jerry's ice cream. . . . I often wait in line for pizza order 104 or so and try to catch some of *The Simpsons*. At the same time, I look around . . . and wonder what it was like to fire those massive Dahlgren guns. At moments like that, I realize what I have become a part of: a long tradition of military leaders who study the art of war along with English and physics.

Sandeep Dasgupta, USNA 2003

Hanging at Dahlgren's seaward end is a model of USS *Antietam*, the largest ship model at the Academy, originally exhibited at the U.S. Centennial Exposition in Philadelphia in 1876 and afterward sent to the Academy for training midshipmen "on the ropes." On the upper deck's landward end is a replica of the B1 Wright Brothers plane originally assembled in 1911 by naval aviator Lt. John Rodgers and midshipmen and flown by Rodgers the next day from Farragut Field; this was the first manned flight in Annapolis. This "aeroplane" and others became part of the flight operation conducted across the Severn at the aerodrome on Greenbury Point, the site of the first U.S. Naval Air Station, established in 1911 and used off and on through 1913.

Dahlgren Hall is named after Rear Adm. John A. Dahlgren (1809–70), an expert in ordnance and the inventor of the smoothbore and rifled cannons, standard armament on naval vessels from 1856 through the Civil War. The smoothbores, with their familiar soda-bottle shape, proved less likely than older guns to explode at the breach when fired, and the larger 11-inch guns also proved effective against the new iron-clad ships of the Civil War. The Confederacy captured many Dahlgren guns and used them in their own defense, and as commander of the blockade off Charleston, South Carolina, Dahlgren received as well as delivered fire from Dahlgren guns. In all, Rear Admiral Dahlgren served in the Navy for over forty-five years, from 1826, when he joined as a midshipman, to his service with ordnance at the Washington Navy Yard in 1847, through his tenure as chief of the Bureau of Ordnance in 1862, to his duty during the Civil War with the South Atlantic Blockading Squadron, to his death on July 12, 1870, while serving as the commander of the Washington Navy Yard. A bust of the admiral by Theodore Mills greets visitors to Dahlgren Hall in the Drydock foyer, and four Dahlgren guns, as well as two Dahlgren boat howitzers, populate the Yard.

> Through the dust and clouds of smoke
> Rings a shot in the dark of clattered hope
> With a barrel gun that explodes with fright
> On enemy sailors who cower in the night.
> Too many sailors had died in battles past,

Battles not won, until one ship had lost its mast
And as dawn approached with the sight of the sun
The fight was won because of Dahlgren's gun.

                                    Patrick J. Bray, USNA 2007

Dahlgren Quotations

The officer should wear his uniform without a stain.

                        Inscription, Mills sculpture, Dahlgren Hall

～❦～

[The captain] will determine and direct when two shot may be fired; when "quick firing" may be permitted; when small arms shall be distributed and loaded; when Boarders shall be called up, and when the ship shall assail an enemy.

[Calls for Assembling at Quarters—Drum Rolls].

1st. The ORDINARY BEAT, will be the call for INSPECTION at general quarters.

2nd. The ordinary Beat, followed by ONE ROLL—EXERCISE at general quarters, without powder.

3rd. The ordinary Beat, followed by two rolls,—ACTION; or EXERCISE AT GENERAL QUARTERS with powder, as though engaged in BATTLE.

                                    Ordnance Instructions, 1802

Burial Site

Laurel Hill Cemetery, Philadelphia, Pennsylvania

Sailor, Scientist, Scholar, Teacher, Author
The Father of Modern Naval Ordnance
His contribution to the design of naval ordnance and ship
construction revolutionized the navies of the world

                        Dedicatory plaque at Laurel Hill Cemetery, 1961

Dahlgren-rifled 30-pounder (Randell Hunt "Doc" Prothro and Gustav F. "Gus" Swainson Jr.)

Guns

On the sea-wall by the river
  Stand the guns of days of yore,
Guns accustomed to deliver
        Volleys with a lion's roar.
Now all useless, they are sitting
        Watching over Severn's side
And their hearts are cold as iron
        As the ships pass with the tide.
Unhappy bits of ornament,
        They know the race is run,
And the glories of the Dahlgrens
        Are the glories past and gone.

George Felix Howland, Labyrinth, 1924

Decatur Road

A gallanter fellow never stepped a quarterdeck—God bless him.

Washington Irving, letter to Henry Brevoort,
August 19,1815

Decatur Road (Randell Hunt "Doc" Prothro and Gustav F. "Gus" Swainson Jr.)

Decatur Road, running between Preble and Sampson halls and alongside Alumni Hall, is named for Commo. Stephen Decatur (1779–1820), who helped define the U.S. Navy's role from its earliest days. He was the son of Stephen Decatur, who commanded privateers during the American Revolution and served as captain from 1789–1801 in the new U.S. Navy. In the 1803–5 Barbary War off Tripoli, Decatur boarded and burned the captured USS *Philadelphia*, an action Adm. Horatio Nelson of the British Navy is said to have called "the most bold and daring act of the age." During the War of 1812, the more powerful British *Macedonian* surrendered to Decatur, commanding USS *United States*. The return to New York of *United States* and her prize, the *Macedonian*, caused a national sensation. In 1820 Decatur agreed to an "honor duel" in Bladensburg, Maryland, with Commo. James Barron, with whom he had had a running feud. Wounded in the duel, Decatur died shortly thereafter.

Decatur Quotations

By good fortune I have risen fast in my profession, but my rank is ahead of my requirements. I went young into the Navy; my education was cut short, and I neglected the opportunities of improvement I had when a boy. For professional knowledge, I hope to get along, expecting to increase it as I grow older; but for other kinds of knowledge, I feel my deficiencies, and want your friendly aid towards getting the better of them. Will you favor me with a list of such books, historical, and others of a standard nature, as you think will best answer my purpose, that I may devote myself at all intervals to the perusal of them?

Reported conversation with Dr. Benjamin Rush, February 1806

In our intercourse with foreign nations, may our country be always right; but our country, right or wrong.

Barbary War victory toast, Norfolk, Virginia, April 1816

Commo. Stephen Decatur, oil portrait (U.S. Naval Institute Photo Archive)

~§~

I do not think that fighting duels, under any circumstances, can raise the reputation of any man, and have long since discovered, that it is not even an unerring criterion of personal courage. Should regret the necessity of fighting with any man, but, in my opinion, the man who makes arms his profession is not at liberty to decline an invitation from any person, who is not so far degraded, as to be beneath his notice.

Letter to James Barron, October 31, 1819

Quotations about Decatur

[M]y orders . . . have been executed in the most gallant and Officer like manner by Lieut Commt Decatur. . . . Their conduct in the performance of the dangerous service assigned them, cannot be sufficiently estimated—It is beyond all praise.

Commo. Edward Preble, on the burning of *Philadelphia*,
February 16, 1804

~§~

During the Action we fired 262 Rounds shot besides Grape double head & Canister from this ship and were several times within 3 cables length of the Rocks & Batteries where our soundings were from 10 to 16 fath[om]s the Officers Seamen & Marines of the Squadron behaved Gallantly throughout the Action. Capt. Decatur in Gun Boat No.4 particularly distinguished himself.

Commo. Edward Preble, USS *Constitution*, August 4, 1804

~§~

Then quickly met our nation's eyes
The noblest sight in nature—
A first-rate frigate as a prize
Brought home by brave Decatur.

Victory song played on arrival of captured HMS *Macedonian*,
New York, December 1812

[Decatur] remarked he did not think it possible to bear so much pain, but never once cried out. . . . Later, he said he would not mind death if it had come on the quarterdeck. "If it were the cause of my country, it would be nothing." Weakly, he thanked the friends who anxiously waited around him, but told his father-in-law, whom he had summoned earlier in the week, "You can do me no service; go to my wife and do what you can to console her."

> *Elizabeth Wilson*, description of Decatur on his deathbed from
> "A Gallanter Fellow Never Stepped a Quarterdeck" (2004)

A hero has fallen! Commodore Stephen Decatur, one of the first officers of our Navy—the pride of his country—the gallant and noble-hearted gentleman—is no more! He expired a few minutes ago of the mortal wound received in the duel yesterday. Of the origin of the feud which led to this disastrous result we know but what rumor tells. The event, we are sure, will fill the country with grief. Mourn, Columbia! For one of the brightest stars is set—a son "without fear and without reproach"—in the freshness of his fame—in the prime of his usefulness—has descended into the tomb.

> *The National Intelligencer*, March 23, 1820

A poor sailor as he wept over him exclaimed that "the Navy had lost her mainmast." With me it is far worse, it is a total, total wreck.

> *Susan Decatur*, describing the funeral services of her husband,
> c. March 1820

Burial Site

St. Peter's Churchyard, Philadelphia, Pennsylvania (Decatur was exhumed from his gravesite in Washington, D.C., in 1846 and moved to St. Peter's.)

Epitaph

He cherished in his heart
And sustained by his intrepid actions
The inspiring sentiment
"Our country right or wrong."
A nation
Gave him in return
Its applause and gratitude

View of the dueling ground near Bladensburg. Engraving by Richardson & Cox (U.S. Naval Institute Photo Archive)

Dewey Field

Dewey Basin, historical postcard (Collection Randell Hunt "Doc" Prothro)

Man of the Hour

There is a story now rarely told
About a man whose deeds were bold.
From a humble start in Vermont he rose,
A career in the Navy was what he chose.
At Annapolis he fought to keep the dream alive,
Even if it took everything just to survive.
Flung into war at a rather young age—
A terrible fight, costly to wage—
During the battles he learned from the best
And awaited the day to put his skills to the test.
Thirty years later: trouble with Spain;
A Commodore now, he had everything to gain.
Given a fleet stationed in Hong Kong,
He finally got what he had wanted so long.
Ordered to Manila—it had to be discreet,
A secret mission, to sink the Spanish fleet—
In the harbor at dawn, enemy within sight,

He said, "You may fire when ready," and the bay was alight.
Throughout the chaos, explosions all around,
He outdid the Spanish; his tactics were sound.
This victory saved the U.S. from attack
And proved to the world that our strength was back.
Even today history's echoes resound,
"Hail the great Dewey, our hero's been found!"

Kenton P. Knop, USNA 2006

Dewey Field, created in the 1959 landfill operation to add space for athletic fields, is a practice field for varsity soccer and lacrosse flanked by the Severn River and Ingram Field (previously Dewey Basin). The field honors "Admiral of the Navy" and "hero of Manila" George Dewey (1837–1917), USNA 1858.

When the conflict with Spain ignited in 1898 after the USS *Maine* blew up in Havana Harbor in Cuba (one of Spain's last New World holdings), Dewey was sent to the Philippines, territory also claimed by Spain, to destroy the Spanish Pacific fleet—which he did. One of the most decisive battles in American history, during which not one American seaman was lost, the Battle of Manila Bay inaugurated the United States as a world power.

George Dewey, born in Vermont, entered the Naval Academy in 1854 and graduated fifth in his class in 1858. As part of Farragut's Western Gulf Blockading Squadron, he saw action during the Battle of New Orleans in April 1862 and at Port Hudson in March 1863. By the age of twenty-eight, he had had command of six naval vessels. After a tour in Annapolis as the officer in charge of plebes and several more tours of duty at sea, he served in Washington as the chief of the Bureau of Equipment, where he oversaw the ongoing transition to the "new Navy" of steam over sail. In 1898 he was promoted to commodore and made chief of the Asiatic Squadron. After the victory of Manila Bay, Congress appointed Dewey "Admiral of the Navy," the first and only such rank ever awarded by Congress, which guaranteed that he remain on the active list in the Navy until death. "Dewey fever" spread across

America, and his image appeared in all the newspapers, in most of the magazines, on glass and china items, toys, furniture, soap, and on about three million commemorative medals and tokens given as souvenirs by governments, patriotic societies, and department stores. Dewey led victory parades in New York City, Washington, D.C., and Vermont and for a month and a half campaigned for president before withdrawing. At his death in 1917, he had served in the Navy for sixty-two years.

Dewey Quotations

You may fire when ready, Gridley.

> Order to Capt. Charles Gridley, US flagship *Olympia*,
> to commence action in Manila Bay, May 1, 1898

Reached Manila at daylight and immediately engaged the Spanish ships and batteries at Cavite. Destroy[ed] eight, including the Reina Christina and the Castilla, also one large steam transport. Anchored at noon off Manila.

> Diary entry, May 1, 1898

Gentlemen, a higher power than we has won this battle to-day.

> Comment to crew on the victory at Manila Bay, May 1, 1898

Quotations about Dewey

I consider that I would be neglecting a most important duty should I omit to mention the coolness of my executive officer, Mr. Dewey.

Capt. Melancton Smith, USS *Mississippi*, in his battle report, as reported
in *The Autobiography of George Dewey, Admiral of the Navy* (1913)

Admiral of the Navy George Dewey, Clinedinst Studios (U.S. Naval Institute Photo Archive)

Be it enacted by the Senate and the House of Representatives of the
United States of America in Congress assembled, That the President is
hereby authorized to appoint, by selection and promotion, an Admiral
of the Navy, who shall not be placed upon the retired list except upon
his own application; and whenever such office shall be vacated by death
or otherwise the office shall cease to exist.

Congressional statute approving office of Admiral of the Navy, 1899

~≈~

It is with feeling of genuine grief that the Secretary of the Navy
announces the death at 5:56 p.m. yesterday at his residence in
Washington of The Admiral of the Navy.

The career of George Dewey "ran in full current to the end."
Vermont was his mother State and there was always in his character
something of the granite of his native hills. Dewey was under fire with
Farragut in the Mississippi River, and bore himself gallantly throughout
the War between the States.

The battle in Manila Bay on 1 May 1898, made him the foremost
naval officer since Farragut and victor of the first American sea fight
with a foreign foe since the War of 1812. . . .

His whole life, 62 years of which were spent in the Navy, was full [of]
honorable achievement, and his service in peace has been hardly less
distinguished than his laurels in war. As president of the General Board
of the Navy since its inception he has played a leading part in making
the Nation ready for war on the seas. The same statesmanlike qualities
which he exhibited in handling the international situation at Manila
after the battle of 1 May 1898, he has shown as the head of this board
of naval experts.

In recognition of his victory in Manila Bay the then commodore was
advanced one grade to that of rear admiral, and in addition received the
thanks of Congress. Later by special act of Congress he was promoted to
be The Admiral of the Navy, a rank never held by an American naval
officer previously, although two, Porter and Farragut, were rewarded with
the rank of full Admiral. He was placed by Congress on the active list
until such time as he might see fit to apply for retirement. But his active
spirit could not rest. He never folded his hands. He chose to die on the

bridge, even until the Pilot came aboard his life craft who should take him across the bar. He died one of the foremost figures of modern times.

Navy Department General Order 258, January 17, 1917

It is pleasant to recall what qualities gave him his well-deserved fame: His practical directness, his courage without self-consciousness, his efficient capacity in matters of administration, the readiness to fight without asking questions or hesitating about any detail. It was by such qualities that he continued and added luster to the best traditions of the Navy. He had the stuff in him which all true men admire and upon which all statesmen must depend in hours of peril. . . . The people and the Government of the United States will always rejoice to perpetuate his name in all honor and affection.

President Woodrow Wilson, January 17, 1917

Since the passing of the civil war heroes no American has enjoyed the adoration of the whole country in the degree to which George Dewey possessed it in the year following the Spanish war. When he returned to New York in September, 1899, bringing with him several of the vessels which had won the battle of Manila Bay on May 1 of the previous year, he received a popular welcome of almost unexampled enthusiasm. . . . [H]is fame was expressed at the time . . . by the naming for him of hundreds of boy babies born in the summer of 1898.

New York Times, January 17, 1917

Burial Site

National Cathedral, Washington, D.C.

Farragut Field

Farragut Field (Randell Hunt "Doc" Prothro and Gustav F. "Gus" Swainson Jr.)

O, how dark the dark ages are
With no sun to brighten up the day
Dark smothering clouds of endless school work
As I sit here at my desk, I glance out the window
Hoping to see sailboats gliding through the wind
Yearning for the morning when I will be awakened
By clashing of football players on the field
The announcement that spring has arrived

Plebe, USNA 2007

F arragut Field, behind Bancroft Hall, is used by both the sprint and varsity football teams as well as for plebe summer training. This field and the Farragut window in the Chapel both honor Adm. David Glasgow Farragut (1801–70), hero of Mobile Bay and the first officer to hold the rank of admiral. Farragut, who had entered the Navy as a young boy, was given command of a prize vessel at twelve years old and brought her safely to shore. In a later assignment, Farragut showed the abilities that would make him one of the Navy's greatest heroes: in 1862, in command of the West Gulf Blockading Squadron, he ran his ships past Confederate defenses to capture the city of New Orleans, an action that led Congress to create the rank of rear admiral especially for him. On August 5, 1864, when he entered the heavily mined Mobile Bay, the last major Confederate port open on the Gulf of Mexico, Farragut defeated the squadron of Confederate Adm. Franklin Buchanan, who had twenty years earlier been the Naval Academy's first superintendent. Farragut is best remembered in that battle for lashing himself to the rigging of his flagship so that he could better observe the action and commanding his fleet to plow through the Confederate mines (then known as torpedoes).

The Battle of Mobile Bay

SIR,—I have the honor to report to the Department that this morning I entered Mobile Bay, passing between Forts Morgan and Gaines, and encountering the rebel ram *Tennessee* and gun-boats of the enemy. . . . The attacking fleet was under way by 5:45 AM, in the following order: The *Brooklyn*, with the *Octoroon* on her port side; *Hartford*, with the *Metacomet*; *Richmond*, with the *Port Royal*; *Lackawanna*, with the *Seminole*; *Monongahela*, with the *Tecumseh*; *Ossipee*, with the *Itasco*; and the *Oneida*, with the *Galena*. On the starboard of the fleet was the proper position of the Monitors or iron-clads. The wind was light from the southwest, and the sky cloudy, with very little sun. Fort Morgan opened upon us at ten minutes past 7 o'clock, and soon after this the action became lively. As we steamed up the main ship channel there was some difficulty ahead, and the *Hartford* passed on ahead of the *Brooklyn*. At 7:40 the *Tecumseh* was struck by a torpedo and sunk, going down very rapidly, and carrying down with her all the officers and crew, with the exception of the pilot and eight or ten men, who were saved by a boat that I sent from the *Metacomet*, which was alongside of me. The *Hartford* had passed the forts before 8 o'clock, and finding myself raked by the rebel gun-boats, I ordered the *Metacomet* to cast off and go in pursuit of them, one of which, the *Selma*, she succeeded in capturing. All the vessels had passed the forts by half past 8, but the rebel ram *Tennessee* was still apparently uninjured, in our rear. A signal was at once made to all the fleet to turn again and attack the ram, not only with guns, but with orders to run her down at full speed. The *Monongahela* was the first that struck her, and though she may have injured her badly, yet she did not succeed in disabling her. The *Lackawanna* also struck her, but ineffectually. The flag ship gave her a severe shock with her bow, and as she passed poured into her a whole port broadside of solid 9-inch shot and thirteen pounds of powder, at a distance of not more than twelve feet. The iron-clads were closing upon her, and the *Hartford* and the rest of the fleet were bearing down upon her, when, at 10 AM, she surrendered. The rest of the rebel fleet, namely, the *Morgan* and *Gaines*, succeeded in getting back under the protection of Fort Morgan. This terminated the action of the day.

Admiral Farragut, battle report to
Secretary of the Navy Gideon Welles,
August 5, 1864

❦

The Has-Beens

[The ship], now obsolete, of which the story,
    In the Annals of the Sea,
    Will always seem to me
Pages writ in never ending glory.
So the Hartford, gallant, brave old sloop of war,
Flagship, she, of Farragut on Southern shore.
    "Damn Torpedoes—go ahead!"
    Words undying, that he said,
As steaming on, the battle's brunt she bore

Lucky Bag, 1910

USS *Hartford*, Farragut's flagship (Special Collections and Archives, Nimitz Library)

Farragut Quotations

Damn the torpedoes. Full speed ahead!

> Most familiar version of the perhaps apocryphal order,
> Battle of Mobile Bay, August 5, 1864

❧

Give me the iron in the men and I care not so much about the iron in the ships.

❧

You should be as ready [for work] in a day as in a year. . . . Even when in port, you should be but waiting for the world to turn round till it comes to your turn to do something to "pitch in"; you should be like cold sauce, always ready.

❧

The safest way to prevent injury from an enemy is to strike hard yourself.

❧

If we had nothing but agreeable things to do in war, everyone would be in the Navy, and no one would be worthy of reward or promotion. We must take the world as it comes. This is a state of war you inhabit.

> *The Life and Letters of Admiral D. G. Farragut* (1879)

Adm. David Glasgow Farragut (U.S. Naval Institute Photo Archive)

Quotations about Farragut

The Secretary of the Navy has the painful duty of announcing to the Navy and the country, the death of the highest officer of the service, David Glasgow Farragut, Admiral of the Navy of the United States. . . . Nearly sixty years of the life of this officer have been spent in the service of the country. The records of his deeds are written on the noblest pages of history; and his death will be mourned by the whole people, who loved while they honored him.

Department of the Navy, August 14, 1870

The story of his brilliant achievements is one of the most frequently told of all the stories of the great war, and the pictorial representations of the heroic old veteran during the novel and remarkable engagement in Mobile Bay, between his fleet and the famous rebel ram Tennessee, lashed in the main rigging near the top of his flag-ship, unmindful of the raining shot and shell, and fire and smoke, glass in hand, grimly watching the movement of the fleet and ordering his officers, have been viewed by thousands; and on the walls of many a modest home highly colored prints representing the scene no doubt are most conspicuously displayed.

New York Times, August 15, 1870

The grade of admiral should now be abolished. It was made for one to whom the country owed a great debt. There is not another naval officer living who is entitled to it. There is not another officer in the navy who has earned a position made for glorious Admiral Farragut.

Brooklyn Daily Union, c. August 1870

Burial Site

Woodlawn Cemetery, Bronx, New York (reinterred in New York on September 30, 1870, after original burial in St. John's Churchyard, Portsmouth, New Hampshire, on August 17, 1870)

During Plebe Summer, no place became more familiar to me than Farragut Field. Every day, after our 0530 reveille, my fellow plebes and I marched down to Farragut Field for our daily physical training (or PT) session. . . . Once formed up by platoons, a drill instructor would mount the elevated platform located in the center of the field. For over an hour, my shipmates and I participated in an arduous workout consisting of numerous pushups, sit-ups, and jumping jacks followed by a "motivating" run. However, none of our workouts was complete without the "Daily Dozen," a series of stretches performed at the beginning and end of the PT session. . . . [T]hese workouts gave my shipmates and me a sense of unity just knowing that we were going through the same pain and rigors. Nevertheless, every day that I pass the vast yet desolate Farragut Field, I can't help but remember the long summer mornings of physical training.

Tyler W. Forrest, USNA 2002

Fitch Bridge

Fitch Bridge . . . is one of my favorite places on the yard. First of all, it represents balance to me . . . between a professional military career and a competitive sports environment. . . . A place for me to see both sides.

Anthony Atler, USNA 2004

Fitch Bridge (Randell Hunt "Doc" Prothro and Gustav F. "Gus" Swainson Jr.)

Fitch Bridge, completed in 1959, is a small footbridge spanning College (formerly Dorsey) Creek, built to link Hospital Point to the Yard's main areas. The bridge has undergone several renovations, most recently in 1995, when the Seabees widened and strengthened it, essentially rebuilding it. Midshipmen make heavy use of it, heading across the creek to attack the obstacle course (known as the O course), to play intramural soccer games, or to complete an "outer," a perimeter run around the Yard.

> Listen to the clippity-clop of feet tromping and stomping across wooden planks, the water swirling, whirling, and lapping against the piles. A slight breeze tends to flow across the center width of the footbridge as you look out over the [water]. A few fishermen line the seawall on the other end as the crew team heaves and hoes, gliding beneath Fitch Bridge. Behind you stand the academic buildings of the Academy and before you the wide open green grasses of Hospital Point.

> *Jason M. Abel*, USNA 2004

The bridge is named for Vice Adm. Aubrey W. Fitch (1883–1978), USNA 1906, "Victor of the Battle of the Coral Sea" and thirty-fourth superintendent of the Academy. As a midshipman, Fitch focused on athletics, playing football and other sports, and he graduated near the bottom of the class. He returned to the Academy, however, for four tours of duty. In World War I Fitch served as the gunnery officer aboard *Wyoming*. In 1930, after his growing interest in aviation, he earned his wings. In 1931 he went on to command the Navy's first aircraft carrier, *Langley*; in 1938, the Naval Air Station in Pensacola; and in 1941, Carrier Division 1 in the Pacific. When Pearl Harbor was attacked on December 7, Fitch was one of the most experienced officers in the Navy. During the Battle of the Coral Sea in May 1942, he commanded Task Force 11 aboard flagship *Lexington*, even as it was sinking. (Struck by the Japanese, it was the first American aircraft carrier to be lost in the war.) The U.S. actions in that battle deterred the planned Japanese attack on New Guinea, and Fitch received a Distinguished Service Medal for his participation. Subsequently he was presented a Gold Star for his role in directing Allied air support in the Solomon Islands and Guadalcanal in 1942 and as air officer next in command to Adm. William Halsey Jr., commander of the South Pacific Fleet. Late in the war, Fitch served as deputy chief of naval operations (air). The day after V-J day, he became the first aviator to be appointed superintendent at the Academy, where he expanded the fledgling aviation program. When he retired in 1947, he had served in the

Navy for more than forty years. His grave on the hillside in the Naval
Academy Cemetery overlooks the bridge named for him.

Fitch Quotations

Better get the men off, Ted.

> To Capt. Frederick Sherman, commanding officer,
> *Lexington*, May 8, 1942

~❧~

The air units we had there [in 1942] consisted of the Navy, Army,
Marine Corps and New Zealand air groups. . . . My job was to operate
these groups against the enemy. . . . If we consider the whole as a
football team, at the center of the line were the heavy bombers and
medium bombers. Included on each side of the center were the torpedo
planes. Then, at the ends, the dive-bombers. Included in the backfield
were the fighter task forces. The quarterback giving the signals was the
commander of the tactical air operations and the coach, the old fellow
on the side line, had the over-all picture making the replacements and
changing the strategy as the situation developed. . . . [I was the] coach,
planning the strategy, picking the teams, and deciding the position each
member was to play.

> Interview regarding South Pacific activities in World War II

Quotations about Fitch

A physical wreck who startled the country first class year with the
announcement that he had refereed nineteen different disputes.
Attained this great distinction by the reputation he made in athletic
contests at the gym. Delights in displaying his entrancing form in any
abbreviated costume. . . . Believes that all successful rough-housing must
be accompanied by numerous casualties.

> *Lucky Bag*, 1906

~❧~

Adm. Aubrey W. Fitch (Special Collections and Archives Division, Nimitz Library, U.S. Naval Academy)

Jake flies over the place. He flies a lot of places where he has no damn business to fly.

Admiral Halsey, on Fitch's late return
from an inspection flight
after taking refuge from bad weather
on a small French island, 1942

The admiral was never aloof. Any junior officer could feel free to come into his quarters to see him about any personal problem.

> Fitch aide, reported by Edward Pinkowski in interview with
> Deputy Chief of Naval Operations (Air) Fitch, c. August 1944

⟿⟾

"COMINCH" corridor, on the second "deck" forward of the Navy Building in Washington, leads to the austere office of the fleet Commander in Chief, Fleet Admiral Ernest J. King. Down this formidable channel, one day recently, steamed Vice-Admiral Aubrey Fitch. He bore with him a topside-shaking plan . . . to create a new office of Deputy Commander in Chief for Air, roughly parallel to the job which five-star General Henry H. Arnold holds down in the War Department. Navy airmen would at last have some of the prestige to which they believe they are entitled.

> *Time*, June 18, 1945

Burial Site

USNA Cemetery

As the hot Annapolis sun beat down on my neck, I was relieved that Plebe Summer was almost finished. I had endured six weeks of training alongside fellow plebes and my exhaustion was showing in our daily drills. Through all of our intense activities, traversing Fitch Bridge had always made my day more bearable. I loved hearing the sound of my feet hit the wooden planks because it reminded me of a pier I fished off when I was younger. A gentle breeze would brush against me as I crossed the bridge, and I would think about my future in the Navy and the challenges ahead. For a few seconds, anyway, crossing Fitch Bridge I had a time to myself that summer, and a cherished sense of freedom.

> Plebe, USNA 2003

Gate 3

Since the unveiling I have visited the new gates repeatedly just
to stand and admire them. At my first view I saw that they were
splendid and my admiration has grown upon me ever since.

Superintendent Thomas C. Hart, 1932

Gate 3, the main gate, 1933–2001 (U.S. Naval Institute Photo Archive)

Gate 3 at Maryland Avenue, once the main gate into the Academy, was designed to stand along a straight path to the sea, and thus to be a symbolic gangplank leading to the decks of the fleet. A 1954 memo in the Records of the Superintendent proposes retaining Gate 3 as the only twenty-four-hour gate into the Academy because "it is the Main Gate by 109 years of tradition," it is "centrally located," and "the security of the Administration Building . . . etc, are predicated on physical presence of #3 Gate guard." The only remaining structures from the original Academy buildings, the old gatehouses, are located just inside the gates.

Ode to the Academy Gates

Those who enter at these gates
Will never more be free

Lucky Bag, 1922

The gates themselves—the granite piers and the bronze grills with rope and anchor motif, designed by Allied Architects of Washington, D.C.—were presented May 28, 1932, by the Class of 1907 as their twenty-fifth anniversary gift to the Academy. At the presentation, the superintendent made some remarks, the class of 1907 gave a speech, and the band played "Anchors Aweigh." The right-hand side of the gate, known as "Bilger's Gate," was traditionally the gate through which passed midshipmen who were "bilging out," or leaving the Academy before graduation.

A Youngster's Soliloquy

To bilge or not to bilge; that is the question:
Whether 'tis better, on the whole, to suffer
The trees and P-works of the Math department,
Or to take pen against a raft of problems
And, by resigning, end them. To bilge: the gate,
No more; and by the gate to say we end
The exams and the thousand awful shocks
That we are subject o, 'tis a consummation
Devoutly to be wished. To bilge, to leave;
To leave, perchance regret; ay, there's the rub;
For in the great outside what things may come

When we have taken off this uniform
Must give us pause; there's the respect
That makes calamity of such a life;
For who would bear the sub and awkward squad,
The special list, the extra duty squad,
The O.A.O.'s neglect, the mail's delay,
The awful laundry, and the spurns
That patient Middies on the tailors take
When he himself might a cit become
With a cold two oh. Who would fardels bare
To bone and groan under an electric light
But that the dread of something on the outside,
That little frequently country from whose bourn
Few travelers return, puzzles the will,
And makes us rather bear those ills we have
Than fly to others that we know not of.

The Log, 1923

After the attacks on September 11, 2001, for security measures, Gate 1 was transformed into the main point of entry into the Academy.

The Gate

We know not what lies beyond. Our lives have changed so much since that fateful day in July. We got haircuts, shots, and new clothes. We were told what to do and have been told what to do ever since. Bedtimes, commands to eat your meals, calls for formation. . . . We are in the military. And then some day, yes, some day, we will leave the Academy and depart through that gate, the gate.

Trevor Felter, USNA 2002

Halsey Field House

Halsey Field House (Randell Hunt "Doc" Prothro and Gustav F. "Gus" Swainson Jr.)

Halsey Bleachers

If only these bleachers
Could talk,
The sweat, the blood, the glory
Of a long day's walk.
In that sea of rubber
I find myself running
To forget my troubles.
"Why do I push myself?"
I sometimes ask.
Then Halsey tells me,
"Because of the extraordinary
Circumstances, my son."

Serge J. Bermudez, USNA 2006

B uilt in 1957, Halsey Field House, home to Navy Men's and Women's Indoor Track and Navy Women's Basketball, houses a two-hundred-meter synthetic track, a five-thousand-spectator basketball court, and squash and tennis courts in addition to a climbing wall and weight rooms. It also fields events such as the high jump, shot put, and long jump.

> Once again I have found myself fighting for space on the locker room floor. The thought of Saturday morning training at 0515 has brought all of us here. We all come early and stay late. To a bystander this could prove to be a pitiful sight: fifteen or so plebes all strewn about the floor in every position imaginable, giving the locker room the look of a war zone. I never really thought that I would be reduced to sleeping in an old, smelly locker room, using my own sweatshirt as a pillow. I usually hide out until 1015 when the liberty bell rings, signifying that it is now safe to return to the hall.
>
> *Charles Dawson*, USNA 2002

The field house is named for Fleet Adm. William F. Halsey Jr. (1882–1959), USNA 1904, renowned World War II officer whose commands included commander, Carriers Pacific; commander, Task Force 16 (which launched the Doolittle raid); commander, South Pacific Force and Area; and, in June 1944, commander, Third Fleet. As a midshipman, Halsey acquired enough demerits to warrant expulsion from the Academy by his youngster year, but he managed to graduate on time, though at the low end of his class. He went on to earn a Navy Cross for his service in World War I, and in 1934, at the age of fifty-two, he earned his wings.

Extremely considerate of others on a personal level, Halsey earned the nickname "Bull" for his aggressive attitude in war. He is best remembered for victories against the Japanese in the South Pacific as he battled up the chain of islands toward Japan in the first part of the war: his participation in the Doolittle Raid on Tokyo on April 18, 1942; his command of the forces that captured Guadalcanal, Bougainville, and other islands in the Solomon Island chain in fall 1942 and winter 1943. After leaving the South Pacific in September 1944, Halsey was placed in command of the Third Fleet and assigned to assist the Seventh Fleet in the Philippines in October 1944. However, Halsey had moved his force north and was unable to render assistance in the October 24–25 battle for Leyte Gulf.

In December the Third Fleet encountered Typhoon Cobra (also known as "Halsey's typhoon") off the coast of the Philippines, which sank three destroyers and severely damaged other ships. These activities damaged Halsey's reputation to some extent, but after turning over command of the Third Fleet (renamed the Fifth Fleet) to Admiral Spruance in January 1945, in May Halsey was once again given command of the Third Fleet. In July his fleet assisted in the invasion of Okinawa and subsequently led attacks on the Japanese mainland. On September 2, 1945, the Japanese signed the articles of surrender aboard Halsey's flagship, USS *Missouri*. In December 1945 Halsey took the oath as fleet admiral; he was the fourth and last officer to hold that rank.

> To the end
> He will go
> From the front he leads
> His people
> Staying true
> Never loosing faith
> Staying true to the Bull
>
> Plebe

Halsey Quotations

Hit hard, hit fast, hit often.

❧

There are no great men. There are just great challenges that men like you and me are forced by circumstances to meet.

❧

Attack—Repeat—Attack.

> Dispatch to the South Pacific Force before
> battle of Santa Cruz Islands, October 26, 1942

❧

Fleet Adm. William F. Halsey Jr. (U.S. Naval Institute Photo Archive)

Send them our latitude and longitude.

> Response to Japanese question intercepted over the radio:
> "Where is the American Fleet?" October 1944

❧

Now that the fighting has ended, there must be no letdown. There must be watchful waiting. Victory is not the end, just the beginning. We must establish peace—a firm, a just, and an enduring peace.

> Broadcast to Third Fleet, August 15, 1945

❧

The sudden change from war to peace can be dangerous at sea; men accustomed to ceaseless vigilance and strenuous duties can become flaccid instead of relaxed if abruptly left idle.

> On the Navy adage
> "Put down the sword and take up the paintbrush"

❧

My life reached its climax on August 29, 1945. I can fix even the minute, 9:25 AM, because my log for the forenoon watch that day contains this entry: "Steaming into Tokyo Bay, COMTHIRDFLEET in *Missouri*. Anchored at 0925 in berth F71." For forty-five years my career in the United States Navy had been building toward that moment. Now those years were fulfilled and justified.

Quotations about Halsey

The only man in the class who can compete with General in the number of offices he has held. . . . A real old salt. Looks like a figurehead of Neptune. . . . Everybody's friend.

> *Lucky Bag*, 1904

❧

You'll never be as good a naval officer as your father!

USNA chief master-at-arms during graduation exercises, 1904

~≈⊱~

Halsey's conduct of his present command leaves nothing to be desired. He is professionally competent and militarily aggressive without being reckless or foolhardy. He has that rare combination of intellectual capacity and military audacity, and can calculate to a cat's whisker the risk involved in operations when successful accomplishments will bring great returns. He possesses superb leadership qualities which have earned him a tremendous following of his men. . . . For his successful turning back of the [Japanese] attempt to take Guadalcanal in mid-November he has been nominated by the President for the rank of Admiral, which reward he richly deserves.

Adm. Chester William Nimitz, Commander in Chief,
Pacific Fleet, October 1942

~≈⊱~

Unconditional surrender of Japan—with Admiral Halsey at sea in command of the greatest combined fighting fleet of all history.

H. E. Stassen, log entry, USS *Missouri*, August 15, 1945

~≈⊱~

For exceptionally meritorious service . . . in a duty of great responsibility as Commander Third Fleet. . . . Admiral Halsey placed in action the greatest mass of sea power ever assembled and initiated attacks on the enemy's naval and air forces, shipping, shipyards and coastal objectives. . . . In operations conducted with brilliant military precision and characteristic aggressiveness, [his] ships and planes . . . bombarded Okinawa, Okino Daito, and Minami Daito in the Ryukyus, they blasted every industry and resource which enabled Japan to make war; gallantly riding out the perilous typhoon of June 5, they effected repairs and went in to knock out remnants of the once mighty Japanese Fleet hiding in camouflage nets. . . . His professional skill and inspiring devotion to the fulfillment of a mission vital to lasting peace reflect the highest credit upon Admiral Halsey and the United States Naval Service.

Gold Star Citation

Burial Site

Arlington National Cemetery, Arlington, Virginia

Like Admiral Halsey, I am a football player. Life at the Academy for varsity athletes requires an extra degree of determination to get through it all. Varsity athletes must be in superb physical shape and be capable of competing with other outstanding athletes from around the country, while training to be officers and college students. It's a heavy burden to bear and it either breaks you down or builds you up. Inspired by Admiral Halsey, I am determined to excel.

Bayard N. Roberts, USNA 2010

Herndon Monument

How many times before has the hat been replaced—
So many generations have climbed for their rights;
One day yearly, all focus on freedom,
On a single cover.
Only a few who know the man
See the broader focus,
Understand the sacrifice—
A monument of example, not of prize.

Plebe

Herndon Monument (Randell Hunt "Doc" Prothro and Gustav F. "Gus" Swainson Jr.)

The gray granite obelisk known as "Herndon" that stands near the Chapel honors Navy Cdr. William Lewis Herndon (1813–57), who lost his life during a storm at sea.

Herndon entered the naval service at age fifteen. He served with his brother-in-law Matthew Fontaine Maury in the Department of Charts and Instruments (later the Naval Observatory) from 1842 to 1846. Then he served with distinction in the Mexican War in command of the brig *Iris*. In 1851, when exploration of relatively unknown parts of the world was considered one of the naval officers' duties, Lieutenant Herndon was given orders to explore the Amazon River basin. Herndon left Lima, Peru, on May 21, 1851, and after a dangerous journey of over four thousand miles through wilderness from sea level to heights of over sixteen thousand feet, he reached Pará, Brazil, on April 11, 1852. In January 1853 he submitted *Exploration of the Valley of the Amazon*, the encyclopedic report of that journey, to Secretary of the Navy John P. Kennedy. (Read by a young Mississippi River steamboat pilot, Samuel L. Clemens, the report became an important literary influence.)

In 1855, when naval officers commanded mail steamers under U.S. register, Commander Herndon was assigned to the mail steamship *Central America*. On September 9, 1857, the steamer was homeward bound from the California gold fields with 474 passengers, including women and children; a crew of 101; and a cargo of two million dollars of gold aboard, when it ran into a hurricane off Savannah, Georgia. For three days Commander Herndon struggled to save the sinking ship, but on September 12 he ordered the boarding of life boats. Sometimes wielding two pistols to keep order, Herndon managed to put all the women and children in lifeboats for transfer to *Marine*, an Indian ship that had come to their rescue. Then, according to eyewitness accounts, knowing he could do no more to save the ship or other shipmates or himself, Herndon donned his ceremonial sword and full dress uniform and, with his gold-braided hat raised in salute, went down with his ship.

> Stand fast, brave crew,
> All is not lost
> Our honor, our courage
> Will be saved at any cost
>
> Plebe

Following his death, Herndon's fellow officers met to raise money for a monument. Created by the Quincy Granite Railway Company, the simple granite obelisk was erected at the Naval Academy in June 1860, one of the first monuments in the Yard. In October 1921 the crew of USS *Herndon* (DD963) paid a visit to the Academy and placed a memorial wreath on the obelisk. In 1988, after years of attempts, *Central America* with its cache of gold was discovered on the sea bottom.

The annual "plebe recognition ceremony," which now takes place during Commissioning Week, marks the promotion of plebes from fourth-class to third-class midshipmen. The ceremony had its origins in 1907, when the recent former plebe class left the graduation ceremony in the Armory (now Dahlgren Hall) and snake-danced to Lover's Lane, a sidewalk forbidden to them as plebes, near the Herndon Monument. Over the years the plebe recognition ceremony has evolved: in the 1940s the "ain't no more plebes" ritual involved the plebes hoisting a classmate to the top of the monument, and by the end of the decade, a hat was left on top to prove Herndon had been conquered.

> The Dixie cup on top of the monument is a final right of passage by fourth class midshipmen. That is why this monument means so much to me, as well as to every other plebe. We count the days until this hard, exhausting year is over. It is almost pointless to think about Herndon as much as I do, but Herndon helps me remember that plebe year—a year of sweat, blood, and tears—does end.
>
> Plebe

In the early 1950s the monument was greased before the climb for the first time. Currently the Herndon ritual involves plebes trying to climb to the top of the twenty-one foot, heavily greased monument to replace the plebe "Dixie cup" with a regular midshipmen cover, or hat. Legend says that the plebe who replaces the Dixie cup will be the first in the class to make the rank of admiral. In 2008, for the first time, in part in homage to a female midshipman who died unexpectedly, a female Dixie cup and a female cover were both placed on top of Herndon.

Toiling bodies slither
And slide, bare arms
And legs strain to climb
The greased obelisk and
Replace the Dixie cup:
No more plebes, no more
Lowest form of human life,
The whole long year
Of sweat and toil and
Tears at an end, almost—
Until the mid at the top
Tumbles and the crowd groans.
Exhausted, determined,
Each plebe digs deep
And tries again
And together they hoist
A classmate to the top.

Herndon Quotations

The citizens of the United States are, of all people, most interested in the free navigation of the Amazon. . . . Our geographical position, the winds of Heaven, and the currents of the ocean, are our potential auxiliaries. Thanks to Maury's investigations of the winds and currents, we know that a chip flung into the sea at the mouth of the Amazon will float close by Cape Hatteras. We know that ships sailing from the mouth of the Amazon, for whatever port of the world, are forced to our very doors by the SE and NE trade winds; that New York is the half-house between Para and Europe.

[If Peru were amenable] then would the mighty river, now endeared to me by association, no longer roll its sullen waters through miles of unbroken solitude . . . but, furrowed by a thousand keels, and bearing upon its waters the mighty wealth that civilization and science would call from the depths of those dark forests [Brazil might say]: "Thus much have we done for the advancement of civilization and the happiness of the human race."

I would strongly advise all travellers in these parts . . . to load their burden mules, saddle and mount their riding-mules, go twice around the

Cdr. William Lewis Herndon (U.S. Naval Institute Photo Archive)

patio or square, on the inside of their dwelling, to see that everything is
prepared and fits properly; and then unload and wait for the morning.

Exploration of the Valley of the Amazon
Made under Direction of the Navy Department, 1854

Quotations about Herndon

The department is about to confide to you a most important and delicate duty, which will call for the exercise of all those high qualities of attainments, on account of which you have been selected.

The government desires to be put in possession of certain information relating to the valley of the river Amazon, in which term is included the entire basin, or water-shed, drained by that river and its tributaries. The desire extends not only to the present condition of that valley with regard to the navigability of its streams; to the number and condition, both industrial and social, of its inhabitants, their trade and products; its climate, soil and productions; but also to its capacities for cultivation, and to the character and extent of its undeveloped commercial resources, whether of the field, the forest, the river, or the mine.

[You are] authorized to employ a cook, servant, guide and interpreter . . . . The geographical situation and the commercial position of the Amazon indicate the future importance, to this country, of the free navigation of that river.

William A. Graham, Navy Department,
to Lieutenant Herndon, February 15, 1851

Burial Site

Atlantic Ocean off the coast of Savannah, Georgia

The Herndon Monument has a special meaning to all plebes at the Naval Academy. It symbolizes the hard work and frustration the plebes have endured in the last year. To me personally it is the culmination of all the work in my life up to this point, including the work that I have done in high school in order to get here. Herndon also shows me that I can do anything if I am determined. There were many times during the summer and during the academic year where I just wanted to quit and go home. Then I would think about climbing Herndon so I could look forward to the years to come.

Christopher D. Bernard, USNA 2004

Hubbard Hall

Hubbard Hall (Randell Hunt "Doc" Prothro and Gustav F. "Gus" Swainson Jr.)

I can still remember my first day of crew practice at the Academy. Instead of rowing, Coach Baker talked about Admiral Hubbard and why he was such a role model. I have been in crew no longer than three months now and can tell a huge difference in my personality, work ethic, and sense of pride. I credit the Academy as a whole, but mostly Hubbard Hall and the lessons I have learned of helping me grow and mature from just a twenty-year-old kid to a man who will be serving his country.

Evan S. Rutherford, USNA 2010

The Spanish-style boathouse was built in 1930 for crew, one of the oldest sports at the Naval Academy. The Academy has sent two crew teams to the Olympics for the United States that have won Gold medals, one in 1920 and the other in 1952.

The boathouse boasts a unique four-dock design for launching and recovering several boats at once. Extensively remodeled in 1993 into a state-of-the-art rowing facility with weight rooms, an indoor rowing tank, bays for fifty shells, and meeting rooms, it was rededicated as the Fisher Rowing Center at Hubbard Hall, after the renovation donors, Zachary and Elizabeth Fisher. An enclosed pavilion next to the boathouse displays life-size sculptures of Zachary and Elizabeth Fisher, known in the military world for their donations of Fisher Houses, guest facilities at military hospitals for the families of wounded servicemen and women.

The building was originally named in honor of Rear Adm. John Hubbard (c. 1849–c. 1932), USNA 1870, an outstanding stroke on Navy

Great White Fleet (U.S. Naval Institute Photo Archive)

Capt. John Hubbard (U.S. Naval Institute Photo Archive)

Crew who helped bring Navy its first team athletic event victory. (This was also a significant rowing event, as the sliding stroke, still in use today, was first used then.) Hubbard grew into a great leader in the fleet. In 1903 he commanded the naval forces during Panama's struggle for independence. For fourteen months, from late 1907 to 1909, he captained USS *Minnesota,* one of the sixteen new battleships of the Atlantic Fleet participating in the around-the-world cruise of the Great White Fleet—so named later on because as a peacetime navy the ships were painted white. This voyage was organized by President Theodore Roosevelt to showcase American naval power. Four squadrons of four ships, served by over fourteen thousand sailors and Marines (including the young Nimitz and Halsey), left Hampton Roads on December 16, 1907, and made twenty ports of call on six continents before arriving back in Hampton Roads on February 22, 1909. Later, Roosevelt gave Hubbard command of the entire Asiatic fleet.

On the nineteenth of April, we are going to dedicate the new boathouse at the Naval Academy which has just been completed. After careful consideration in the selection of a name for the boathouse, it has been decided to name it Hubbard Hall, after you who were the father of race-boating at the Naval Academy. This name seems particularly appropriate to me, and I hope that it meets with your approval, and that we have your consent to so name it.

On that day, the Naval Academy crews are racing Columbia University and Massachusetts Institute of Technology. Before these races, it has been decided to hold a short dedicatory service at the boathouse. As a part of this service, there will be two or three five-minute addresses, and it would give me great pleasure if you would consent to make one of them.

> *Adm. S. S. Robison*, USNA superintendent,
> letter to Admiral Hubbard, April 1, 1930

≈୧≫

The purpose of your letter of yesterday was an immense surprise to me—equally it gave me immense gratification. Of course I cannot but consent to the naming the new boathouse at the Naval Academy as has been decided. It is a distinction as welcome as it is unexpected. While I am flattered that you think the name is particularly appropriate, I can lay no claim to that merit. I was only one of several who were equally interested and active in the promotion of race-boating at the Naval Academy in those now long past days of its infancy. It was my fortune to have had the most prominent position in the boat —the stroke oar—that is all. Now as to being present at the dedicatory service on April 19th, needless say that it would give me great pleasure to do so. And to make the short address if you so desire—provided that I feel myself at that time physically able to do so. The fact is that I have been having rather a mean time of it lately with that wretched ailment called "shingles," of which I hope that I am now in the last stages. I am expecting to get away for a week or ten days from the 7th of April with the hope that change will finish the cure. If as the 19th draws near I should not feel able to being at the service I am sure you will understand, as you will also the necessity of this conditional acceptance.

John Hubbard, letter to Admiral Robison, April 2, 1930

Burial Site

Probably in Washington, D.C., but unable to locate

Ingram Field

Ingram Field (Randell Hunt "Doc" Prothro and Gustav F. "Gus" Swainson Jr.)

As I set out for crew practice, the hall was quiet and empty, the fluorescent lights providing an unnatural glow and humming. Heading toward Ingram Field where we met every morning for captains' practices, I stepped outside, where the dark night was lightened only by the occasional street light. I could smell that indescribable, fresh scent of a new morning and inhaled it like perfume. The air was invigorating and bracing for the long day ahead. These morning workouts, considered a hassle to most, provide peace and energy lasting the whole day for those willing to appreciate them. I fell in with the flow of people heading down the barely visible stairs, every step a step in faith into the new day.

Erin E. Arthur, USNA 2009

ngram Field, where the varsity track team holds its meets, is located between Dewey Field and the Michelson-Chauvenet complex. It is named for Vice Adm. Jonas H. Ingram (1886–1952), USNA 1907, USNA football coach (1914–17) and director of athletics (1926–30), and commander of the U.S. South Atlantic Fleet during World War II. Earlier in his career, during the Mexican War of 1914, Lieutenant (jg) Ingram, on board USS *Arkansas*, distinguished himself in command of the artillery and machine guns during the second day of the battle of Veracruz, for which he later received a Medal of Honor. For his service in

Midn. Jonas H. Ingram, 1907 (Special Collections and Archives Division, Nimitz Library, U.S. Naval Academy)

World War I while on the staff of the Division Three commander of the
Atlantic Fleet battle force, Ingram received a Navy Cross. During World
War II he steadily rose in rank and command: in 1941, as rear admiral, he
served as commander, Task Force 3; in 1942, as vice admiral, he served as
commander, South Atlantic Force, U.S. Atlantic Fleet; and in 1944, promoted to admiral, he served as commander in chief, U.S. Atlantic Fleet.
As commander in chief, he was responsible for the safe shipment of troops
and supplies to Europe and the destruction of the German U-boat fleet.

Quotations about Ingram

> Give him room, and stand from under! Can go through anything short
> of a stone wall, and woe betide anyone in his path.
>
> *Lucky Bag*, 1907

～℮⑨〜

> For distinguished conduct in battle, engagement of Vera Cruz, 22 April
> 1914. During the second day's fighting the service performed by him was
> eminent and conspicuous. He was conspicuous for skillful and efficient
> handling of the artillery and machineguns of the Arkansas battalion, for
> which he was specially commended in reports.
>
> Medal of Honor Citation

The Battle of Veracruz, 1914

During the Mexican Revolution, which had begun as an armed struggle against the dictator Porfirio Díaz in 1910 and lasted into 1920, relations between the United States and Mexico were increasingly strained.
In April 1914, in response to growing concern over the military dic-
tatorship of Victoriano Huerta, President Woodrow Wilson sent three
Navy vessels to Veracruz under the command of Rear Adm. Frank Friday
Fletcher. On April 21 nearly fifteen hundred American combat troops
were put ashore, and another fifteen hundred reinforcements landed
that night. By noon on April 22 the American forces had taken control of the city. In the two-day action Fletcher lost only a few men, while

the Mexicans had nearly eight hundred dead or wounded. Following this initial landing, the United States occupied Veracruz for several months, but the men who landed on April 21–22 accomplished their mission in two days and returned to their ships.

> [Admiral Ingram is granted this award] for taking a major part in the flow of United States troops across the Atlantic. . . and in the successful combating of the German submarine menace.
>
> Gold Star Citation, 1944

Burial Site

Arlington National Cemetery, Arlington, Virginia

Japanese Monument
(The Pagoda)

Japanese Monument (Randell Hunt "Doc" Prothro and Gustav F. "Gus" Swainson Jr.)

The sun catches the eastern and western faces of the four-sided monument with full force. The light then glances over the other sides, and trickles through the slabs of stone to make shadows at precise angles. It is a work of precision and clean, simple beauty.

Andrew R. Wing, USNA 2006

A four-sided, thirteen-tiered stone pagoda representative of the Fuji-wara period of eighth- and ninth-century Japan rises serenely in front of Luce Hall across from the Warner Soccer Pavilion. The Japanese Monument was donated to the Academy in 1940 by the widow of Hirosi Saito, the Japanese ambassador to the United States. Saito's devotion to the cause of friendship between the two countries in part reflected the popular reverence in Japan for such Americans as Commo. Matthew C. Perry and General of the Army Douglas MacArthur. Perhaps it also reflects the general interest of the Japanese in America at that time, as evidenced by the many students who were admitted to the United States between 1868 and 1906. The remains of Ambassador Saito, who had died in the United States, were returned to Japan on USS *Astoria*, partly as an exchange favor for the earlier return to the United States of Ambassador Bancroft, who had died in Japan. In 1941, when war against Japan was declared, demonstrators demanded the monument be removed, but Academy authorities decided to keep the pagoda in place as a reminder of the sometimes fragile nature of international friendships.

Pagodas, which usually serve a religious function, are often associated with a Buddhist temple. In Buddhist tradition, both four and thirteen are significant numbers. The four sides of the Naval Academy pagoda display Sanskrit characters representing the Four Buddhas, or "enlightened ones": those who experience enlightenment or Nirvana through self-knowledge; those who experience enlightenment through teaching, or historical examples; those who preach enlightenment; and those who have attained Nirvana but are silent. The four sides could also signify the four "signs" in Buddhist thought, representing the four "sights" seen by Siddhartha Buddha (also known as Guatama Buddha, the Buddha most familiar to Westerners), which brought him to enlightenment: an old man, a sick man, and a corpse, all representing the prevalence of suffering in the world; and a holy man or *sadhu*, representing one who is at peace with the world. The four signs reflect the four truths of Buddhism: *dukkha*, affliction (the diagnosis); *tanha*, desire (the cause); *nordha*, cessation (the prognosis that we can be well); *magga*, the path of practice (the cure). Pagodas range from one to thirteen and even fifteen tiers, but five is the most common; the number thirteen, considered an image of perfection, also represents the thirteen disciples of Guatama Buddha.

Pagoda Inscription

In memory of Japanese Ambassador Hirosi Saito, who died at Washington on February 26, 1939, and whose remains were, by order of Franklin D. Roosevelt, conveyed on board the USS *Astoria* to his native land, and in grateful appreciation of American sympathy and courtesy, this pagoda was presented by his wife and children to the United States Naval Academy, Annapolis, in October 1940.

Selections from Buddhist Sutras

Form does not differ from the void,
and the void does not differ from form.
Form is void and void is form.
No ignorance and also no ending of ignorance
Until we come to no old age and death
And no ending of old age and death.

Heart Sutra

Make abundant offerings.
Repent misdeeds and evil actions.
Rejoice in others' merits and virtues.

Avatamsaka Sutra

Pagoda

O

how

serene-

ly into the

sky the stone

pagoda uprises,

thirteen tiers piled

stone on stone, small-

er and smaller, higher

and higher, into an image

of perfection; and how daunt-

less at anchor nearby *Intrepid*

and *Valiant*, ever-vigilant, ride the

tides, as though to

remind us that

detachment also

has its limits.

Jeannette Monument

Jeannette Monument (Randell Hunt "Doc" Prothro and Gustav F. "Gus" Swainson Jr.)

Standing here in bitter cold
I have a feeling
That remains untold,
An emptiness unreal—
The pain that they must have felt
Alone in that dark land
Hoping all the snow would melt
By some unearthly hand.

Philip Galindo, USNA 2006

Officers and men of the U.S. Navy donated the ice-dripping cross rising from a high boulder base in the cemetery on Hospital Point in 1890 to commemorate the men of the *Jeannette* Arctic Expedition in 1879–81. This scientific expedition, to explore the movement of the polar ice cap and search for a navigable waterway through the ice, was placed under Navy command, as were similar expeditions of the time. USS *Jeannette*, formerly *Pandora*, a Royal Navy steam gunboat, had been outfitted as an ice-cutter and renamed in honor of the sister of James Gordon Bennett, owner of the *New York Herald* and an Arctic enthusiast who financed the *Jeannette* Expedition. She set sail from San Francisco on July 9, 1879, with thirty-two men under the command of Lt. George Washington De Long. On September 6 she became trapped in the Arctic ice, where she remained for almost two years. During this time, De Long maintained order by keeping his men at their tasks, and he kept up their spirits with football games, hunting and fishing expeditions, religious services, navigation classes, and storytelling sessions.

On June 11, 1881, when the ice started to break *Jeannette* apart, Lieutenant Commander De Long (he had been promoted November 1, 1879) gave the order to abandon ship. The men watched through the night as the boat sank, and the next morning set off for the coast of Siberia in three boats: a whaleboat under the command of Lt. George Melville; a cutter under the command of Lieutenant Commander De Long; and a second cutter under the command of Lt. Charles W. Chipp. However, storm winds soon separated the three boats. De Long's and Melville's boats made shore, separately, but Chipp's boat disappeared. Melville and his crew made it back to civilization, as did two of the crew members of De Long's boat, but the rest perished.

The story of the *Jeannette* Expedition, told in dramatic detail in the ship's logs, De Long's ice journal, Melville's official report, and other documents, offers outstanding examples of duty to mission and to shipmate in unrelentingly trying circumstances. Lt. George Colvocoresses, head of the Department of Drawing at the Academy in 1890, designed the *Jeannette* Monument based on descriptions in Melville's report of the burial site he constructed on the shores of the Lena River, a rock cairn surmounted by a cross. De Long's ship journal, his ice journal after he left the ship and up to the time he froze to death, and the contents of his pockets when his body was recovered are all in the USNA Museum collection.

It is for their bravery in the face of disaster and their resilience in peril that the crew of the USS *Jeannette* is immortalized. And their cross will be a continuous reminder to us that survive them that there are no boundaries for human courage.

Aaron D. Dixon, USNA 2010

Journal of the *Jeannette* Expedition

Oct. 28th (1879): This is a glorious country to learn patience in. We are securely held as in a vice [between two ice floes].

[Winter routine, to begin Nov. 1]:

6 AM —Call executive officer.
7   —Call ship's cook.
8:30 —Call all hands.
9   —Breakfast by watches.
10   —Turn to, clear fire-hole of ice, fill barrels with snow,
          clean up decks.
11   —Clear forecastle. All hands take exercise on ice.
11:30 —Inspection by executive officer.
12 PM —Get soundings.
1 PM —one watch may go below.
2   —Fill barrels with snow. Clear fire-hole of ice.
3   —Dinner by watches.
4:30 —Galley fire out. Carpenter and boatswain report
          departments to executive officer.
7:30 —Supper by watches.
10   —Pipe down. Noise and smoking to cease, all lights to be out
          except one burner of bulkhead lantern. Man on watch to
          report to the executive.

Dec 4th —Were it not for our daily walking exercise of 2 hours I fear we should stagnate. From 11-1, however, all hands are sent out of the ship. The officers generally walk, and the men go hunting, without success, or kick foot-balls. . . . Danenhower started a school of elementary navigation for the crew.

Dec 9th—We are continually standing by . . . with everything ready for an emergency. We seem to feel as if we were living on the edge of a crater.

July 18th [1880]—This kind of life is most discouraging! If we were only drifting toward our goal we would be somewhat content; but alas! We are steadily drifting away from it: or, in our enforced idleness we were accomplishing anything for the good of science or human nature, it would be a comfort—but instead of either we are simply burning coal to cook food to consume day after day. . . .

July 26th—We have failed, inasmuch as we did not reach the Pole; and we and our narratives together are thrown into the world's dreary waste-basket, and recalled and remembered only to be vilified or ridiculed. . . . Yet I would not wish to be understood to imply we have given up the fight. We look for to-morrow with just the same faith and with as great expectations as we did on the 1st of June. . . . A full meteorological record is kept, soundings are taken . . . birds shot and skinned . . . ship's routine carried out. . . . Occasionally a trip is proposed somewhere—to Paris, to Naples, to the West Indies—to come off "one of these days when we get back."

[Oct 21st—Another day has come and gone, and here we are yet; and the only thing which has disturbed the regular monotony may be described as the stupendous discovery of a fox-trot.]

Nov 7th—The arrival of the first Sunday in the month involves the reading of the Articles of War and the mustering of the crew. The reading is conducted with all the seriousness and decorum that would prevail in a frigate.

March 11th [1881]—At midnight brilliant flashing of an aural mass of curtain segments west between horizon and zenith. At the same time I remarked what I have frequently heard before, noises from the ice all around me like the singing which a whiplash makes in cutting through the air. . . .

June 11th—At four PM the ice came down in great force all along the port side, jamming the ship hard against the ice on the starboard side. . . .

[I]t was feared that the ship was about to be seriously endangered, and orders were accordingly given to lower the starboard boats, and haul them away. . . . At six PM it was found that the ship was beginning to fill. From that time forward every effort was devoted to getting provision, etc., on the ice. . . . [A]t eight PM everybody was ordered to leave the ship.

June 12th—At one AM the mizzen mast went by the board, and the ship was so far heeled over that the lower yard-arms were resting on the ice. At three AM the ship had sunk until her smoke-pipe top was nearly awash. At four AM the Jeannette went down. First righting to an even keel, she slowly sunk. . . . When she finally sank, the foremast was all that was standing. . . . Crew engaged in getting sleds ready for boats. . . . Lauterbach serenaded us . . . with a mouth harmonica. . . . Danenhower lively. Alexy "plenty good."

Lt. G. W. De Long

◈

Report to William E. Chandler, Secretary of the Navy

SIR: I have the honor to report my return to the United States, and to respectfully submit the following detailed statement of my movements subsequent to the separation, during a gale, from Lieut. George W. De Long, commanding the Arctic Steamer Jeannette and her shipwrecked crew, on our way toward the coast of Siberia. All acts prior to that time are fully entered in the ship's logs. . . .

[Sept. 12–18, 1881] The three boats left Simonoski Island about 8 AM on the 12th September, 1881, and remained in company until noon, when all three boats were brought to the edge of the ice-floe, where we had our dinner in company, and filled our pots and kettles with snow to be used as drinking-water and for tea. The wind had been gradually freshening since early morning, and when we shoved off from the ice-floe we had a fresh breeze and the boats were carrying full sail. . . .

[B]y 7 PM the wind had increased to a full gale and all three boats were making pretty bad weather, all hands in my boat being constantly employed in pumping or bailing out the water. . . .

Shortly after that time we lost sight of our fellow ship-mates and their boats, with but little hope of seeing them again before reaching the

Lt. George Washington De Long, J. Dupont, c. 1879 (U.S. Naval Institute Photo Archive)

coast. As our future progress was a mystery to be solved by experience alone, the elements being unpromising, I deemed it prudent to reduce our ration from one and a half pounds of pemmican to three-quarters of a pound for each person, per day. The sea, which nearly swamped us, dissolved the snow which we had gathered for quenching thirst, and from that time we were without drinking water. . . .

[T]he morning of the 16th September . . . I made the coast line. . . . Toward evening we landed and made a fire for the purpose of drying our clothing and securing some sleep. By this time I found that most of the people, myself included, were suffering with frosted feet and legs; so badly were we frozen that we were barely able to walk. During the 17th I made another good day's work, considering our condition, and turning a headland to the southward, camped during the night. . . .

[Nov. 5–21: By early November, Melville's party had made it to Belun, a Russian outpost. Ninderman and Noros, from De Long's cutter, had also reached Belun. Melville made immediate preparations for a rescue party, leaving on November 5 with two dog teams, two native guides, and food for ten days.]

[T]hat night I slept at Ku Mark Surka, and on the day traveled 50 versts (33 miles) to Balcour, the hut in which Ninderman and Noros were found. The next day was so stormy that the dogs could not face the gale. . . . [On November 8] I traveled about 60 versts (40 miles), and at dark dug a hole in the snow-bank and slept there during the night.

[Nov. 11] The weather was terribly stormy and very cold, and upon my arrival in North Belun I was so benumbed by cold that I was unable to walk or speak. After being carried to one of the huts I found that my feet and legs were so badly frost-bitten that it was necessary to have foot and leg mittens made to cover my limbs in lieu of moccasins.

[Nov. 12] In the evening a native came into the hut and gave me a paper which, upon reading, I found to be a record left by De Long at a hut on the river. . . . The next morning [another] paper and a Winchester rifle were brought to me, and after reading the papers I found where De Long had landed on the coast and where he had made a cache for his log-book, chronometer, navigation-box, instruments, and such other articles as he could no longer carry. . . .

[Nov. 13] Got 3 sleds and driver, returned to trail. . . . I was frozen so badly as to be unable to walk without assistance, and finally the natives and the dogs were unable to work, the latter howling and lying down in the snow in such a manner that it was impossible to make them move. I had but three days' provisions left, and was depending upon offal, such as fish-heads, horns, hoofs, and decayed entrails, found in some of the huts, to make my provisions last.

[Nov. 20–21] On the next morning I ran for Qu Vina, 40 versts (26 miles), the storm meanwhile raging furiously. We found considerable deer-scraps and fish-heads in this hut, where we waited two days for the storm to abate. Monday morning, the 21st day of November, came out clear and cold, so I started with the intention of making all the distance I could. . . . I arrived at Belun after midnight . . . having been absent twenty-three days, during which time storms and darkness almost constantly prevailed, and was so badly frozen in feet, legs, and hands that I could not stand alone, but had to be assisted or to crawl upon my hands and knees.

[Nov. 28. Back at Belun, Melville was informed that neither De Long nor any of his party had been heard of; in December, he secured approval and funds for another search attempt, and in January, he set out again. However, after four sled dogs died and the native sled drivers suffered frozen limbs, he once again turned back. Two weeks later, Melville set off on his final attempt to find De Long's party].

[Dec. 23, 1881] William H. Hunt, Secretary of the Navy, telegram to Melville:

Omit no effort, spare no expense, in securing safety of men in second cutter. Let the sick and the frozen of those already rescued have every attention, and, as soon as practicable, have them transferred to milder climate. Department will supply necessary funds.

[March 23–April 17, 1882. Melville report continues:]

[I]ntending to follow the bay around from the westward with Ninderman and dog-sleds, in hopes of finding the river along which Ninderman & Noros had come after leaving De Long and his party . . . I started on along the river bank, and Ninderman, being 300 yards in advance, found an old flat-boat. . . . In proceeding towards the point I [was startled] by the sight of three bodies, partially buried, one left arm being raised clear above the snow. . . . [I] immediately recognized them as the bodies of Lt. De Long, Dr. Ambler, and Ah Sham, ship's cook. . . .

By the 27th of March I had found all the people of De Long's boat except Ericksen and Alexy [who had been buried previously by De Long]. I gathered up what small articles lay around, placed the bodies together, and covered them with a piece of tent cloth. . . . I made a box, twenty-two feet long, seven feet wide, and two feet deep of 7-inch planks, mortised together and wedged. Out of the center of the box, and with its foot placed in the rock, I raised a cross 22 feet high, made of a spruce spar, 13 inches in diameter at the base, with a large cross-arm, faced to a width of 13 inches. By April 7 I had buried the bodies within this tomb and raised a pyramid of stone over the structure to a height of nine feet.

[Melville searched for the second cutter all along the coast, but found no evidence of it. Returning to civilization with the news of the fate of the expedition, Melville arranged to bring back the remains of the *Jeannette* explorers.]

Lt. George W. Melville, Chief Engineer, October 17, 1882

It is with the sincerest grief and the deepest respect that the ancient Russian City of Smolensk greets the honored remains of the members of the American expedition on board the steamboat, "The Tanet," of these heroes who met a tragical end in wrestling with the blind and rough elements of our northern boundary's cold and uncongenial climate— who fell victims to their love of science, light and humanity. It is to those noble champions of a noble idea, those indefatigable workers, who for science's sake laid down their very lives, that we offer here our last duty, our last homage. . . . May their heroic deed live in the memory of the remotest posterity as an ever present example of the valor, the self-denial, that always characterize the American nation in her strife for truth, light, and genius—those pillars that are the surest foundation of all human happiness.

Alexander Engelhardt, Mayor of Smolensk, January 1884

Address at the Unveiling of the *Jeannette* Monument

We have come here to-day to pay the final tribute to a little band of officers and seamen of the Navy, who, nine years ago, gave up their lives, in a toilsome and difficult enterprise, an arduous labor of exploration and scientific research. . . . Their expedition made its contribution to our knowledge of the lands within the Arctic Circle, but, like so many others that had gone before it, failed of its great and ultimate purpose.

Commodore George Melville (U.S. Naval Institute Photo Archive)

But this same expedition, failure though it was in its attempt to penetrate to the Pole, or even to gain a latitude beyond its predecessors, yet, in its bright example of sustained effort, of lofty steadfastness of purpose, of dangers met unflinchingly and hardships borne without complaining, was crowned with a success far surpassing the triumphs of scientific discovery, and worthy of all that we can do to commemorate and celebrate it here. . . .

We need not dwell upon the events of that fatal journey. . . . [D]ying as they did, [these men] left behind them a renown that to the Service they loved and died for remains, and will remain forever, a priceless heritage. That long retreat, over five hundred miles of drifting ice and open ocean, a retreat matchless in the records of Arctic achievement, shines out, even through the dark tragedy at its close, with the triumphant splendor of a victory won. On the long roll of the world's explorers are no brighter names than those of De Long and his gallant company of the *Jeannette*. They fell not, warriors though they were, in war, nor was the fate of nations trembling upon the issue of their struggle. But it is not in war alone that martyrs win their crowns; nor is it only in the clash of arms and the din of battle that is revealed the beauty of heroic death.

It matters not whether their bones lie here, or at their homes, or on the bleak Siberian coast, where they gave up their lives: "the whole earth," said Pericles, "is the sepulcher of illustrious men." But it is fitting that here should be their monument. It stands here for us Americans, who hold our Navy and our Country dear, as a memorial of what her sons have done, and as an earnest of what they will do hereafter. It stands here for you, the comrades of those young officers who fell, to give you added strength and courage, when you too find yourselves the victims of relentless fate and driven to the edge of the black chasm of despair. It stands here, last of all, for you, Cadets of the Navy, that daily you may have before your eyes this bright example of heroic virtue— . . . virtue which in the past has been the pride and glory of your Service, and which it will rest with you to transmit in undimmed luster to the generations yet to come. . . . There they stand, the martyrs of the Lena Delta, the men who, through high courage, overcame disaster; surrounded by that goodly company of brave explorers, whose memory, like theirs, remains enshrined [here] illumined by the brightness of their own imperishable fame.

J. R. *Soley*, Assistant Secretary of the Navy, October 30, 1890

Jeanette Crew Burial Site

De Long and others reburied in Woodlawn Cemetery, Westchester County, New York

Memento

Marble ice drips from the marble cross,
memorial to officers and crew lost
in the expedition to the Pole,
failed experiment that shows

how hopelessness can be faced
with hope: day after icebound day,
to take soundings, toss footballs,
plan trips to Paris, France;

to name the sled (the ship
now sunk) without irony or pity
(but with such spirit in adversity!)
Nil Desideratum, Never Despair.

In our own struggles on the ice—
or anywhere!—may we learn to dare
more for others than for self,
to rise to such sacrifice.

King Hall

King Hall exterior (Randell Hunt "Doc" Prothro and Gustav F. "Gus" Swainson Jr.)

Upperclassmen appear relaxed in the noisy atmosphere, chatting with classmates about classes and sports games. As a plebe, however, my emotions when entering King Hall are of a different caliber. . . . I stand at my table at attention, waiting for the upperclassmen to arrive and begin quizzing me incessantly on daily rates. This feeling of anxiety before meals is a reason I look forward to the day I can stroll into King Hall as a relaxed upperclassman.

Brandi N. Olson, USNA 2004

K ing Hall, the vast T-shaped dining area inside Bancroft Hall, seats the entire brigade of over four thousand midshipmen at once, in squads of twelve at over four hundred tables. After the command "Brigade, seats!" is called at noon meal, the most formal meal of the day, the staff prides itself on serving all the mids lunch within just a few minutes.

A tender breaded chicken strip smothered in honey mustard served in between a hot biscuit is the right way to start a day. About every other week King Hall serves up this delicious delicacy. Why they do not serve Breakfast Chicken Sandwiches more often is a mystery to my fellow classmates and me. In fact this breakfast sandwich is the only thing that will inspire my roommates and me to wake up when given the opportunity to sleep in.

Travis E. King, USNA 2008

King Hall doors (Randell Hunt "Doc" Prothro and Gustav F. "Gus" Swainson Jr.)

The mess is named for Fleet Adm. Ernest J. King (1878–1956), USNA 1901, commander in chief of the U.S. Fleet and chief of naval operations in World War II. As a junior officer, King served on a variety of large and small ships and held instructor duty at the Academy. In the early teens, he commanded a torpedo flotilla. From 1915 through World War I, he served on the staff of Adm. Henry Mayo. After the war he commanded a submarine flotilla and the submarine base at New London, Connecticut. In 1930, after flight training and further sea duty, he was given command of aircraft carrier USS *Lexington*. In 1941 he was appointed commander of the Atlantic Patrol Force and then commander of the newly created Atlantic Fleet. After the attack on Pearl Harbor, King returned to Washington as commander in chief, U.S. Fleet. In 1942 he received a dual appointment as CNO. As a member of the Joint Chiefs of Staff, Admiral King lobbied successfully for resources for Pacific offensive operations against Japan, despite a war strategy of concentrating resources and efforts in the European and Atlantic theaters.

Midshipmen's Mess Hall, 1945 (U.S. Naval Institute Photo Archive)

Adm. Ernest J. King (U.S. Naval Institute Photo Archive)

In 1944 he was promoted to fleet admiral. When the war was won on all fronts, King retired from active duty.

> When serving twelve thousand people a day, there is quite a bit of foresight that must be involved. Each meal is another battle that must be thought through carefully and planned accordingly to avoid the slightest mistake. King Hall is an example of the efficiency that Admiral King embodied and the Navy strives to achieve every day.

Plebe

King Quotations

Do all that we can with what we have.

Hold what you've got and hit them where you can.

No fighter ever won his fight by covering up, merely fending off the other fellow's blows. The winner hits and keeps on hitting even though he has to be able to take some stiff blows in order to keep on hitting.

Learn to think—learn to analyze—learn to look before you leap—apply scientific method in all things. . . . [P]ostgraduate technical education . . . has more than mere engineering knowledge as its aim. . . . [It has been presented] for the purpose of broadening your viewpoint, and, frankly, with the hope that you will, on your own initiative, begin to look about you and see what is going on in the world.

"Education of Naval Officers," Naval Postgraduate School lecture,
May 16, 1925

It is particularly important to comprehend the enemy point of view in all aspects.

> "Establishment of the Combat Intelligence Division of Fleet Headquarters," July 1, 1943

[I]t is important to realize that there can be no hard and fast rule for setting up commands in the field. . . . It was fortunate that the War Department and the Navy Department, working together for many years . . . had instituted, not rigid rules, but a set of principles for joint action in the field which proved sufficiently flexible to meet the varying conditions that were encountered during the war.

> *Third Report to the Secretary of the Navy*, December 8, 1945

We must, if you like, paraphrase the phrase, "waging war." Why should we not "wage peace"? Why should we not make as much effort to win the peace as we do to win the war? Why should there not be a militant peace, and not for a few weeks or a few months or a few years, but always?

> *The Evening Bulletin*, October 14, 1946

Quotations about King

> A man so various that he seems to be,
> Not one, but all mankind's epitome.
> Temper? Don't fool with nitroglycerin.
>
> *Lucky Bag*, 1901

Lord, how I need him.

Secretary of the Navy Frank Knox, December 23, 1941

❦

Admiral King, commander in chief of United States fleet, and directly subordinate to the president, is an arbitrary, stubborn type, with not too much brains and a tendency toward bullying his juniors. But I think he wants to fight, which is vastly encouraging.

President Dwight D. Eisenhower, diary entry, February 23, 1942

❦

[King] was an exceptionally able sea commander. He also was explosive, and at times it was just as well that the deliberations of the Joint Chiefs were a well-kept secret.

William Leahy, I Was There (1950)

Burial Site

USNA Cemetery

Leahy Hall

Leahy Hall (Randell Hunt "Doc" Prothro and Gustav F. "Gus" Swainson Jr.)

Built in 1939 as a medical clinic, Leahy Hall was later home to the Aviation Department, then the Modern Languages Department, from 1952 to 1973. In 1973 Leahy Hall became the home of the Registrar's Office (recently relocated to Nimitz Library) and the Admissions and Candidate Guidance offices.

The building is named for Fleet Adm. William D. Leahy (1875–1959), USNA 1897, chief of naval operations, governor of Puerto Rico, ambassador to France, chief of staff of the commander in chief, and Fleet Admiral of the U.S. Navy. In World War I Leahy commanded the dispatch boat that was used by Assistant Secretary of the Navy Franklin Delano Roosevelt and won the Navy Cross in 1918 for transporting troops to France.

After achieving flag rank in 1927, he became chief of the Bureau of Ordnance. In 1937 he served as the chief of naval operations until his retirement from the Navy in 1939. He became governor of Puerto Rico in 1939. Then, beginning in 1940, he served for two years as U.S. ambassador to France, where he attempted to persuade the Vichy government to rejoin the war against Hitler. In July 1942 Leahy returned to active duty as the chief of staff to the president, and in December 1944 he was appointed to the newly created rank of fleet admiral, becoming the first five-star in the U.S. armed forces.

Leahy Quotations

The aspect of the Pearl Harbor disaster which is really surprising is that so many people failed to do either the obvious or sensible things.

~~~

[The bombings of Hiroshima and Nagasaki were] of no material assistance in our war against Japan. . . . In being the first to use [the atomic bomb] we had adopted an ethical standard common to the barbarians of the Dark Ages. I was not taught to make war in that fashion, and wars cannot be won by destroying women and children.

I Was There, 1950

Quotations about Leahy

Bill, if we have a war, you're going to be right back here to help me run it.

President Franklin D. Roosevelt on Leahy's retirement, 1939

Fleet Adm. William D. Leahy (U.S. Naval Institute Photo Archive)

❦

One of the architects of victory in World War II and of the peace that followed.

NY Times editorial, July 21, 1959

❦

In the passing of Admiral William D. Leahy, the nation has lost an outstanding American. . . . As a naval officer and as a diplomat, Leahy dedicated his life to the service of his country in war and in peace.

President Dwight D. Eisenhower, July 21, 1959

❦

With the customary ceremony and honors, Admiral Leahy's casket was carried to the grave, where Chaplain Zimmerman read the burial service. A final cannon salute, the traditional three volleys, and the sounding of taps closed the final rites for the five-star admiral.

"Former Chief of Naval Operations Fleet Admiral William D. Leahy Special Military Funeral, 21–23 July 1959"

Burial Site

Arlington National Cemetery, Arlington, Virginia

Lejeune Hall

A ship without Marines is like a garment without buttons.

Adm. David D. Porter

Lejeune Hall (Randell Hunt "Doc" Prothro and Gustav F. "Gus" Swainson Jr.)

Midshipmen have to learn to face their fears head on. Lejeune Hall, dedicated to United States Marine Corps Lieutenant General John A. Lejeune, is the place where many do. The Marines earned their nickname, the Devil Dogs, during World War I. The Germans, amazed by their ferocity and their relentless pursuit of victory, named the Marines after the mythical hounds of hell. This was the spirit that General Lejeune represented as a commander and commandant, making his name live on in history. Now in this building that commemorates this great man, mids are trained in swimming and wrestling as well as in confidence, so that the devil dog spirit may be passed on. Sometimes, though, we can use a little luck; so every time I pass the bronze relief that hangs in the inside hallway, I make a point to buff the nose for good luck.

Tyler W. Forrest, USNA 2002

L ejeune Hall, a 95,000-square-foot steel and concrete building built in 1982, houses a diving pool and Olympic-size swimming pool and other facilities for the swimming, diving, and water polo teams. The large pool is also used for the required "forty-year swim," a forty-minute test of a midshipman's ability to swim while fully clothed; and the diving pool is used for the leap from the ten-meter platform, required of every midshipman for graduation.

General Lejeune

The spirit of a man who never died
With skill to erase doubt from our eyes
In battle he was never a stranger
Offered laughs in the face of danger

Always prepared to carry out any task
To handle any job he was asked
First Marine to command an Army division
His calm decisive attitude made this a good decision

Today as midshipmen we remember him
As a kind of demon, evil and grim
Who tortures us with the "forty-year" swim
Required by all to acquire a piece of him

Perfect example of endurance and determination
He dedicated forty years of his life to his nation
John Lejeune—in this world, man without compare
Whose place in history no one could share

Nelson B. Diggs, USNA 2007

The only building at the Academy named for a Marine Corps officer, Lejeune Hall honors Lt. Gen. John Archer Lejeune (1867–1942), USMC, USNA 1888. The Personnel Act of August 5,1882, had opened the Marine Corps to Academy graduates, and on commissioning, Lejeune joined up. Often referred to as "the greatest of all Leathernecks," Lejeune spent more than forty years in the service. During the Mexican War, he took part in the April 21, 1914, landing at Veracruz, and during World War I, he first commanded the new Marine base at Quantico, then led the Army Second Infantry Division (consisting of both Army soldiers and U.S. Marines). Lejeune personally designed the division's Indian head insignia patch, which is still used today. After the war, Lejeune served as the Marine Corps commandant from 1920 to 1929. As commandant, Lejeune, believing that the Navy needed Marines—troops familiar with naval ways and able to conduct land operations in support of naval actions—developed the amphibious warfare techniques that make the Marines unique. He was the man most responsible for creating the Marine Corps of today, with its traditions of discipline, loyalty, and integrity and its ability to accomplish the most arduous and dangerous of missions. From 1929 until 1942 he served as superintendent of the Virginia Military Institute.

A statue of Lejeune stands humbly, with gloves off, in front of Lejeune Hall. Created in 2000 by Louisiana sculptor Patrick Dane Miller and donated to the Academy by Patrick Taylor (1937–2004, USMC), the statue was dedicated on May 3, 2002. Other castings of the statue are located at Lejeune's birthplace in New Roads, Louisiana; the Marine

Corps Base Camp, Lejeune, North Carolina; Marine Corps Base Quantico, Virginia; the USS *Kidd* Memorial, Baton Rouge, Louisiana; and the Marine Corps Heritage Museum near Quantico, Virginia.

> It is bronze.
> And it is stone.
> But there are truths
> Held under the surface.
> Many pass by
> But few ever notice.
> His figure is there
> Standing in glory.
> I will remember
> How his work transformed the corps,
> Kept it alive.
> Without him
> There would be no corps,
> No need for so great a commandant.

Brendon P. Smeresky, USNA 2006

~≫~

Dedication of Lejeune Hall

Accomplishing the mission of the Naval Academy—to prepare young men and women morally, mentally, and physically to be professional officers in the naval service—requires equal and unrelenting attention to this triad. No officer better represents a successful blend of these attributes than Lieutenant General John A. Lejeune, an 1888 graduate of the Naval Academy who became the 13th Commandant of the Marine Corps. It is most fitting that the first building to be named after a Marine at the United States Naval Academy be dedicated in his honor. Designed to hone physical fitness and survival skills through a focus on swimming, martial arts training, and wrestling, Lejeune Hall formally opens it doors today after three years of construction. I cannot but think that General Lejeune—pugnacious, aggressive, and competitive—would approve and applaud our efforts to fulfill our commitment to physical excellence with the help of this beautiful new athletic facility.

Vice Adm. Edward C. Waller, Superintendent, April 28, 1982

Lt. Gen. John Archer Lejeune, Patrick Miller statue (Randell Hunt "Doc" Prothro and Gustav F. "Gus" Swainson Jr.)

Marine Corps Birthday Message (Marine Corps Orders No. 47, Series 1921)

The following will be read to the command . . . on the 10th of November of every year:

On November 10, 1775, a Corps of Marines was created by a resolution of Continental Congress. Since that date many thousand men have borne the name "Marine." In memory of them it is fitting that we who are Marines should commemorate the birthday of our corps by calling to mind the glories of its long and illustrious history. . . .

In every battle and skirmish since the birth of our corps, Marines have acquitted themselves with the greatest distinction, winning new honors on each occasion until the term "Marine" has come to signify all that is highest in military efficiency and soldierly virtue.

This high name of distinction and soldierly repute we who are Marines today have received from those who preceded us in the corps. With it we have also received from them the eternal spirit which has animated our corps from generation to generation and has been the distinguishing mark of the Marines in every age. So long as the spirit continues to flourish Marines will be found equal to every emergency in the future as they have been in the past, and the men of our Nation will regard us as worthy successors to the long line of illustrious men who have served as "Soldiers of the Sea" since the founding of the Corps.

Be kindly and just in your dealings with your men. Never play favorites. Make them feel that justice tempered with mercy may always be counted on. This does not mean a slackening of discipline. Obedience to orders and regulations must always be insisted upon, and good conduct of the men exacted. Especially should this be done with reference to the civilian inhabitants of foreign countries in which Marines are serving.

Lejeune Quotations

The major factor of true military discipline consists of securing the voluntary cooperation of subordinates, thereby reducing the number of infractions of the laws and regulations to a minimum [and] by laying down the doctrine that the true test of the existence of a high state of discipline in a military organization is found in its cheerful and satisfactory performance of duty under all service conditions.

The spirit of comradeship and brotherhood-in-arms which has traditionally existed throughout the ranks of the Marine Corps is a vital characteristic of the Corps. It must be fostered and kept alive and made the moving force in all Marine Corps organizations.

It will be necessary for officers not only to devote their close attention to the many questions affecting the comfort, health, morals, religious guidance, military training, and discipline of the men under their command, but also to actively enlist the interest of their men in building up and maintaining their bodies in the finest physical condition; to encourage them to improve their professional knowledge and to make every effort by means of historical, educational, and patriotic address to cultivate in their hearts a deep abiding love of the Corps and Country.

Reminiscences of a Marine, 1930

⁓ℰℊ⁓

True education may be divided into three main branches. These may be described as the up-building of character; the development of faculties of the mind; and the physical training of the body. They are stated in the order of their importance.

Man has always been and still is a fighting animal, and our safety and happiness require that substitutes for war or for armed conflict should be found.

Address to VMI students, 1937

Burial Site

Arlington National Cemetery, Arlington, Virginia

My heart pounded in my throat. Through the eyes of what should have been a bird, I stood high above that ocean of space beneath me, a little pool of water waiting for me miles below. Standing in line to jump off the ten-meter platform, my anxieties grew. . . . My turn drew nearer. Thoughts racing in my head began to focus on my predicament; how would I survive this matter? "Just as I always have," I kept telling myself; "just leap out in faith." If completed, this task would signify more than just the accomplishment of the jump. With the end of plebe summer approaching, the jump would stand as a symbol of my confidence in my ability, a main objective in this ordeal. . . . My turn came. Without hesitation, I took a deep breath and leapt out into space. The weightless sensation surged into an adrenaline rush, and I slammed into the water as gracefully as everyone else. My day became a success. Soon after everyone had jumped, a chant began, encouraging our senior enlisted leader, Gunnery Sergeant Bradley, to jump as we just had. "GUNNEY, GUNNEY, GUNNEY . . ." He obliged, and with his splash down into the cool pool water below, we were accepted.

Jared M. Sutherland, USNA 2009

Uriah P. Levy Center
and Jewish Chapel

May the Jewish midshipmen use this chapel to deepen their love for our country and their quest for learning, tradition and identity.

Elie Wiesel

Uriah P. Levy Center and Jewish Chapel (Randell Hunt "Doc" Prothro and Gustav F. "Gus" Swainson Jr.)

The Levy Center and Jewish Chapel, named in honor of Uriah Phillips Levy (1792–1862), the first Jewish-American naval officer to reach flag rank, was dedicated September 18, 2005, to help fulfill the Academy's mission of the moral development of midshipmen. Nestled between the seventh and eighth wings of Bancroft Hall, it was designed in the octagonal, domed style of Thomas Jefferson's Monticello, which Levy once owned and restored. The chapel, composed of wood and Jerusalem stone with a soaring four-story atrium, serves both as a place of worship and a fitting monument to American Jews who have served in the country's defense since the inception of the Navy and Marine Corps. Housing the Honor Court and Ethics Center, the building also functions as a training ground in ethics for all midshipmen.

> The Center is named for Commodore Uriah Phillips Levy (1792–1862), whose crusading efforts led to the abolishment of corporal punishment and the professional enhancement of naval officers. His vision of leadership led him to purchase Monticello, Thomas Jefferson's home, as a public tribute to the country's third president. Despite six court-martials, primarily for charges stemming from anti-Semitism, Levy dedicated fifty years service to the Navy, rising through the ranks to become Commodore of the Mediterranean Fleet in 1860. He was the first American Jewish officer in the Navy to reach flag rank. In honor of Levy's dedication to the navy, his country and his faith, the Levy Center stands as a source of education and religious inspiration for midshipmen of all faiths and nationalities.

> The Commo. Uriah P. Levy Center and Jewish Chapel Brochure

Burial Site

Cypress Hills Cemetery, Brooklyn, New York

> The Levy Center embodies the best our midshipmen's future has to offer outside of the academic classroom—in soul and spirit. History is replete with cases of doom because of leadership without ethics. What the Levy Center means to me: a future where midshipmen lead men and women into battle courageously and ethically.

> *Lt. Matthew B. Krauz*, USNA 2001, 20th Company Officer

Commo. Uriah P. Levy (U.S. Naval Institute Photo Archive)

Luce Hall

. . . where under flashing lights we were imbued with the envolumed arcana of an entrancing sea-lore.

Lucky Bag, 1929

Luce Hall (Randell Hunt "Doc" Prothro and Gustav F. "Gus" Swainson Jr.)

In Luce learn the laws of the Navy,
Recall the rules of the road,
Don't forget *red right returning*
Nor the difference between ebb and flow.

Timothy C. Steiner, USNA 2010

Head of the Class

An innovative mind
That thought only of the future,
Admiral Luce did in life
What all men wish to do,
Challenging what life has in store,
Always pushing to be better,
Always encouraging those around him.
Memorialized not for his character
Or work; memorialized
For his encouragement of others.

Daniel S. Sherman, USNA 2007

Rear Adm. Stephen B. Luce, c. 1885 (U.S. Naval Institute Photo Archive)

L uce Hall, the seamanship and navigation building constructed in 1920, honors Rear Adm. Stephen B. Luce (1827–1917), USNA 1847, one of the Navy's outstanding officers in the fields of strategy, seamanship, education, and professional development. His book *Seamanship*, first published in 1866, served as the Academy's seamanship text for thirty-five years, until it was replaced in 1901 by Austin M. Knight's *Modern Seamanship*. Luce first entered naval service as a midshipman in 1841, one of the "forty-oners," the first Naval School class to move from Philadelphia to Annapolis. He taught seamanship at the Academy in 1860–61 and again at Newport in 1862–63, when the Academy was relocated there during the Civil War. During the war, he also commanded the monitor *Nantucket* and the gunboat *Pontiac*. After the war, he led the 1865 summer cruise back to Annapolis and served as commandant of midshipmen until 1868. From 1878 to 1881 he was inspector of training ships, and from 1881 to 1884 he commanded the U.S. Training Squadron. He organized the first "no notice" amphibious landing with two infantry battalions, one made up of sailors. Luce was instrumental in establishing the Naval War College, a school designed specifically for the professional development of naval officers after a tour at sea, giving them the opportunity to develop administrative as well as tactical skills. He served as the first president of the Naval War College from 1884 to 1886 and as special adviser from 1901 to 1910. Luce was also one of the founders of the U.S. Naval Institute and served as its president from 1887 to 1898.

Burial Site

St. Mary's Church, Portsmouth, Rhode Island

Leadership laboratory
Laborious law
Seamanship studies
Notorious nav
Enticing ethics
Monotonous MO-boards
Determined discussion
. . . vague recollection

Ryan P. Keller, USNA 2009

❦

In Luce I sit, staring at my hand,
as halyards clank and deep-throated warnings
of passing vessels sound. With diligence
I bend my head toward the printed charts
and strain to hear the veteran lieutenant
retelling stories from beyond the view of land.

Andrew L. Lewis, USNA 2009

Macdonough Hall

Feeling the call to war
He was compelled
To fight for his country
The beliefs that he held
Raised up a fleet
To counter the threat
And an infant nation
Was left in his debt.

Isaiah D. Gammache, USNA 2006

Macdonough Hall (Randell Hunt "Doc" Prothro and Gustav F. "Gus" Swainson Jr.)

M acdonough Hall, originally conceived as a boathouse and sited on the Severn River's shoreline, opened in 1903 as a gymnasium with space on the upper floor for the Seamanship Department. In Ernest Flagg's grand symmetrical design for the training facilities of the Academy, it flanks the east side of Bancroft Hall, while its twin, Dahlgren, the original Armory, flanks the west. Expansion of the Academy on land reclaimed from the Severn changed its relationship to the water and transformed its function. Today it is a physical training facility, with a pool, a basketball court, and other athletic training areas.

Built in 1924 as a separate building for aquatics, though now architecturally connected to Macdonough, Scott Natatorium was named for Rear Adm. Norman Scott (1889–1942), USNA 1911, who was killed in action in the naval battle of Guadalcanal (also referred to as the third and fourth battles of Savo Island and the Battle of the Solomons). One of the islands in the Solomon Islands chain in the southern Pacific, Guadalcanal became the staging area for the first major offensive launched by the Allied forces against the Japanese. The hard-fought campaign, lasting from August 7, 1942, to February 9, 1943, provided the Allies a strategic victory. For his actions in the naval battle on November 13, Scott was awarded a Medal of Honor posthumously.

> In Macdonough, past the pool, and up two flights of stairs there is a place where ghosts walk. The smell of sweat and worn leather is testament to the champions who trained here. In patches, the yellow floor is worn grey from jumping rope and dancing feet. The bags sway silently, beaten to submission. . . . Spanning a century the brigade champions line the walls on blue plaques, their names in gold. In the back of the locker, above the gloves worn by a hundred fists, are the tattered words of "Gentleman Jim": "The man who always fights one more round . . . is never whipped."
>
> *Steven Podmore*, USNA 2005

Macdonough Hall honors Capt. Thomas Macdonough (1783–1825), the "Hero of Lake Champlain" (or the "Hero of Plattsburg"), known for defeating the British on Lake Champlain in 1814. Macdonough joined the Navy as a midshipman at age sixteen and soon saw action in the

West Indies during the undeclared war with France (1798–1801). During the Barbary War of 1803–5 off the coast of Tripoli (see the Tripoli Monument entry), he proved his mettle. After pirates had captured the U.S. frigate *Philadelphia*, Macdonough joined Stephen Decatur in boarding the vessel in February 1804 and, setting it afire, preventing its use by the enemy. One story tells how, during gunboat actions that August, Macdonough, his cutlass broken and useless, boarded a Barbary ship and wrestled a pistol from a pirate in order to shoot and kill him. From 1810 to 1812, Macdonough left active duty, but as hostilities rose between the United States and Britain in 1812, he rejoined the Navy. Secretary of the Navy William Jones ordered Macdonough to take over the crippled fleet in Lake Champlain and protect the nation from British invasion from the north. In his letter of June 17, 1813, reminding Macdonough that the Navy relies upon "your efficient and prudent use of the authority vested in you . . . and for which you are held responsible," Jones commanded him to "regain by every possible exertion the ascendancy which we have lost."

The September 11, 1814, Battle of Lake Champlain (known by the Army as the Battle of Plattsburg, as it involved land as well as naval actions) is considered one of the most significant battles in U.S. history. Knowing that the British ships outgunned his, especially at long range, Macdonough forced the British to engage at close quarters. By positioning his flagship *Saratoga* so that it could be turned around without relying on the wind, he was able to renew the attack despite grave losses. The battle forced the British Army to retreat into Canada and helped demolish British territorial claims to the region at the 1814 peace conference in Ghent, Belgium. Macdonough's transformation of the fleet and his brilliant battle strategy helped save the nation.

> Thanked for freedom upheld
> Remembered by ships of his name
> Thought of as prince of the sea
> American hero, he lies in fame

> Plebe, USNA 2007

Capt. Thomas Macdonough, c. 1815 (Massachusetts Historical Society)

Macdonough Quotations

On October 3rd 1803 I was ordered on shore by Lieutenant Tarbell for fresh provisions takeing in the boat 6 men, when the boat got on shore I took two men up to the markett for the purpose of bringing down the provisions leaving John Cox, Thomas Green and William Hughes with another to take care of the boat with orders not to leave it, but on my return to the boat three of the men were gone. I was from the boat about one half hour. October 6th 1803 I went on shore for the same purpose takeing four men in the boat and three up to the markett leaving John Tuck to take command of the boat and on my return found he had made his escape.

Letter to Commo. Edward Preble, October 16, 1803

⤚⤙

Sir: The United States now being at war, I solicit your order for service in the Navy and hope you will favor me with such a situation as in your opinion I am suited to hold. I have the honor to be, your most [obedient servant], T. Macdonough

Letter to Secretary of the Navy , Paul Hamilton, June 26, 1812

⤚⤙

Macdonough, Plattsburg gun (Randell Hunt "Doc" Prothro and Gustav F. "Gus" Swainson Jr.)

The Army Secretary has been pleased to grant us a signal victory on Lake Champlain in the capture of one frigate, one brig, and two sloops of war with the enemy.

Letter to Secretary of the Navy Jones, September 11, 1814

〜✦〜

SIR, I have the honor to give you the particulars of the action which took place on the 11th instant on this lake. For several days the enemy were on their way to Plattsburgh by land and water, and it being understood that an attack would be made at the same time by their land and naval forces, I determined to await at anchor the approach of the latter.

At eight AM the lookout boat announced the approach of the enemy. At 9, he anchored in a line ahead, at about three hundred yards distance from my line; his ship opposed to the SARATOGA his brig to the EAGLE, Captain Robert Henley; his galleys, thirteen in number, to the schooner, sloop, and a division of our galleys; one of his sloops assisting their ship and brig, the other assisting their galleys; our remaining galleys with the SARATOGA and EAGLE. In this situation, the whole force, on both sides, became engaged, the SARATOGA suffering much from the heavy fire of the CONFIANCE.

I could perceive, at the same time, however, that our fire was very destructive to her. The TICONDEROGA, Lieutenant Commander Cassin, gallantly sustained her full share of the action. At half past 10 o'clock, the EAGLE, not being able to bring her guns to bear, cut her cable, and anchored in a more eligible position, between my ship and the TICONDEROGA, where she very much annoyed the enemy, but unfortunately, leaving me exposed to a galling fire from the enemy's brig. Our guns on the starboard side being nearly all dismounted, or not manageable, a stern anchor was let go, the bower cable cut, and the ship winded, with a fresh broadside on the enemy's ship, which soon after surrendered. Our broadside was then sprung to bear on the brig, which surrendered in about 15 minutes after. The sloop that was opposed to the EAGLE had struck some time before, and drifted down the line; the sloop which was with their galleys having struck also. Three of their galleys are said to be sunk, the others pulled off. Our galleys were about obeying, with alacrity, the signal to follow them, when all the vessels were reported to me to be in a sinking state; then it became necessary to annul the signal to the galleys, and order their men to the pumps. I could only look at the enemy's galleys going off in a shattered condition, for there was not a mast in either squadron that could stand to make sail on; the lower rigging being nearly shot away, hung down as though it had been just placed over mastheads. The SARATOGA had fifty-five round shot in her hull, the CONFIANCE one hundred and five. The enemy's shot passed principally over our heads, as there were not twenty whole hammocks in the nettings at the close of the action, which lasted, without intermission, two hours and twenty minutes. . . .

I close, sir, this communication with feelings of gratitude, for the able support I received from every officer and man attached to the squadron which I have the honor to command. I have the honor to be, with great respect, sir your most obedient servant, T. MACDONOUGH

Letter to Secretary of the Navy William Jones, September 13, 1814

Burial Site

Riverside Cemetery, Middletown, Connecticut

Epitaph

He was born in the State of Delaware December 1783 & died at sea of pulmonary consumption while on his return from the command of the American Squadron in the Mediterranean on the 02nd Nov 1825. He was distinguished in the world as the hero of Lake Champlain.

Macdonough Athlete

Twisting and turning on the rings,
Known to do amazing things,
He trains constantly for meets,
Where he must be the best to compete.
He flips until he reaches his peak,
Then twists and lands on his feet,
A gymnast, an amazing athlete.

David O. Jones, USNA 2010

Macedonian Monument

Macedonian Monument (Randell Hunt "Doc" Prothro and Gustav F. "Gus" Swainson Jr.)

Emulations

Honor, courage and commitment.
Values sacred to our calling,
Values embodied in your name.

Your monument stands proudly at the
Heart of the Academy.
Your spirit is emulated in the
Hearts of a class of warriors.

We shape stone to model your
Achievements,
We shape Midshipmen to model your
Character.

                                                    Plebe, USNA 2007

At the end of Stribling Walk, just a few yards from Flagg's academic
group of buildings, including Sampson, Mahan, and Maury halls,
stands the Macedonian Monument, a white figurehead atop a concrete pedestal, guarded by a cannon on each of four corners. The helmeted figurehead, originally located at the bow of HMS *Macedonian*
and erected at the Naval Academy in 1924, represents Alexander the
Great (356–323 BC), the powerful Macedonian king who conquered an
empire stretching from Egypt to India. HMS *Macedonian*, built in England in 1810 to combat the Napoleonic fleet, was loaded with thirty-eight
18-pounders (cannons firing 18-pound shot). In 1812, when the United
States declared war on Great Britain for impressing U.S. sailors, Stephen
Decatur, commanding USS *United States*, engaged the *Macedonian* in a
fierce battle. After the British frigate had lost both its mizzenmast and
mainmast and a good number of sailors, Capt. John Surman Carden of
the Royal Navy struck colors. When he went aboard the *United States*
to deliver his sword, Decatur tried to lessen the pain of surrender, saying
that he could not accept the sword of such a gallant commander. Decatur took the captured vessel to the United States to great acclaim, and it
was then entered into the U.S. fleet as USS *Macedonian*. The ship saw
action in the Barbary War of 1815, a renewal of naval actions against the
Barbary Coast powers. The *Macedonian* figurehead continued as the figurehead of USS *Macedonian* (1812–38), then as the figurehead of USS
Macedonian II (1836–52), after which it was affixed to a building at the
New York Navy Yard. In 1875 it was sent to the Academy, where it was
exhibited on the porch of the Seamanship Building from 1875 to about
1900. Then it was likely moved to Macdonough Hall from 1903 to 1918
and to Luce Hall from 1918 to 1924, before it was mounted on its current
pedestal and called the Macedonian Monument.

Every time I pass by the figurehead of the Macedonian I am struck with pride. The thought of a young, highly unprofessional navy without hesitation taking on and defeating the most powerful navy at the time always inspires me to do my best no matter what the odds.

Matthew E. Danielson, USNA 2010

~≈9≈~

The Battle between USS *United States* and HMS *Macedonian*

A strange noise, such as I had never heard before, next arrested my attention; it sounded like the tearing of sails, just over our heads. This I soon ascertained to be the wind of the enemy's shot. The firing, after a few minutes' cessation, recommenced. The roaring of cannon could now be heard from all parts of our trembling ship, and, mingling as it did with that of our foes, it made a most hideous noise. By-and-by I heard the shot strike the sides of our ship; the whole scene grew indescribably confused and horrible; it was like some awfully tremendous thunderstorm, whose deafening roar is attended by incessant streaks of lightning, carrying death in every flash and strewing the ground with the victims of its wrath: only, in our case, the scene was rendered more horrible than that, by the presence of torrents of blood which dyed our decks. . . .

I have often been asked what were my feelings during this fight. I felt pretty much as I suppose every one does at such a time. That men are without thought when they stand amid the dying and the dead is too absurd an idea to be entertained a moment. We all appeared cheerful, but I know that many a serious thought ran through my mind: still, what could we do but keep up a semblance, at least, of animation? To run from our quarters would have been certain death from the hands of our own officers; to give way to gloom, or to show fear, would do no good, and might brand us with the name of cowards, and ensure certain defeat. Our only true philosophy, therefore, was to make the best of our situation by fighting bravely and cheerfully. I thought a great deal, however, of the other world; every groan, every falling man, told me that the next instant I might be before the judge of all the earth. For this, I felt unprepared; but being without any particular knowledge of religious truth, I satisfied myself by repeating again and again the Lord's prayer and promising that if spared I would be more attentive to religious duties than ever before. This promise I had no doubt, at the time, of keeping;

but I have learned since that it is easier to make promises amidst the roar of the battle's thunder, or in the horrors of shipwreck, than to keep them when danger is absent and safety smiles upon our path. American sailors, HMS *Macedonian* fell into American hands.

Samuel Leech, British sailor in the U.S. Navy,
Thirty Years from Home, 1843

~~~

Macedonian Reflections

Into night-dark waters off Tripoli
To burn the captured vessel free,
Decatur boldly led his men.
All I ask is that you follow me!

Later in the bright Azores,
Fighting till the decks flowed red
And *Macedonian* struck her colors,
Decatur, ever gracious, said

To the defeated British captain,
"I cannot accept the sword
Of so gallant a commander,"
And took off his hat and bowed.

Two centuries later now
The prized figurehead,
A helmeted Greek warrior,
Gazes not into blue horizons

But toward stone structures
Of academic instruction
That teach the importance of reflection
As well as of action.

Mahan Hall

O great portal! . . . O massive doors! . . . intriguing our souls
into the splendid deepnesses that lie beyond.

Lucky Bag, 1929

Mahan Hall, rear view (Melissa Jo Keevers Bridges)

He defined Navy's role—power—no matter the place,
Gave us a purpose and pushed harder our pace
Of building the Navy so all can sense our power
And fear the thought of war's dreadful hours.

This building, this monument stands for all to see
The clock at the summit unraveling history.
The walls within echo thoughts of the past,
We all can hear Mahan's advice to the last.

The bells enclosed keep rhythm and time,
Inspire thoughts and emotions, sublime.
The hall stands through the day and the night,
A beacon of hope, a beacon of light.

Scott A. Simpson, USNA 2010

Mahan Hall with its "great portal" and tall clock tower, completed in 1907, is the central building of Flagg's academic group. Situated on Stribling Walk at the far end from Bancroft Hall, it is designed in similar Beaux-Arts style, with high-relief facade sculpture, large elaborate windows, and graceful curves. Mahan houses an auditorium on the lower level, where the Academy's theatrical organization, the Masqueraders, performs; and on the upper level is the Hart Room, an informal study area that was once the library, as revealed by the low-relief sculpture of an open book over the interior doorways.

As the last class bell sounds, and students retreat to Bancroft Hall, the single dormitory on the Yard, I quietly wander down the walk alone, eyes fixed upon the doors of Mahan Hall as they enlarge before me. I imagine the marble floors, the delicate carvings, the lofty ceilings, and the plush red seats of the theater. This is a vision that I carry with me throughout the day, to alleviate the stress of life as a midshipman. As a first year student at the Naval Academy and a new member of the Masqueraders, the long-established guild of Naval Academy actors, I have found Mahan Hall to be a place where I can escape from the trials of plebe year. As I enter the elegant marble hall, the darkened auditorium, and step on the stage, I feel the tradition of theater that has

Mahan Clock Tower (Special Collections and Archives Division, Nimitz Library, U.S. Naval Academy)

become deeply rooted in the culture of the Academy. For over a century, theater has enriched the leadership experience of midshipmen, while at the same time providing a release for their emotions. Admiral Mahan may never have guessed that a theater would be named in his honor, but he would be proud of the way the Masqueraders have contributed to the development of fine naval officers.

Robert P. Wall, USNA 2004

The clock tower, which rises 140 feet from the center of Mahan Hall, provides a perfect location for hanging "spirit banners," or sheets decorated by midshipmen to inspire athletic teams to victory. A "new" bell, cast at the Philadelphia Navy Yard from the bells of four scrapped battleships (*Alabama*, *Indiana*, *Massachusetts*, and *Michigan*, which had served in midshipmen summer cruises), was installed in the tower in 1923 and connected to a Seth Thomas Clock. The bell rings every fifteen minutes.

Bell Tower Haiku

Tick—tock
Can't stop staring
Doesn't the minute hand ever stop?

Ryan G. Beall, USNA 2008

The clock tower bell tolls.
My heart skips another beat.
Still the bell tolls
Whether my weather is sunny or dark.
It tolls indifferently, neutrally passing
The time.

David A. Pilko, USNA 2006

Mahan Hall was named for Rear Adm. Alfred Thayer Mahan (1840–1914), USNA 1859. During the Civil War, Mahan served with the South Atlantic and Western Gulf blockading squadrons. He also served two tours as president of the Naval War College (1886–89 and

Adm. Alfred Thayer Mahan, 1904 (U.S. Naval Institute Photo Archive)

1892–93). After retiring in 1896, he was recalled during the Spanish-American War. In 1899 he was a delegate to the first Peace Conference at The Hague, convened to ban certain types of modern technology in warfare. A persuasive writer, Mahan argued in his 1890 text *The Influence of Sea Power Upon History 1660–1805* that a nation's greatness depended on its control of the seas. His major proposals included using the Caribbean Islands, Hawaii, and the Philippines for bases to protect U.S. commerce; building a canal for ocean-to-ocean fleet mobility; and raising a "great white fleet" of stream-driven armor-plated battleships, painted white to signify a peacetime force. A radical thought at the time in a country focused on westward expansion, Mahan's thesis proved a major influence on Theodore Roosevelt and other proponents of a powerful Navy and overseas expansion. Mahan is also credited with coining the term "Middle East" in his 1902 article discussing the significance of American interest in all areas of the world.

Mahan Quotations

Wars may cease, but the need for heroism shall not depart from the earth, while man remains man and evil exists to be redressed.

⟶⟞⟡⟝⟵

[Americans must turn their] eyes outward, instead of inward only, to seek the welfare of the country.

⟶⟞⟡⟝⟵

To communicate to others that which one's self has acquired, be it much or little . . . is not only a power but a duty. . . . If it be in any measure a reproach to a man to die rich, as has been somewhat emphatically affirmed, it is still more a reproach to depart with accumulations of knowledge or experience willingly locked up in one's own breast.

President's Address, American History Association, 1902

Quotation about Mahan

Alfred Thayer Mahan, the great advocate and visionary of American seapower.

Secretary of the Navy John H. Dalton, 1988

Burial Site

Quogue Cemetery, Quogue, Suffolk County, New York

Clock Tower

The white face stares
relentless as an eye.
Every fifteen minutes
bells mark the time
between class and drill
and meals and study hour.

Only sometimes—
as when a youngster
climbs the tower
to drape a Beat Army!
banner there, retold in tales
in the bright, fleet days
of October homecomings—
does time relent, the climber remain
forever young.

꧁ꫝ꧂

I stare at the tower at the end of Stribling Walk every Tuesday, Thursday, and Friday as I head to English class. Many times an inspirational banner has been hung atop the tower by some mischievous midshipmen. These spirit-inducing banners have been hung by midshipmen for decades prior to home football games. Of all the banners that I have viewed in my time at the Academy the one that sticks out the most in my mind is the one from the class of '73. I remember wondering how these men, who are older than my father, were able to successfully "recon" a banner atop Mahan. This task is one that many midshipmen who are much younger, faster, and maybe a little more daring, have been caught performing several times. In order to successfully perform this task one must break into Mahan Hall, then avoid the video cameras, and finally watch out for the Yard police. With a successful "recon" these alumni proved to me that although with age one may lose speed and strength, one gains knowledge.

Charles Dawson, USNA 2002

Maury Hall

Do not strive to be content . . . but be content to strive.

Professor Matthew Maury, 1870

Maury Hall (Randell Hunt "Doc" Prothro and Gustav F. "Gus" Swainson Jr.)

Maury Hall, the third building of Flagg's academic group formerly housing the English and Law Department and the Modern Languages Department, is now part of the Division of Engineering and Weapons. The building is named after Commo. Matthew Fontaine Maury (1806–73), the "pathfinder of the seas" who pioneered the use of wind and current charts that revolutionized shipping around the world. Maury joined the Navy in 1825 with an appointment as midshipman by Sam Houston, then a U.S. senator from Tennessee. Three voyages from

1825 to 1834 and Psalm 8 ("whatsoever passeth through the pathways of the seas") inspired Maury to study ships' logs and whaling records to chart sea and ocean wind currents. To determine the speed and direction of ocean currents, Maury released weighted "drift bottles" with instructions sealed inside for whoever found them. From the locations and dates of discovery, Maury developed charts of the ocean currents, publishing *Wind and Current Charts* in 1847.

Seriously injured in a carriage accident at age thirty-three and unable to serve at sea, Maury continued to serve in the Navy in a primarily academic and research capacity. A strong advocate for strengthened naval education, Maury pushed for an organized Naval Academy with a curriculum in chronometry, natural history (physics and chemistry), mathematics, and international and maritime law. He joined the staff of the U.S. Naval Observatory (formerly the Depot of Charts and Instruments) in 1842 and, on the completion of a new observatory in 1844, became superintendent, a position he held until 1861. During this time he also initiated the first international conference in oceanography, meteorology, and navigation and published the first textbook of modern oceanography, *The Physical Geography of the Sea* (1855). When his home state of Virginia seceded from the Union in 1861, Maury resigned from the U.S. Navy. Appointed a commander in the Confederate navy, he developed electric mines (known as torpedoes) and spent most of the war years in England, Ireland, and France trying to obtain ships and supplies for the Confederacy. The last five years of his life were spent as a professor of physics at the Virginia Military Institute. For many years after the war, his name was expunged from official U.S. records, yet all sailors today are indebted to him for his service in charting the oceans.

Maury Quotations

I hold the right of copy to a theoretical and practical treatise on Navigation. I should be pleased to receive from you proposals for publication.

The work comprises a treatise on Algebra, on Geometry, Logarithms, Plane Trigonometry, Spherics, Nautical Astronomy, and Navigation, with a set of Logarithmic and other tables, useful to the Navigator. . . . Such a work as this purports to be, is much requested in the Marine of our

Country. It is elementary, and designed well for the use of those who are being educated for the . . . Naval Service. And strange as it may appear, there is not in the English language, a nautical work, which professes to be an Elementary, theoretical & practical treatise on Navigation.

Letter to Cary, Lea & Co., February 13, 1835

Your letter of the 11th inst. has been received and read with a high degree of satisfaction. In it you have the kindness to inform me that His Majesty the King of Denmark, to testify his high appreciation of the services rendered by myself in the cause of science, has signified his wish to confer upon me the Cross of the Order of the Dannebrog. I consider myself fortunate, so to have wrought in my humble office that my labours in the service of my own country should have commended themselves to the favourable consideration of His Majesty; and I feel myself highly honoured that he should deem them worthy of such a signal mark of royal favour.

The organic laws of my country, however, will not allow one of its officers to accept a title from any foreign potentate. Permit me, therefore, to plead this in excuse of the request that you will proceed no further in carrying out the honourable and friendly intentions expressed in your letter.

Letter to Torbin Bille, Legation of Denmark, November 14, 1856

The calm belts of the sea, like mountains on the land, stand mightily in the way of the voyager. Like mountains on the land, they have their passes and their gaps.

Sailing Directions, 1847

Cdr. Matthew Fontaine Maury, 1853 (U.S. Naval Institute Photo Archive)

Our planet is invested with two great oceans; one visible, the other invisible; one underfoot, the other overhead; one entirely envelopes it, the other covers about two thirds of its surface.

[A]s for the general system of atmospheric circulation which I have been so long endeavoring to describe, the Bible tells it all in a single sentence: "The wind goeth toward the South and returneth again to his circuits."

The Physical Geography of the Sea, 1855

Last Words
All's well.

Quotations about Maury

Maury's life consisted of an endless and exhaustive search for knowledge—facts which were undetermined and which no man had taken the patience and trouble to ascertain before him. The benefits resulting from the compilation of the data obtained were denied to no mariners. They soon became of immense value. All nations were stimulated by his energy to join in the exploration. The charting of the seas grew to world-wide extent under Maury's guidance. Crowned heads of all Europe bestowed their highest honors and medals upon him, moved by the debt of gratitude which they owed to him. His place among the great is suggested by his sobriquet—"Pathfinder of the Seas."

Class of 1929 Commemoration, Lucky Bag, 1929

It affords me great pleasure to hand you, in the name of my Government, the accompanying gold medal; its German inscription may be thus rendered in English:

"To the Promoter of Science, to the Guide of Navigators, Lieutenant M. F. Maury, an honorary acknowledgment of the Senate of the Republic of Bremen."

This inscription, better than could any of mine, shows the sense of high appreciation in which your eminent merits, in regard to all maritime interests, are held in my country—the citizens of which are perhaps more generally engaged in navigation, and therefore more benefited by your valuable discoveries and directions than those of any other country. Your name, which has so long been an ornament of the U.S. Navy, is, and will ever be, gratefully remembered in Bremen.

R. Schlieden, Minister of Bremen, December 28, 1856

I have great pleasure in informing you, by order of my Government, that His Majesty the King of Denmark, being desirous of testifying his high sense of the eminent services you have rendered to science by your important and comprehensive researches with reference to the physical geography of the sea, its winds and currents, recorded in the valuable publications of the National Observatory under your superintendence, His Majesty has been pleased to confer on you the Cross of a Knight of the Dannebrog.

Torbin Bille, Legation of Denmark, November 11, 1856

Burial Site

Hollywood Cemetery, Richmond, Virginia

Mexican War Monument

The Center Piece

A group of plebes marches by
The walkway surrounding the monument
Ideal for squaring corners,
No time to stop and admire.
The bell rings.
I walk rapidly to class,
Halt in my tracks
Before the four green cannons,
The beautiful centerpiece
Dedicated to Navy men
That has stood the test of time,
Watching over plebes being transformed
By obstacles overcome, knowledge acquired,
Into what the armed forces require.

Plebe

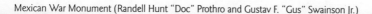

Mexican War Monument (Randell Hunt "Doc" Prothro and Gustav F. "Gus" Swainson Jr.)

Prominently placed at the intersection of Chapel and Stribling walks and midway between Mahan and Bancroft halls, the Mexican War Monument (originally known as the Midshipmen's Monument) commemorates four midshipmen—H. A. Clemson, J. R. Hynson, J. Wingate Pillsbury, and Thomas B. Shubrick—who lost their lives in the Mexican War of 1846–47. The longest-standing monument in the Yard, as well as one of the oldest, this Egyptian-style obelisk was sculpted of Pennsylvania marble and donated in 1848 by "passed and other midshipmen," including the midshipmen of the Class of 1846. It is the first in a long tradition of class gifts.

> The focused midshipmen stream briskly by the white marble memorial in the bustle of the ten-minute class change, not pausing to consider the four midshipmen who sacrificed their lives at Veracruz. . . . Realizing the sacrifices the four men made for their country, I now know better than to walk past this important memorial, giving it only a cursory glance. I recognize the example set by those midshipmen is an ideal, much like a distant island on the high seas: oft dreamed about, but difficult to attain.
>
> J. Adam Pegues, USNA 2003

None of the four midshipmen honored by the monument actually attended the Naval School at Annapolis. Clemson and Hynson, who had attended the Asylum School and passed their exams, were already passed midshipmen. Midshipman Shubrick was ordered to the Naval School, but then his orders were changed to report to the steamer *Mississippi*, being prepared as Commo. Matthew C. Perry's flagship. Midshipman Pillsbury was already aboard *Mississippi* when it joined the naval force off Veracruz at the Mexican War's outbreak in 1846. *Mississippi* later returned to Norfolk, then to Veracruz in March 1846 with Passed Midshipman Clemson aboard. On May 13, 1846, just months after the opening of the Naval School in Annapolis in 1845, Congress declared war against Mexico. The United States ordered a blockade of the coast and an amphibious landing at Veracruz with twelve thousand soldiers, the largest such operation until the landing at Gallipoli in World War I. Shubrick was decapitated by an enemy round shot while at the Naval

Battery at Veracruz. When his launch, sent from *Mississippi* in pursuit of a blockade runner, capsized, Pillsbury gave his place on the upset boat to his crew member and was swept away and drowned. Hynson went down with the vessel. Park Benjamin, midshipman author and Naval Academy historian, records their deaths: "Before aid could reach them the vessel sank. Hynson went down with it; Clemson clung to a spar which he deliberately abandoned when he saw it could not support all who were hanging to it."

Hynson, Clemson, Shubrick, and Pillsbury. These are the names immortalized by the Mexican, or Midshipmen's, Monument. They are the names of midshipmen who valiantly gave their lives at Veracruz during the Mexican War. These words seem so simple and straightforward, yet they serve as an example of what it means to be an officer in the Navy. Although the stone is chipped and the bronze letters have oxidized over time, the steadfastness of the monument symbolizes the spirit of these brave men. Sitting in the middle of Stribling Walk, the main pathway of midshipmen, the monument is a daily reminder of why we chose to come to this institution and to serve our country.

Plebe, UNSA 2003

Michelson Hall

He may not have earned his fame
By desecrating other men,
But as a graduate he brought fame
To the Academy once again.

Matthew E. Charles, USNA 2007

uilt in 1965–68 as part of the Michelson-Chauvenet complex to enhance math and science instruction at the Academy, Michelson Hall houses the Physics and Chemistry departments. It is dedicated to Albert A. Michelson (1852–1931), USNA 1873, physicist and first American scientist to be awarded the Nobel Prize (1907). Born in Poland, Michelson immigrated at an early age to the United States with his family. After graduation from the Academy, he served on the North

Michelson Hall (Randell Hunt "Doc" Prothro and Gustav F. "Gus" Swainson Jr.)

Atlantic Station before returning to the Academy, where he gained international recognition for his paper, "On a Method of Measuring the Velocity of Light." Some of the tools Michelson used in his experiments are on display in Michelson Hall, and bronze discs on the outside plaza mark the line of sight that he used in measuring the velocity of light.

> As I walk through Michelson Hall on my way to chemistry class, the reason for the boldness and perfection of the building becomes evident. Michelson was a man who always wanted to excel at everything he did. "My greatest inspiration is a challenge to attempt the impossible," he said. However, what he strived for did not just better himself or those immediately around him, but impacted the whole world. "Worldwide confidence in his ability, his judgment and honesty is indicated by the fact that, in his work, no one ever attempted to repeat his experiments or check his results except himself," said biographer Carleton James. Michelson's legend lives on at the Academy to inspire others with the motivation he possessed throughout his four years as a midshipman and beyond. His dedication, knowledge, and ability to impact the world push me to do well.

> *Michael A. Byrd*, USNA 2010

Michelson's creative spirit shone through at a young age. When he did not receive an appointment to the Naval Academy, he traveled to Washington, D.C., to convince President Ulysses S. Grant to give him a special appointment—which Grant did, even though he had already used all of his appointments. As a midshipman, Michelson stood first in his class in optics and acoustics and second in mathematics but received numerous demerits for infractions such as whistling and "skylarking." As a faculty member in physics at the Academy, he first accurately calculated the speed of light in demonstrations with his students. After several more years of Navy service, Michelson resigned to pursue his study of physics: in 1883 he became a professor of physics at Case Western Reserve in Ohio; in 1890, a professor at Clark University in Massachusetts; and in 1892, professor of physics and head of the Department of Physics at the new University of Chicago. During World War I Michelson rejoined the Navy. After the war, he resumed his physics career, first at Chicago, and then at the Mount Wilson Observatory in Pasadena in 1929. Unlike most of the other figures commemorated at the Academy, Michelson did not achieve fame on the battlefield, but his name and his accomplishments continue to bring light to the world.

At night I leave the Hall and travel down Chapel Walk and go to the two places that give me peace. Not the peace that comes with rest or spirituality, but instead the peace that is gained by understanding. The two places that provide this intellectual tranquility are Michelson and Chauvenet halls. In the day both appear as large, powerful houses of academia: square, grey, and of plain design. However, at night they glow and shine in the orange lights that cast pools of citrus luminescence onto the coarse granite walkways, and the small silver discs used by Albert Michelson to refract light still do their job, tossing the contents of the spectrum throughout the night sky. The two houses, both alike in dignity, are my saviors, for they sort the spinning numbers and equations and turn them into silver, gold, and pi.

Plebe

Plaza Commemorative Plaque

The markers on the Plaza paving follow the line of sight for the optical experiments measuring the speed of light carried out by Ensign Albert A. Michelson, USN, between 1877 and 1879 while serving as instructor of Physics at the United States Naval Academy. This distinguished graduate of the Naval Academy was the first American scientist to be awarded the Nobel Prize.

Groundbreaking Ceremony, Michelson Hall

Today marks another new beginning in the long and vital life of our nation's naval academy. Today as we break ground for the new home of the science and mathematics department, the physical facilities of the Naval Academy begin to catch up with the academic revolution that commenced here in 1959 and which is making such splendid progress. . . .

Some may shed a tear for the landscape they once knew but five years from now the undergraduates will enjoy vastly improved facilities not only in Michelson Hall but throughout the academic complex.

Probably never has a name for a new building been so obvious. Albert Michelson, Class of 1873, won world fame for his work here on this campus. As an ensign, after a very short tour of sea duty, he returned to the Academy to teach in the science department and on the very ground [on] which we are now standing and sitting, which was in those days a seawall, he conducted his measurements on the speed of light to accuracies far beyond anything previously achieved. And if we'd stood where we are now standing in the early dawns or the late evenings of that June of 1879 Ensign Michelson would have made us move. For we would have obstructed his line of sight. And in those days, I am told, people moved even when Ensigns spoke. Michelson went on to achieve greatness as a renowned research physicist and teacher and in 1907 he became the first American to win the Nobel Prize for Physics. . . . The midshipmen who will work and learn in Michelson Hall are now only youngsters and plebes or still in high schools across the nation. But let us be confident that they will pursue their dreams with the same inspiration and energy that Albert Michelson displayed. Everyone who devotes himself to excellence as did Michelson will repay the nation's investment in this great hall for which we are about to break the ground.

Adm. Horacio Rivera Jr., Chief of Naval Operations,
December 16, 1965

༺ঌༀঌ༻

Dedication Ceremony of Michelson and Chauvenet Halls

The Naval Academy exists for the purpose of educating and training young men to be professional officers in our Navy and Marine Corps. The education provided by the Academy grows in scope and sophistication each year as the tasks and technology of the naval service become even more complex. As scientific knowledge expands in both scope and depth, the facilities for imparting that knowledge to each new generation must likewise expand.

Vice Adm. James Calvert, 1968

Midn. Albert Michelson, 1873 (U.S. Naval Institute Photo Archive)

The honor, discipline, prestige, and challenge of naval service has always intrigued me, yet my perception of the military was deeply colored. I never saw the Naval Academy as an academic institution until I learned about Albert Michelson. He represents a balance between all things military and all things academic at the Academy. His story showed me that I could be an officer and a man of intellect at the same time.

Plebe

The Chemists of Michelson

Many think we have no fun,
Experimenting till day is done
In Michelson, our second home.
But in the lab we're in the zone.
Beakers, scales, all tell tales;
We can't stop, our work prevails.
Reactions, titrations provide information,
But sometimes complications make us frustrated.
Six hours a week, thirty weeks a year,
We've come to love what plebes fear.
Determined to make this a career
Though we often feel like quitting, we persevere.

David O. Jones, USNA 2010

Michelson Quotations

Let S, Fig 1, be a slit through which light passes falling on R, a mirror free to rotate about an axis at right angles to the plane of the paper . . .

From a handwritten draft of a paper on the velocity of light,
written during U.S. Navy service

My greatest inspiration is to attempt the impossible.

It is the pitting of one's brains against bits of iron, metals and crystals and making them do what you want them to do. When you are successful that is all the reward you want.

New York Times, January 18, 1929

It seems to me that scientific research should be regarded as a painter regards his art, a poet his poems, and a composer his music.

Quotations about Michelson

[Demerits received for] skylarking and whistling in the corridor, laughing on guard, reading a novel on duty, playing a musical instrument on Sunday, receiving visits after taps, smoking in his room, and visiting the cake stand during study hour.

USNA Midshipmen Records, 1873

It was you who led the physicists into new paths, and through your marvelous experimental work paved the way for the development of the theory of relativity. Without your work this theory would be scarcely more than an interesting speculation.

Albert Einstein, quoted in Michelson Hall
Dedication Ceremony brochure

Professor Albert Einstein today expressed his sorrow at the death of Professor Albert Michelson, whom he had once characterized as the man who inspired in him the concept of the theory of relativity. "Dr. Michelson was one of the greatest artists in the world of scientific experimentation. His investigations were of decided significance to the theory of relativity."

New York Times, May 12, 1931

~≈~

We lose in Dr. Michelson one whose work has been of the highest credit to American science. But greater than his scientific contributions have been his examples of skillful workmanship and the inspiration of his unflagging joy in scientific research.

Shapley Harlow, Director, Harvard Observatory, c. May 1931

Burial Site

Cremated. His ashes are probably spread at Mount Wilson Obervatory, Los Angeles County, California.

The Master of Light

Gather 'round students
And ye shall hear
Of the Master of Light
Who worked through the years

To unlock the secrets,
The treasures, the knowledge
Of science mysterious
To those in college

Of Polish descent,
Michelson was his name,
His work and experiments
Shot him to fame

He grew up in America
Patriotic as well
His life a success story
Waiting to tell

Of the exploits and failures
Not even he could foresee
All starting with
The Naval Academy

Demerits came fast
During plebe year
The list runneth over
Giving no reason to cheer

Washbasin untidy
Living quarters unsat
Skylarking, whistling, and
Singing at that!

He found his niche
In science indeed
Optics and physics
Were calls he would heed

Commissioned at last
He set sail on the sea
For years he would learn
What a mariner be

After the Navy
He went into lab
To solve everyday problems
We all knew we had

How fast does light go?
We all wondered back then
Is it twenty or thirty
Or forty or ten?

With much persistence
He dove into his work
Learned the ways of the photon,
Electron, and quark,

Found the speed of light
At last, question answered
The problem was solved
Never to be reversed

And now we look back
And remember his name
And cherish the science
That brought him his fame!

And Michelson Hall
Stands proudly today
For the Master of Light
Who showed us the way.

Steven A. Vuleta, USNA 2006

Midway Memorial

The Class of 1942, U.S. Naval Academy, sponsors this monument so that the Battle of Midway may be studied, appreciated and remembered by future midshipmen and all who pass here by.

Dedicatory plaque

Midway Memorial (Randell Hunt "Doc" Prothro and Gustav F. "Gus" Swainson Jr.)

The Midway Memorial is situated beside the Submarine Centennial Memorial at the intersection of Blake and Buchanan roads on the Dahlgren side of Bancroft Hall's second wing. The memorial is a grouping of two smaller granite stones and a larger polished granite marker engraved with the map of Midway Island and the trajectories of Japanese and American fleet operations on June 3–7, 1942 (including preliminary air attacks against the Japanese approximately six hundred miles from Midway on June 3, before the actual battle for the island itself began on June 4). Designed by the International Midway Memorial Fund and based on a monument erected at Midway Island, the stone was carved by John Kinnard of Thurmont, Maryland. Donated by the class of 1942, the Midway Memorial is dedicated to the battle that is often called the turning point of the war in the Pacific. The American victory boosted flagging morale among U.S. troops. In October 1996 Senator John McCain gave the keynote address to the eight hundred veterans of World War II and other guests who attended the presentation of the Midway Memorial. Each spring Battle of Midway veterans gather at the Academy for dinner and an evening with the midshipmen.

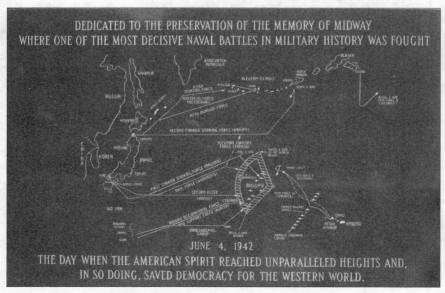

Midway Memorial close-up (Randell Hunt "Doc" Prothro and Gustav F. "Gus" Swainson Jr.)

The historical commentary engraved on the memorial plaques and stones highlights the strategy of the small American naval force under Adm. Chester W. Nimitz and its successful execution by two rear admirals, Jack Fletcher and Raymond Spruance, against the much larger and formerly dominant Japanese force. The plaques on the smaller granite stones chronicle the actions of U.S. warships and planes, as well as Japanese losses. In his address at the commemoration of the sixty-fifth anniversary of Midway at Patuxent River Naval Air Station in June 2007, Rear Adm. Steven Eastburg succinctly describes the importance of this battle:

> Midway was the last American base in the Pacific outside of Hawaii, and Japan's control of the Pacific would have certainly been enhanced by defeating the United States at this location. [Instead, what] the world witnessed during those four days at Midway was fundamentally a clash between naval war strategies—Japan, with the centuries-old strategy of surface warfare, and the United States, with a fresh strategy relying on naval aviation and the carrier fleet. [This] new aviation warfare concept proved both swift and decisive. . . . As a result of [our] victory, [r]enewed confidence swept through American and Allied forces, both in the Pacific and European theatres. There's little doubt that subsequent Allied victories such as D-Day would not have occurred when they did—or at all—if not for the Battle of Midway victory.

Monument Inscriptions

> They had no right to win. Yet they did, and in doing so they changed the course of a war. More than that, they added a new name—Midway—to the small list that inspires men by example . . . like Marathon, the Armada, the Marne. Even against the greatest of odds, there is something in the human spirit—a magic blend of skill, faith and valor—that can lift men from certain defeat to incredible victory.
>
> *Walter Lord, Incredible Victory*

The day when the American spirit reached unparalleled heights and, in so doing, saved democracy for the Western world.

Commemoration of the June 4, 1942, commencement of the attack

⁓ළ⁓

The battle that doomed Japan.

Plaque inscription, from a Japanese account

⁓ළ⁓

Action Report, Battle of Midway (June 3–6, 1942)

In numerous and widespread engagements lasting from the 3rd to 6th of June, with carrier based planes as the spearhead of the attack, combined forces of the Navy, Marine Corps and Army in the Hawaiian Area defeated a large part of the Japanese fleet and frustrated the enemy's powerful move against Midway that was undoubtedly the keystone of larger plans. All participating personnel, without exception, displayed unhesitating devotion to duty, loyalty and courage. This superb spirit in all three services made possible the application of the destructive power that routed the enemy. . . .

LESSONS AND CONCLUSIONS FROM THE ACTION

Combined training is needed by land based aircraft and Fleet units to provide for better exchange of information and coordination of attack. . . . All units require more training in sending clear, complete and accurate reports that will give a commander all the information he needs to know, completely correct, without repeated questioning.

The performance of officers and men was of the highest order not only at Midway and afloat but equally so among those at Oahu not privileged to be in the front line of battle. I am proud to report that the cooperative devotion to duty of all those involved was so marked that, despite the necessarily decisive part played by our three carriers, this defeat of the Japanese arms and ambitions was truly a victory of the United States' armed forces and not of the Navy alone.

Fleet Adm. Chester W. Nimitz, June 28, 1942

~~ঞ্চ~~

Action Report, Battle of Midway (June 4–6, 1942)

Torpedo 8, led by Lieutenant Commander John C. Waldron, U.S.N., was lost in its entirety. This squadron flew at 100 knots below the clouds while the remainder of the group flew at 110 knots, climbing to 19,000 feet. Lieutenant Commander Waldron, a highly aggressive officer, leading a well trained squadron, found his target and attacked. . . . This Squadron is deserving of the highest honors for finding the enemy, pressing home its attack, without fighter protection and without diverting dive bomber attacks to draw the enemy fire. Ensign G. H. Gay, A-V(N), U.S.N.R., is worthy of additional praise for making a torpedo hit and for the presence of mind he showed in hiding under his seat cushion, after being shot down, for several hours, thereby probably saving his own life and giving us an excellent eye-witness picture of the damage caused by the attack on the enemy carriers.

Capt. Marc A. Mitscher, commanding USS *Hornet*, June 13, 1942

~~ঞ্চ~~

Sole Survivor: Torpedo Squadron Eight, Battle of Midway

Torpedo 8 had a difficult problem, we had old planes and we were new in the organization. We had a dual job of not only training a squadron of boot [inexperienced] Ensigns, of which I was one of course, we also had to fight the war at the same time, and when we finally got up to the Battle of Midway it was the first time I had ever carried a torpedo on an aircraft and was the first time I had ever had taken a torpedo off of a ship, had never even seen it done. None of the other Ensigns in the squadron had either.

Quite a few of us were a little bit skeptical and leery but we'd seen [Lt. Col. James H.] Doolittle [USA] and his boys when they hadn't even seen a carrier before and they took the B-25s [twin-engine "Mitchell" bombers] off, we figured by golly if they could do it, well we could too. It turned out the TBD [Douglas "Devastator" Torpedo Bomber] could pick up the weight, so it was easy. We learned everything that we knew about Japanese tactics and our own tactics from Commander Waldron and Lieutenant Moore and Lieutenant Owens as they gave it to us on the blackboards and in talks and lectures. We had school everyday and although we didn't like it at the time, it turned out that was the only way in the world we could learn the things we had to know, and we exercised on the flight deck, did all kinds of things that we'd have to do artificially because we couldn't do our flying most of the time.

As I said, we had had no previous combat flying . . . but when we finally got into the air on the morning of June the 4th, we had our tactics down cold and we knew organization and what we should do. We could almost look at the back of Comdr. Waldron's head and know what he was thinking, because he had told us so many times over and over just what we should do under all conditions.

I didn't get much sleep the night of June the 3rd, the stories of the battle were coming in, midnight torpedo attack by the PBY's [twin-engine patrol bomber seaplane, known as "Catalina"] and all kinds of things, and we were a little bit nervous, kind of, like before a football game. We knew that the Japs were trying to come in and take something away from us and we also knew that we were at a disadvantage because we had old aircraft and could not climb the altitude with the dive bombers or fighters and we expected to be on our own. We didn't expect to run into the trouble that we found of course, but we knew that if we had any trouble we'd probably have to fight our way out of it ourselves.

Before we left the ship, Lieutenant Commander Waldron told us . . . not to worry about our navigation but to follow him as he knew where he was going. And it turned out just exactly that way. He went just as straight to the Jap Fleet as if he'd had a string tied to them and we thought that morning, at least I did when I first saw the Japanese carriers, one of them that was afire and another ship that had a fire aboard and I thought that there was a battle in progress and we were late. . . .

The Zeros [Japanese fighter-bomber planes] jumped on us and it was too late. I don't think that any of our planes were damaged, even touched by anti-aircraft fire, the fighters, the Zeros, shot down everyone of them, and by the time we got in to where the anti-aircraft fire began to get hot, the fighters all left us and I was the only one close enough to get any real hot anti-aircraft fire, and I don't think it even touched me and I went right through it, right over the ship. . . .

Personally, I was just lucky. I've never understood why I was the only one that came back, but it turned out that way, and I want to be sure that the men that didn't come back get the credit for the work that they did. They followed Comdr. Waldron without batting an eye. . . . I know that if I had it all to do over again, even knowing that the odds were going to be like they were, knowing him like I did know him, I'd follow him again through exactly the same thing because I trusted him very well. We did things that he wanted us to do not because he was our boss, but because we felt that if we did the things he wanted us to do then it was the right thing to do. The Zeros that day just caught us off balance. We were at a disadvantage all the way around. . . .

I dropped down after going over these ships, I didn't feel very badly, I had a left leg that was burned and a left arm that was gone, the plane was still flying and I felt pretty good and I didn't see any sense in crashing into those planes. I thought maybe I'd get a chance to go back and hit them again someday and as long as there's life there's hope, so I pulled up and went over them, dropped back down next to the water, just after I passed over the fantail and then I heard the torpedo go off. Just a little bit after that the anti-aircraft fire hadn't picked up anymore, but the Zeros jumped on me and I was trying to get out of the fleet. Before I got away from them though, the five Zeros dived right down on me in a line and about the second or third one shot my rudder control and ailerons out and I pancaked into the ocean. The hood slammed shut, I couldn't keep the right wing up. It had hit the water first and snapped the plane in, and bent it all up and broke it up and the hood slammed shut and it was in the sprained fuselage. I couldn't hardly get it open. That's when I got scared. I was afraid I was going to drown in the plane. . . .

I [did get] out of there and thought about my rear gunner, made a dive to try and pick him up, but I couldn't get to him. The first thing I saw after I came to the surface was the other of those two large carriers headed right straight for me and she was landing planes. . . . They went right by me about 500 yards to the west of me and the cruiser that was with her was only a thousand yards, screen and I presume, went by about 500 yards to the east of me headed north and they circled back.

After the [U.S. Navy] dive bombers came in and beat those carriers up and got them burning good and they lost control of them and they stopped pretty close to me, there was another [Japanese] cruiser that patrolled up and down on the north and south line that came by me first to the east [then back south]. The next time she came up, she went by me much closer . . . and then the third time that she came up, she came almost to me and made her 180 degree turn and went back, and on her way back that time, a patrol plane came by over to the west and she circled around the [Japanese aircraft carrier] Kaga to get on the other side and help throw up a screen against the patrol planes. They were trying to knock her down and she didn't come back anymore.

Then during the afternoon, there was a [Japanese] destroyer came pretty close to running me down. It came closer to me than any other ship. If there had been anybody aboard that I knew I could have recognized them as they went by. Of course, I was hiding under this cushion and instead of having my head above and out of the water, I presented the side of this little black cushion to him and hoped that they'd figure out that I was a piece of the wreckage. . . .

My main troubles in the water, outside of my leg burning very badly in the salt water . . . was keeping my eyes open. The salt water finally got in my eyes to such an extent that I could only with very great difficulty open my eyes and I would open them and scan the horizon 360 degrees and then shut them again and leave them that way unless I heard something or unless I figured it was maybe a ship might have gotten close since I looked the last time and I'd force them open and look again. . . .

The cushion just came floating out [of the plane] and Commander Waldron had always told us that he insisted that we have knives on our belts and everything else and he always told us that if we ever got in a spot like that never to throw anything away. I saw this cushion and at first I had no idea what I'd do with it but I figured I'd keep it. It turned out that it, I think, saved my life. I am very sorry that we didn't have time when Pappy Cole came along in his P boat [PBY seaplane?] and picked me up, I would like to have, rather, gotten that life boat, the cushion and all that stuff brought back, but he asked me if I'd seen any planes that day and I told him I'd seen a couple of Jap cruiser planes, so he didn't stay there very long. I was so tickled to be picked up along about that time that I wasn't worried very much about souvenirs anyway.

Lt. George Gay (1917–1994), 1980

Midway Memorial Sixty-Fifth Anniversary Commemoration, Patuxent River Naval Air Station, June 7, 2007

Midway is a lesson in the greatest tradition that the Navy has: service over self, duty over self, shipmate over self. Midway tested the Navy's core values of honor, courage and commitment, and it now stands as the standard by which we conduct ourselves.

Capt. Glen Ives

~~≈✦≈~~

Let's cherish the important memory of the Battle of Midway, but let's also remember in our thoughts and prayers the safety, security and success of our brave servicemen and women who, in the same spirit, fight today for American ideals. Let's never take our freedom or our democracy for granted. . . .

Rear Adm. Steven Eastburg, Keynote Address

Mitscher Hall

The stern-looking face of this whitened patriarch belies his true nature. Often Pete endeavors to frown upon the light and happy side of life, but he never really succeeds. . . . Pete is a man who never says much, and his smiles gain by their vary rarity. We know him for a true friend and a man on whom one can depend.

Lucky Bag, 1910

Mitscher Hall (Randell Hunt "Doc" Prothro and Gustav F. "Gus" Swainson Jr.)

Mitscher Hall was completed in 1961 as the Brigade Library and Auditorium, or "L and A" as it was known at the time. It is situated between Bancroft's seventh and eighth wings. When Nimitz Library was completed in 1973, the Mitscher library space was converted into the Chaplain's Center, and when the Levy Center and Jewish Chapel was completed in 2005, adjacent to Mitscher Hall, the chaplains' offices were moved there.

The building is named in honor of Adm. Marc A. "Pete" Mitscher (1887–1947), USNA 1910, one of the Navy's great battle commanders. Mitscher spent six years at the Academy as a midshipman, resigning after his first youngster year because of disciplinary problems, reentering as a plebe in the class of 1910, and finally graduating at the low end of his class. However, he soon developed an interest in flying, earned his wings in 1916, and became a pioneer in naval aviation. In 1919 he was awarded the Navy Cross for his participation in the world's first successful transatlantic flight as pilot of the "flying boat," NC-1.

Over the next twenty years, Mitscher held a number of important aviation positions in Washington and aboard ship. During World War II he launched Lt. Col. Jimmy Doolittle's raids against Tokyo from the deck of USS *Hornet*. As commander of Task Force 58, he pioneered the use of fleets of aircraft carriers for a single operation, conducting campaigns with this force in the battles for the Marshall Islands in February 1944, the Philippine Sea in June 1944, Leyte Gulf in October 1944, and Okinawa in 1945. Offered the position of chief of naval operations at the end of the war, he opted instead to command the Eighth Fleet and later the Atlantic Fleet. While serving as commander in chief, Atlantic Fleet, he died of a heart attack.

Mitscher Quotations

The kids who do the flying and shooting deserve the credit for any success.

Adm. Marc A. Mitscher, directing battle against Japan, 1944 (U.S. Naval Institute Photo Archive)

I'm an old man now; I spent my youth looking ahead. . . . Only a damned fool would sit facing the wind.

On a photograph of himself facing aft on a carrier deck

Quotations about Mitscher

A valiant and inspiring leader, bold and decisive in carrying the fight to the enemy.

Distinguished Service Medal

❧

One obvious candidate for the new big air job [deputy commander in chief for air] would be wizened, frail-looking 58-year-old Vice-Admiral Marc A. Mitscher, a naval aviator since 1915, pilot of the NC1 on the first Navy transatlantic flight in 1919, commander of the carrier *Hornet*, which launched the Doolittle raiders against Tokyo, best known as the boss of famed Task Force 58, which has swept the Pacific from Pearl Harbor to Tokyo. Last week "Pete" Mitscher came home from the Okinawa campaign. He was "embarrassed" by rumors that he had been killed; he was tired but very much alive. He had fought long & hard for the past five months in the Pacific.

Time, June 18, 1945

❧

He did not die in action. It is one measure of a sea fighter's success not to die in action. But he died of wounds as surely as any hard-hit soldier ever did. He grew old, at 60, in his country's service, and the heart that beat so valiantly from Kwajalein to the waters of Japan was prematurely stilled.

New York Times, February 4, 1947

❧

I always had a sense of confidence and security when Admiral Mitscher was out with Task Force 58. I always had the feeling that whatever he had to do would be done and in full measure. He needed no detailed instructions. All he needed was the opportunity and he always made the most of it.

[Mitscher] spoke in a low voice and used few words. Yet, so great was his concern for his people—for their training and welfare in peacetime and their rescue in combat—that he was able to obtain

their final ounce of effort and loyalty, without which he could not have
become the pre-eminent carrier force commander in the world.

Fleet Adm. Chester W. Nimitz, Armed Forces Staff College,
February 4, 1947

～✦～

A bulldog of a fighter, a strategist blessed with an uncanny ability to
foresee his enemy's next move. He was above all else, a Naval Aviator.

Adm. Arleigh A. Burke

Burial Site

Arlington National Cemetery, Arlington, Virginia

> He was a quiet guy;
> Everyone knew that.
>
> A Navy Cross for attempting
> To be first across the Atlantic,
> "For distinguished service in the line
> Of his profession."
> This was always his intent.
>
> Responsible for development
> Of the carrier task force,
> He gained control
> Of the sea and air
> During the Second World War
> And others had no choice
> But to follow.
>
> Ever striving for improvement
> Toward the end of the war,
> He experimented
> With formations and maneuvers,
> Leading attacks
> Against the Japanese.

Deputy Chief of Naval Operations
Was his title at the conclusion of the war,
Then Admiral in command of
The Eighth Fleet,
Then the entire Atlantic Fleet.
His heart stopped
On February 3, 1947.

He contributed forty-one years
To the establishment
Of Naval Aviation;
He served up until his death.

He was a quiet guy;
Everyone knew that.

His actions did all the talking.

Jamison L. Lupo, USNA 2006

Adm. Ben Moreell Monument

Moreell Monument (Randell Hunt "Doc" Prothro and Gustav F. "Gus" Swainson Jr.)

Working Bee

Not rough waters of the sea
Or hailing hostile bullets
Dissuade the Navy Seabees
From undertaking their best.

Brilliance of their deeds
Distinguishes them from the rest
And has helped build up
Our military preparedness.

A gun in one hand
And a hammer in the other:
The Navy Seabees,
Builders and defenders.

Joseph H. Manaloto, USNA 2007

The monument honoring Adm. "King Bee" Ben Moreell, the father of the Seabees, stands behind the Levy Center on Brownson Road. It consists of a bust of Admiral Moreell and a replica of a panel of the Seabee Memorial at Arlington National Cemetery, designed by Iwo Jima sculptor (and sculptor of the USNA busts of Nimitz and Rickover) Felix de Weldon, himself a former Seabee.

Admiral Moreell (1892–1978) joined the Navy in World War I as part of the Civil Engineering Corps and served for thirty years, including his years as chief of yards and docks and chief of the Civil Engineering Corps, from 1937 to 1946. He initiated dry dock construction at Pearl Harbor and construction projects on Wake and Midway islands in the Pacific long before the United States entered the war. By January 1942 he had organized a naval construction battalion, initially formed with volunteers from the construction trades, to provide the Navy with sailors who could construct roads, airfields, dry docks, and other facilities for the war effort. He gave the Seabees, whose name comes from the initial letters of Construction Battalion, their motto: *Construimus, Batuimus* (We Build, We Fight). He retired after the war to chair President Herbert Hoover's Task Force on Water Resources and Power and join the Board of Visitors at the Academy, where he helped oversee the major renovation project in the mid-twentieth century.

Moreell Quotations

High morale, expert skills, versatile ingenuity, strong devotion to duty and deep sympathy for the needy are the hallmarks of [the Seabees'] record.

"About the Seabees," plaque inscription

[The awards and honors given me] are all very meaningful and deeply appreciated by me. I accepted all with pride and humility. . . . [T]he citation for the Distinguished Service Medal presented in 1945 for World War II service gives me the greatest sense of a job "well done."

Quotations about Moreell

Displaying great originality and exceptional capacity for bold innovation, he inspired in his subordinates a degree of loyalty and devotion to duty outstanding in the Naval Service, to the end that the Fleet received support in degree and kind unprecedented in the history of naval warfare.

Distinguished Service Medal, 1945

Ben Moreell possessed a warmth for people. Born of his belief in the value of each individual, he left a legacy of creativity. He was a blessing to all who knew him and to countless others.

Monument inscription

Adm. Ben Moreell, Felix de Weldon bust (Randell Hunt "Doc" Prothro and Gustav F. "Gus" Swainson Jr.)

Seabees—Can Do

With willing hearts and skillful hands, the difficult we do at once, the impossible takes a little longer. With compassion for others we build—we fight for peace with freedom

Seabees Memorial inscription,
Arlington National Cemetery,
Arlington, Virginia

Burial Site

Arlington National Cemetery, Arlington, Virginia

The Song of the Seabees

We're the Seabees of the Navy—
We can build and we can fight—
We'll pave a way to victory
And guard it day and night
And we promise that we'll remember
The Seventh of December—
We're the Seabees of the Navy
Bees of the Seven Seas

Lyrics by Sam M. Lewis, music by Peter De Rose

Navy-Marine Corps Memorial Stadium

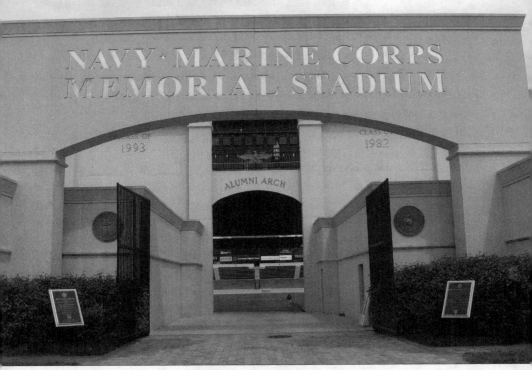

Navy-Marine Corps Memorial Stadium, main entrance (Randell Hunt "Doc" Prothro and Gustav F. "Gus" Swainson Jr.)

There are many traditions that involve the stadium at the Academy. The most obvious is the football games themselves. Football at Navy starts over an hour before the players even get on the field, with March Over. The entire brigade marches from the Academy, through the streets of Annapolis, and onto the field.

The people of Annapolis line the streets and cheer on the midshipmen by clapping and throwing them candy as they march
by. Then the brigade enters the field and stands at attention
as the National Anthem plays. Following the National Anthem
the brigade tips hats to the crowd and forms the spirit tunnel
for the football team, which runs out on the field as jets scream
overhead in an adrenalin-rushing flyover. Throughout the game
the brigade sits together in a corner of the stadium, cheering
the team on, and the plebes run on the field to do pushups
after every Navy score.

Plebe

Although not in the Yard itself, Memorial Stadium is so integral to
Academy life that it must be included in this survey of monuments
and memorials. Built as the home of Navy football to honor the

Jack Stephens Field (Randell Hunt "Doc" Prothro and Gustav F. "Gus" Swainson Jr.)

men and women of the U.S. Navy and Marine Corps who have fought for our country for over two hundred years, the stadium opened in 1959 with 350 memorial plaques and over six thousand seats dedicated to individual members of the armed forces. Since that time, hundreds of nameplates and plaques have been added, and beginning in 2002 the stadium was completely renovated into a multipurpose, year-round facility. Lacrosse games as well as football games are played on the field's weather-resistant FieldTurf. Over eight thousand chair-back memorial plates were removed for refurbishing and reinstalled. The memorial plaques were similarly treated, then installed on a memorial wall. Battle arches and class arches were constructed to illustrate the story of the Naval Service. According to an official announcement of the Naval Academy Varsity Athletics,

> Each combination of battle arches contains a history lesson on the left arch and a description of the particular battle on the right. Each and every battle fought by either the Navy or Marine Corps is depicted through the use of color-coded battle streamers allowing visitors to chronologically view the story of the brave men and women who we honor for their service to our country.

As the stadium was being built in 1958, it was proposed that the bridge tower from the Enterprise, the most decorated carrier of World War II, be incorporated into the new stadium. This proved impossible at the time, so instead the stadium's elevator tower was named for the ship.

The stadium was rededicated on October 8, 2005, after the Navy–Air Force game, which Navy won 27-24. The field is named Jack Stephens Field after a 1947 alumnus and important donor to the renovation project. Before the stadium was built, football games were played on Thompson Field, on land near Lejeune Hall.

Nimitz Library

A sanctuary of mind, a sanctuary for thought
This is the place which I have sought.

Plebe

Nimitz Library (Randell Hunt "Doc" Prothro and Gustav F. "Gus" Swainson Jr.)

Children of the day,
Have you no courage to stand?
Educate yourself with the finest,
Study with the greatest,
Teach one another to lead,
Endure and push to the final goal.
Remember those who have gone before you,
Not those who stand in your way
Inhibiting you . . .

Keith R. Jackson, USNA 2007

L ocated at the corner of the seawall where College Creek joins the
Severn River, Nimitz Library sits looking over a postcard water view.
Designed by John Carl Warnecke and Associates (architects of the
Chauvenet-Michelson complex) as a modern complement to Flagg's
grand structures, it was dedicated in 1973. In addition to library facili-
ties, Nimitz also houses the Academic Center, the Multimedia Support
Center, the Academic Research Center, and the Economics, Language
Studies, and Political Science departments.

The sign reads "Nimitz Library," but it would be more appropriately
labeled "Nimitz Refuge." In its official capacity it is the primary library
on campus; in an unofficial capacity Nimitz serves as a makeshift refuge
camp for banished plebes, "unsat" upperclassmen, and a myriad of others
looking for a place to be left alone. It's a quiet place where plebes can
relax and upperclass can work free of distractions. Whether it is to peruse
old books in the rare book collections, edit a spirit spot in the media lab,
or just hide away for a few hours, Nimitz, full of endless possibilities, is
inarguably the best place to go.

Darby C. Driscoll, USNA 2009

The library building is named in honor of Fleet Adm. Chester W.
Nimitz (1885–1966), USNA 1905, Pacific Allied Forces commander
and chief of naval operations. Originally determined to join the Army,
Nimitz was admitted to the Naval Academy at the age of fifteen. He

got seasick his first time out on a boat but excelled at math and graduated near the top of his class. As an ensign he was court-martialed and given an official reprimand when *Decatur* ran aground under his command, but less than two years later he was promoted to lieutenant (skipping the rank of lieutenant junior grade). Ordered to the First Submarine Flotilla in 1909, he was then given command of the flotilla at age twenty-four. He subsequently went on to develop the Navy's first diesel engines. In World War I he commanded the submarine force in the Atlantic Fleet and later served as chief of the Bureau of Navigation. He also established the first NROTC unit, at the University of California–Berkeley in 1926.

As five-star fleet admiral in World War II, with combat teams commanded by Adms. Frank J. Fletcher, William Halsey, Marc A. Mitscher, Stansfield Turner, Raymond A. Spruance, John S. McCain Sr., and T. C. Kincaid, Nimitz developed much of the U.S. naval strategy that led to U.S. victory against Japan. Ten days after the attack on Pearl Harbor, Nimitz was given command of the U.S. Pacific Fleet. Known as the "Island Hopper," he led the fleet in defeating the Japanese navy in major battles of the war in the Pacific. His successful attack strategy terminated with the assaults on Iwo Jima and Okinawa. On September 2, 1945, the Japanese formally surrendered aboard his flagship *Missouri*.

Nimitz is remembered as a kind and considerate boss who took responsibility for his actions. He died at age eighty, never having retired from the Navy. His memorials include, in addition to the library, the first nuclear-powered aircraft carrier, dedicated in 1975. A bust of Admiral Nimitz by Felix de Weldon, sculptor of the Iwo Jima memorial, resides just inside the library's foyer.

Nimitz Quotations

God grant me the courage not to give up what I think is right even though I think it is hopeless.

Fleet Adm. Chester W. Nimitz, c. 1944 (U.S. Naval Institute Photo Archive)

Is the proposed operation likely to succeed? What might the consequences of failure [be]? Is it in the realm of practicability in terms of material and supplies?

❧

Among the Americans who served on Iwo Island [Jima], uncommon valor was a common virtue.

> CINCPACFLT Communique 300, March 17, 1945

❧

The very gallantry and determination of our young commanding officers need to be taken into account here as a danger factor, since their urge to keep on, to keep up, to keep station, and to carry out their mission in the face of any difficulty, may deter them from doing what is actually wisest and most profitable in the long run.

> On the Pacific typhoon, December 1944

❧

It is an axiom that in preparing for any contest, it is wisest to exploit—not neglect—the element of strength.

> "Who Commands Sea—Commands Trade," March 1948

Quotations about Nimitz

"A man he seems of cheerful yesterdays and confident tomorrows"

> —Wordsworth

. . . Possesses that calm and steady going Dutch way that gets at the bottom of things. "Now see here." Delights in a rough house. One of the cave-dwellers but is determined to be a fusser. . . . Mixer of famous punches.

> *Lucky Bag*, 1905

❧

He was the calmest man in the face of great problems that I have ever known.

> Rear Adm. Thomas C. Anderson,
> interview published in
> A Cluster of Interviews, 1969

For exceptionally meritorious service to the Government of the United States as Commander in Chief, United States Pacific Fleet and Pacific Ocean Areas, from June 1944 to August 1945. Initiating the final phase in the battle for victory in the Pacific, Fleet Admiral Nimitz attacked the Marianas, invading Saipan, inflicting a decisive defeat in the Japanese Fleet in the First Battle of the Philippines and capturing Guam and Tinian. In vital continuing operations, his Fleet Forces isolated the enemy-held bastions of the Central and Eastern Carolinas and secured in quick succession Peleliu, Angaur and Ulithi. With reconnaissance of the main beaches on Leyte effected, approach channels cleared and opposition neutralized in joint operations to reoccupy the Philippines, the challenge by powerful task forces of the Japanese Fleet resulted in a historic victory in the three-phased Battle for Leyte Gulf, October 24 to 26, 1944. Accelerating the intensity of aerial offensive by pressure exerted at every hostile strong point, Fleet Admiral Nimitz culminated long-range strategy by successful amphibious assault on Iwo Jima and Okinawa. A wise, steadfast and indomitable leader, Fleet Admiral Nimitz, by his daring strategy and his faith in the courage and skill of the officers and men under his command, finally placed representative forces of the United States Navy in the harbor of Tokyo for the formal capitulation of the Japanese Empire. Through his mastery of naval warfare, his strategical skill, his sound judgment and his inspiring leadership, he demonstrated the highest qualities of a naval officer and rendered services of the greatest distinction to his country.

Gold Star Citation, October 5, 1945

Admiral Nimitz loved his country and the sea. His devotion to one inspired his mastery of the other, earning for his quiet courage and resolute leadership the undying gratitude of his countrymen and an enduring chapter in the annals of naval history.

President Lyndon B. Johnson,
statement on Nimitz's death,
February 10, 1966

Burial Site

Golden Gate National Cemetery, San Bruno, California

Nimitz Library is a special place to me because I feel the inspiration and embodiment of leadership of Nimitz there. His example of dedication, persistence, and compassion demonstrate the most important parts of his leadership. Nimitz once was in the same shoes I am, a plebe at the Naval Academy. Maybe one day, through hard work, I will rise to high command like Nimitz.

Scott A. Simpson, USNA 2010

Porter Road

Whenever I pass the homes of Porter Road I cannot control my urge to slow down and soak in as much of the beauty as possible. When I go on a jog, I always make it a point to pass along the backsides of the duplex houses where I peek over the short wall that separates the alley from the backyard. [The] sight of the residences spawns feelings of wonderment and awe. . . . Someday I could be living there.

Jason M. Abel, USNA 2004

Porter Road (Randell Hunt "Doc" Prothro and Gustav F. "Gus" Swainson Jr.)

T ree-lined Porter Road, which runs from Lejeune Hall near Gate 1 past the garden at Buchanan House, is also known as "Captains Row" for the residences there of such high-ranking officers in the Yard as the commandant of midshipmen, the Academy's senior marine officer, the senior chaplain, the academic dean and provost, the athletic director, and the heads of academic divisions who are Navy captains and Marine Corps colonels. The large three-story brick duplexes are both formal and inviting with their blue-and-white striped canopies shading wrap-around screened porches.

Porter Road is named for Adm. David Dixon Porter (1813–91), Civil War gunboat commander and superintendent of the Naval Academy from 1865 to 1869. The son of Commo. David Porter, David Dixon Porter entered the naval service in 1829, serving in his early years on the coastal survey and then in the Mexican War. During the Civil War, he rose rapidly through the ranks: he first commanded the mortar flotilla on the Mississippi River under Farragut; then as acting rear admiral in the Vicksburg Campaigns of 1862–63, he commanded the Mississippi Squadron; and finally, as head of the North Atlantic Blockading Squadron, he led naval forces in two attacks against Fort Fisher, North Carolina, the most powerful Confederate fort on the Atlantic. After the war, as superintendent of the Naval Academy, he was instrumental in improving instruction and in dramatically expanding Academy acreage. He introduced team sports and improved student social life (so much so that locals referred to the Academy as "Porter's dancing school") and also oversaw the introduction of significant and long-standing traditions such as the Color Parade, the Farewell Ball, class rings, and June Week (the precursor to Commissioning Week, the weeklong series of activities culminating in the graduation and commissioning ceremony). In 1866 Porter was promoted to vice admiral, and in 1870, as chief of the Bureau of Navigation and the senior officer in the postwar Navy, he achieved the rank of full admiral. From 1877 until his death, he served as head of the Board of Inspection in Washington, D.C.

Porter Quotations

No commander will permit any one under his command to land for the purpose of taking property of any description from plantations along the river within the limits of this squadron.

The duties of commanders will be confined to seizing rebel property afloat.

No person shall be allowed to pillage, burn or destroy (unless from military necessity, which must be shown) under penalty of the severest punishment.

General Order No. 44, Mississippi Squadron, April 10, 1863

The following qualifications will be required in officers who are applicants for promotion, viz:

> Good moral character
> Good physique
> Good professional knowledge
> Good mental qualities.

They must write and read *well*; have a good knowledge of the management of great and small guns, and stationing of the men.

General Order No. 95, September 25, 1863

It is in the increasing horrors of war that I look for its abolition. War will finally grow so terrible that the nations will not want to engage in it. . . . We will then have great national congresses who will continually sit and decide upon the differences of nations.

Interview, April 8, 1885

Quotations about Porter

Porter is probably the best man [to be placed in charge of the blockade of Fort Fisher]. . . . [Although he] is impressed with and boastful of his own powers . . . he [combines daring with] great energy, great activity and abundant resources.

Secretary of the Navy Gideon Welles,
diary entry, September 1864

⁓⁓

[For] all the eminent skill, endurance and gallantry exhibited by him and his squadron, in cooperation with the Army, in the opening of the Mississippi River.

Congressional Commendation, 1864

⁓⁓

[To] Rear Admiral David D. Porter, and to the officers, petty officers, seamen, and Marines under his command, for the unsurpassed gallantry and skill exhibited by them in the attacks on Fort Fisher, and the brilliant and decisive victory by which that important work was captured from the rebel forces and placed in the possession of the United States; and for their long and faithful services and unwavering devotion to the cause of the country in the midst of great difficulties and dangers.

Congressional Commendation, 1865

⁓⁓

Ode to Our Naval Heroes

Your Record to time shall not yield,
Bright emblazoned on river and main,
With those deeds for the flag shown on deck and on field,
That defied aught of rending or stain.
As great billows now swell—now are gone—
Pealing long on their reach to the shore,
Your life-forms recede, but your fame surges on,
And in memory resounds evermore.

Hymn, Porter Memorial Service, May 14, 1891

Capt. David Dixon Porter, attributed to John Trumbull, 1863 (U.S. Naval Institute Photo Archive)

Burial Site
Arlington National Cemetery, Arlington, Virginia

Preble Hall

(U.S. Naval Academy Museum)

[The museum] houses the mementos of by-gone generations and wars. . . .

Here . . . we have Navy tradition in a nut-shell.

Lucky Bag, 1944

Preble Hall (Naval Academy Museum)

The primary mission of [the] Museum . . . is to inspire the midshipmen; and to attempt to give them an understanding and appreciation of the Navy's contribution, in war and peace, to the highest ideals of our country, and to show how the Navy has defended and preserved these ideals. Accordingly, the displays consist largely of those tangible things which tend to build

loyalty to the Service and an appreciation of its noblest ideals—
important visual aids in the teaching of naval history and ever
present reminders of the midshipmen's heritage, the Navy's
long record of loyalty, integrity, and service to the nation.

Capt. Wade De Weese, Director, USNA Museum, 1920

P reble Hall, housing the U.S. Naval Academy Museum, was built
1938–39 to provide a permanent location for the exhibition and
storage of artifacts and mementos related to the Navy's history and,
in particular, the Naval Academy's history. The original museum, known
in its early days as the Naval School Lyceum, was first housed on the
second deck of the new mess hall completed in January 1846. The first
major collection, the Navy's Trophy Flag Collection, begun by Act of
Congress in 1814, was transferred to the Academy in 1849 by executive
order of President James K. Polk. After the Civil War the Lyceum was
located in the building that housed the first chapel. In the early twentieth century, many of the historic treasures were displayed in Memorial
Hall, Mahan Hall, and the Seamanship Department. In 1922, with the
acquisition of the Boston Naval Library and Institute collections, the
museum moved to the ground level of Maury Hall; officially renamed
the U.S. Naval Academy Museum, the collections served as a laboratory
for history classes taught on the upper level of Maury. In the mid-1930s
President Franklin Roosevelt agreed that the museum needed more
space, and in September 1938 the cornerstone was laid for Preble Hall.
F. W. Southworth, architect of the Navy's Bureau of Docks and Yards,
designed the building of white-pressed brick with granite facings.

[The museum offers] important visual aids in the teaching of naval
history and ever present reminders of the deeds of valor of our youthful
Navy's heroes.

Capt. Harry A. Baldridge, USNA Museum curator, 1945

Museum curator Captain Baldridge wrote in his historical survey of the museum that the museum curator was also the first chaplain and that the missions of the two were the same: "the inculcation of moral and spiritual values in the midshipmen during their formative years." Among the most notable objects in the collection are the John Paul Jones Commission, signed by John Hancock in 1776; the cutlass of Thomas Macdonough, who served under Commo. Stephen Decatur at Tripoli and later led the American fleet to victory over the British at Plattsburg in the War of 1812; Oliver Hazard Perry's "Don't Give Up the Ship" battle flag and sword from the War of 1812; the seal ring of Capt. James Lawrence, who, mortally wounded, uttered the command not to give up the ship; the bullet that killed Commodore Decatur in the "honor duel" in Bladensburg, Maryland; and Thomas Moran's oil painting of the burning of USS *Philadelphia*. The museum also displays, in the Class of 1951 Gallery of Ships exhibition space, two of the country's most significant ship model collections: the Rogers collection of "admiralty models" of the 1650–1850 sailing ship era, submitted to the British Admiralty; and the Ships of Bone collection, crafted during the Napoleonic Wars by French prisoners, who were held in such land-based prisons as Dartmoor and Norman Cross as well as aboard British prison ships. The Beverley R. Robinson Collection of Naval Prints offers outstanding examples of Marine prints. Another significant collection of Marine art is the collection of World War II watercolors painted by American landscape artist Jason Schoener as a Navy ensign stationed at Eniwetok Atoll in the Marshall Islands in 1944–45.

The Preble Hall Museum is an amazing collection of naval artifacts and exhibits. To a tired, hungry plebe in the middle of plebe summer, it is nothing more than another opportunity to duck the detailers and sleep. My company was marched down Stribling Walk one morning and straight to Preble Hall. We had just finished breakfast and had already had our morning training session. Upon entering the museum we were introduced to our guide. From the start I could tell that this guy enjoyed what he was doing and wanted to share it. I personally had another idea than that of a tour. Since I had been to the museum before, I knew of the ship exhibit downstairs. In particular there is a section that has a dark, air-conditioned corridor that would serve my purposes exactly. I managed to detach myself from the crowd around the guide. I quickly looked for any detailers, then made my way to the stairs. Unfortunately I was intercepted before I reached them and forced to return to the crowd for the remainder of the tour. Sleep would have to wait for another day.

Charles Dawson, USNA 2002

Commo. Edward Preble, oil portrait c. 1805 (U.S. Naval Institute Photo Archive)

The museum building was named in 1970 for Commo. Edward Preble (1761–1807), an inspiring early Navy leader whose bold thinking and insistence on training established the Navy as a powerful force in American diplomacy. Preble had been an officer in the Massachusetts navy in the early 1780s and was held as a prisoner of war during the struggle for independence. After independence, he served in the merchant marines for fifteen years until commissioned into the U.S. Navy in 1798. Within two years, he commanded USS *Essex*, the first American warship to sail in both the Indian and Pacific Oceans. In 1803, in command of the Mediterranean Squadron, he brokered a peace treaty with the emperor of Morocco, but when the other Barbary Coast powers would not agree to the treaty, he blockaded the well-fortified Tripoli harbor (see the Tripoli Monument entry). Then, with his small fleet of seven ships and a thousand men, he attacked the heavily defended harbor, inflicting severe casualties. When the corsairs captured USS *Philadelphia*, Preble masterminded the famous burning of the ship. Many of the officers serving under Preble, including Stephen Decatur and David Porter, unofficially known as "Preble's Boys," went on to become famous naval leaders themselves in the War of 1812. Preble's insistence that ships be kept in a state of readiness while under sail and that tight discipline be maintained helped establish the rules and regulations of the modern Navy.

Burial Site

Eastern Cemetery, Portland, Maine

> There is no doubt in my mind that [the museum] should be extended so as to display more models and prints and paintings of the United States Navy ships.
>
> *President Franklin D. Roosevelt*, c. 1930

Ship bone model (Naval Academy Museum)

Ships of Bone

How white shine
These ships of bone
Carved by French prisoners
From meal rations,

What masterpiece
Of art and patience
Each plank and pulley!
And these POW rations—

Bread and ashes—
From a more recent war,
Molded into a pair of dice,
Speak with simple artifice

But equal eloquence
Of suffering mastered.

Ricketts Hall

Ricketts Hall (Randell Hunt "Doc" Prothro and Gustav F. "Gus" Swainson Jr.)

Weight Room Poem

Pumping iron all the time
Biceps, triceps
Pumping iron
Chest, back, even neck
Pumping iron all the time
Calf, thighs, also hamstrings
Pumping iron all the time
The weight room is a favorite place
That most meatheads call their home
To me this place is my own
Pumping iron all the time

Plebe, USNA 2006

Ricketts Hall was built in 1966 to replace USS *Reina Mercedes* as enlisted housing and lodging for visiting athletic teams. In 1981, when Naval Station headquarters and personnel were moved across the Severn, where much of their work area had been since World War II, Ricketts Hall became the headquarters for Naval Academy Athletic Association (NAAA).

> Demanding time to promote success
> Never relenting in its quest for perfection
> The vast weight room
>
> Adds to the unflinching work ethic
> Of our Navy football brotherhood.
>
> *Jeffrey Lenar*, USNA 2010

Now home to varsity football as well as NAAA, Ricketts Hall was named for Adm. Claude V. Ricketts (1906–64), USNA 1929, who played defensive end for the varsity football team. A "prior-enlisted," he rose through the ranks to attain the Navy's highest rank. At the Academy, he served as First Battalion commander. During the attack on Pearl Harbor in 1941, as the gunnery officer on USS *West Virginia*, he initiated "counterflooding" efforts to stabilize the damaged ship, an action often credited with saving the ship. In the 1950s he commanded the Second Fleet. Promoted to vice admiral in 1961, he was serving as vice chief of naval operations when he died in 1964.

Report from USS *West Virginia*

At about 0755 on 7 December, 1941, I was sitting at breakfast table in wardroom when assembly was sounded and fire and rescue party called away. Almost immediately thereafter as I was leaving the wardroom general quarters was sounded. As I went up the ladder to the starboard side of the quarter deck, I heard the word being passed by word of mouth that, "The Japs are attacking." As I reached the quarterdeck I felt the ship being hit. . . . I went up the starboard side of the boat deck to the AA battery, which was being manned [by] Ensign Hunter . . . and I told him to open fire as soon as possible. . . . I then went to the Fire Control tower as I was the senior officer in the gunnery department aboard. The tower was locked so we broke it open. The Captain then appeared and as the ship was listing rapidly to port and I knew probably few C&R officers were aboard I said, "Captain, shall I go below and counterflood." He replied, "Yes, do that." I went down through times square where I picked up Billingsley, B.M.1/c., to help. We went to the main deck and aft on the starboard side and down to the second deck through the escape scuttle in the hatch in front of the Executive Officer's Office. The hatches in this vicinity were closed with escape scuttles open. Wounded were being brought up the hatches forward. The ship was now listing so heavily that on the linoleum decks it was impossible to walk without holding on to something. I reached the third deck . . . and went forward to the first group of counterflood valves. Billingsley went aft and got a crank for operating the valves. When he came back, Rucker and Bobick, shipfitters from Repair III, came with him. . . . When I was assured that counterflooding was well underway, I told Rucker to counterflood everything on the starboard side until the ship was on an even keel. It was not long before the excessive list to port began to decrease. . . . A considerable number of men were in the starboard passageways on the third deck and I ordered them forward to A-420 to supply ammunition. From information received shortly afterwards I don't believe these men ever got to A-420.

I then went to the AA battery on the boat deck and found that all ammunition from the ready boxes had been expended. I went to time square and formed an ammunition train, opening hatches as necessary. However, when the hatch to the third deck A-420 was opened we found it to be flooded. This hatch was again closed and further attempts to obtain ammunition were abandoned. Ensign Ford, who was assisting me in this attempt then very properly used the ammunition train and other personnel available to evacuate the wounded from the second deck. At about this time someone told me that the Captain was seriously wounded. . . . I then went to the flag bridge myself and found Ensign Vail and Ensign Delano with the Captain who was lying in the starboard doorway leading to the Admiral's walk. Lieut.(jg) F. H. White arrived shortly afterwards. I sent Ensign Vail to the boat deck with orders to send all our AA guns crews to the TENNESSEE to assist in firing. The Captain had a serious abdominal wound, a large piece of metal or other similar object apparently having passed through his abdomen. Leak, Chief Pharmacists Mate, arrived with a first aid kit and dressed the wound as best he could.

We put the Captain on a cot and moved him under shelter just aft of the conning tower. He remained here during the second air attack. We had no stretcher but we obtained a wooden ladder about 8' long and put the Captain on it and lashed him to it and tied a line on each corner intending to lower him over the port or starboard side of the conning tower down to the boat deck. By that time however a serious oil fire had started, apparently in the galley, and heavy black smoke poured up over the bridge and boat deck forward. The boat deck had to be evacuated so we could not lower the Captain there. Neither could we lower him aft of the bridge because it was covered with fire. I went to the after part of the bridge to see if there was any avenue of escape. The starboard after corner of the flag bridge was clear most of the time and I could see that the starboard side of the ship aft of the boat crane was clear of fire and smoke. By this time the fire had spread to the life jacket stowage under the after part of the bridge and flames were coming up through the bomb hole in the port side of the flag bridge deck. The signal flags caught on fire and I cleared out those in outboard end of the starboard flag bag. The personnel I had left with the Captain had been forced to leave him and come aft for air, and a knife to cut the Captain's lines loose from the ladder. As I was comparatively fresh I went forward and found him still lashed to the ladder, one end of which was up against the shield where the latest attempt had been made to lower him. He was still partially conscious. I returned aft and got Lieut.(jg) F. H. White and two men and we went forward again, unlashed the Captain from the ladder, brought him aft and took him up to the navigation bridge, port side, where there was no fire and comparatively little smoke. On this trip to recover the Captain the area was completely obliterated with heavy black smoke except where a puff of wind would blow it aside. We got aft none too soon as fire from the lumber stowage shortly broke out and covered this area with flames. I left Leak with the Captain and the rest of us went to the starboard side of the flag bridge. . . . I attempted to fight the heavy fire on the forward part of the bridge but the pressure was not enough to have much effect. A party under the direction of Ensign Graham was by this time fighting the fire on the boat deck and after side of the bridge structure. About this time Leak came to me and said, "Mr. Ricketts the Captain is about gone." Knowing that we could do him no more good we, with the help of Ensign Graham, passed a line between the starboard boat crane and the flag bridge, secured it, and I ordered

Adm. Claude V. Ricketts, 1929 (U.S. Naval Institute Photo Archive)

the men to go to the crane via this line. In the meantime Leak had gone back to the Captain but he was then dead. . . . I went down the fire hose to the crane. From that time on until relief fire fighting parties arrived we fought the fire on the boat deck, starboard casemates, and port side of the main deck forward. . . .

The personnel that worked with me on the bridge I cannot commend too highly. They carried out every order promptly and enthusiastically, even when it meant danger to themselves. They did not attempt to abandon the bridge until ordered to do so. . . .

The Captain deserves the highest praise for his noble conduct to the last. Although in great pain he kept inquiring about the condition of the ships, whether or not we had any pumps running, etc. He was particularly concerned about the fires on board and the oil on the surface of the water. . . . He did not want to be moved and after the fire started kept insisting that we leave him and go below. . . .

ADDENDA:

Looking backwards I can see that I should have utilized more time between the first and second attack in attempting to get ammunition to all machine guns. It might have been possible to get some from the TENNESSEE for the after guns. Also I should have broken out marines with rifles and their ready ammunition. Such action might have helped repel the second attack.

Lt. Cdr. Claude V. Ricketts, December 7, 1941

❧

The Navy League's Admiral Claude V. Ricketts Award for Inspirational Leadership

To a Navy enlisted person who, by traditional performance of duty, has demonstrated outstanding leadership and the professional competence required by his or her rank.

Quotation about Ricketts

After a short term [in the Navy] at San Diego, he brought his ambitions to the Academy, along with a willingness to work to their achievement. During Plebe year, Rick was, as usual, very modest and retiring, and attracted no particular attention. . . . Next year, steady application showed result; and he began to find himself academically and at fisticuffs. . . . Second Class year he . . . likewise showed the old Navy fight as a boxer, and was chosen skipper. Not content with these achievements, Rick reached the Academic top flight, and made a spotless record that belied his earlier fall from grace. . . . First Class year found him . . . First Batt Commander. The latter job is a tough assignment, but Rick has the knack of tackling unlikely jobs and carrying them through. His quiet good nature and sincerity have won him many friends, and will win him more in the future. He keeps his own counsel, and one might be deceived by his modest disposition as to the quality of man present; but make no mistakes—the man is all there.

Lucky Bag, 1929

Burial Site

Unable to locate

When I walk into Ricketts Hall, whether it's through the front, side, or back door, the first thought that runs through my mind is that it's time to get better today.

Nathaniel T. Frazier, USNA 2010

Rickover Hall

Rickover Hall (Randell Hunt "Doc" Prothro and Gustav F. "Gus" Swainson Jr.)

Principles of Electricity . . . just three little words. Those three
little words were a pain in the neck for Midshipmen who didn't
have the knack for things electrical. We blew circuit breakers,
fuses and meters . . . and went back to Bancroft Hall with our
hair singed and our fingers tingling. . . . Juice we called it . . .
and stewed in it.

Lucky Bag, 1953

Rickover Hall, built to replace the Flagg-designed Isherwood Hall, is the home of the Division of Engineering and Weapons offices. Three of the five departments in that division—Aerospace Engineering, Mechanical Engineering, and Naval Architecture and Ocean Engineering—are also housed here. The sculpture of Rickover in the main lobby was created by Paul D. Wegner, who also designed the Submarine Centennial Memorial. On the second deck terrace overlooking the hall's main entrance, the Challenger Memorial honors the seven members of the lost NASA space shuttle team, including teacher Christa McAuliffe and pilot Michael J. Smith, USNA 1967.

Lived Lives Lost

A voyage to lead the way,
A feat of might, dawn of a new day,
Seven were chosen, pioneers of the time
Whose moment in history books surely would shine.

Gathered together for a single task,
Gathered due to feats of the past,
Stars shining brightly they embarked for space.
Now they are symbols of the human race.

Stephen P. Kelly, USNA 2006

Rickover Hall pays tribute to Adm. Hyman G. Rickover (1900–1986), USNA 1922, architect of the nuclear Navy. Born in Russia, Rickover immigrated to Chicago when he was six and entered the Naval Academy at age eighteen. From 1929 to 1933, he served in the submarine fleet. In 1937 he took command of USS *Finch*, his last fleet command. For the next forty years, Rickover guided the Navy into nuclear propulsion. His determination led to the development of the first nuclear-powered submarine, USS *Nautilus*, and the construction (which he oversaw) of 150 nuclear vessels. Rickover's sixty-four years of service earned him numerous awards, including the Distinguished Service Medal and two Congressional Gold Medals. In addition to establishing a nuclear Navy, Rickover advocated forcefully for civilian use of nuclear power.

Father of the Nuclear Navy
Hard as a Nautilus shell,
Bright as an atomic explosion,
His legacy continues on the Yard:
Pursuit of engineering perfection.

Alexander D. Hagness, USNA 2007

Rickover Quotations

More than ambition, more than ability, it is rules that limit contribution; rules are the lowest common denominator of human behavior.

Sit down before fact with an open mind. Be prepared to give up every preconceived notion. Follow humbly wherever and to whatever abyss Nature leads, or you learn nothing.

Free discussion requires an atmosphere unembarrassed by any suggestion of authority or even respect. If a subordinate always agrees with his superior he is a useless part of the organization.

Success teaches us nothing; only failure teaches.

U.S. Navy Postgraduate School, March 16, 1954

Did you do your best?

Quoted in Jimmy Carter's *Why Not the Best?* 1975

Adm. Hyman G. Rickover (U.S. Naval Institute Photo Archive)

Quotations about Rickover

As water seeks its level, so has "Rick" sought to bring himself up to the plane of a worth-while and credit-bestowing profession. Neither a star on the gridiron nor a terror in the pool, yet did he loom large through the chalk screens.

Lucky Bag, 1929

[Rickover was] not too easy to get along with . . . not too popular [but very dependable] no matter what opposition he might encounter.

Adm. Earle Mills, head of the Bureau of Ships

Sharp-tongued Hyman Rickover spurred his men to exhaustion, ripped through red tape, drove contractors into rages. He went on making enemies, but by the end of the war he had won the rank of captain. He had also won a reputation as a man who gets things done.

"The Man in Tempo 3," *Time*, January 11, 1954

Admiral Rickover

Possessed of a purpose
He forged a path
Across a frontier
Untried and new
Clinging to his course,
He met the task
Three score and more
He served for you

Ronald W. Bell, dedication on plaque, USS *Rickover*

Burial Site

Arlington National Cemetery, Arlington, Virginia

Prayer to Rickover

Rickover, debater
Stern and sleek
How can one so strong look so meek?
Those beady eyes, that hoarse uninviting
Lack of a smile
Why could you not have had fun
Every once in a while?

No uniform, that's OK
You just wore regular clothes everyday
That gold, those stripes
And ribbons too,
If I were you I would wear
What I was due. . . .

With your knowledge to spare
You set us atop
The rest of the world
You made sure your voice was heard
Always in charge
Never at large

Never asleep
Yet never upbeat
Admiral Rickover
"Sometimes I wish you had fallen over"
Because of you now I must pay my dues
Engineering test tomorrow
Come on you can follow

Rickover, Rickover, be with me now
Rickover, Rickover, don't let me fail

David R. Lawrence, USNA 2006

Sampson Hall

The Department of English, History, and Government attempts to indoctrinate the midshipmen with those characteristics which belong to a gentleman, namely, an effective and intelligent use of words, a knowledge of the best literature, a knowledge of the history and the government of the United States and foreign countries, and the ability to speak before an audience. That this task is accomplished by the Department is evidenced by the fact that naval officers are welcomed in any society.

Lucky Bag, 1939

Sampson Hall (Randell Hunt "Doc" Prothro and Gustav F. "Gus" Swainson Jr.)

Who needs Humanities? We have machines
They can think, and we their tenders stand

Benjamin M. Gallo, USNA 2009

S ampson Hall, part of Ernest Flagg's academic triad, which also includes Mahan and Maury halls, originally housed the Science Department but is now home to the Division of Humanities and Social Sciences offices and two of its departments, the Department of English and the Department of History.

The building is named for Rear Adm. William T. Sampson (1840–1902), USNA 1861, the Academy's thirteenth superintendent and a hero of the Spanish-American War of 1898. As superintendent from 1886 to 1888, Sampson, formerly a faculty member and head of the Department of Physics and Chemistry at the Academy, vigorously prosecuted hazing offenses, encouraged the study of technical subjects, strengthened the athletic program, and created the "aptitude for the service" grade. In February 1898 he presided over the Board of Inquiry charged with investigating the destruction of USS *Maine*, which had blown up in Havana Harbor. Although the findings proved inconclusive, the explosion precipitated the Spanish-American War. During the war with Spain, Sampson served as commander of the North Atlantic Squadron, defeating the Spanish fleet under Adm. Pascual Cervera at the Battle of Santiago, Cuba, on July 3, 1898. A few years later, as part of the Great White Fleet's round-the-world voyage from late 1907 to 1909, Sampson captained the armored cruiser *New York*.

Journal, Battle of Santiago

A true account of the Naval battle as seen by me on board the *Iowa*. I have a couple of boys writing this with me and I am writing for the benefit of my wife. . . .

At daylight one bright morning, July 1, the fleet steamed in front of the batteries and again silenced the enemies' guns and then for one time we started in to destroy Morro Castle altho[ugh] no guns were mounted there and it was a harmless piece of architecture as the old stone mill at Newport yet its appearance was tempting and an eyesore to the entire fleet and besides the colors of Castile floated from its flagstaff which seemed to aggravate the not over meek temperament of the gunners and Blue Jackets. The combination of Masionery was logically harmless but sentiment sways the reason in war times and acting on the impulse, the *Oregon* sent a 13 in[ch] shell towards the flag on that inoffensive flagstaff. When the smoke had cleared away, a great breach could be seen in the parapets of Morro and the flag and staff could be seen nowhere. Many a man in the fleet wished he could get his fingers on that striped piece of bunting; to secure it was out of the question. However, the colors were down and Morro was a smoking ruin and if not as whole at least as pictures as one so nothing remained for the fleet but to steam out to their old stations and resume the blockade on Saturday the 2nd. The *Massachusetts* went to Guantanamo to coal and to remain there for several days. The *New Orleans* and *Marblehead* had departed on a cruise and in the evening the Flagship *New York* and *Indiana* steamed to the eastward leaving only the *Iowa*, *Texas*, *Oregon*, [&] *Brookline* [Brooklyn] to watch the entrance.

Early on Sunday morning, July 3rd, Auxiliary Cruiser *Gloucester*, was seen along the shore and the torpedo boat Eric[c]son steaming lazily along. Everything was as quiet and monotonous as ever and in consequence the routine was taken up and, therefore, we were to have the usual Sunday morning inspection. At 9:15 the bugle sounded quarters and every man went to his division and fell in for inspection by the Captain. The men were not in a very amiable mood for quarters is not a very cherishing period on board a man of war and is cursed at softly and stiffly below and aloft forward and aft. The executive officer was on the last lap of his inspection when a voice from the bridge yelled out the news that sent a thrill through everyone in the ship for that yell was the long looked for one. "The ships are coming out." No time for formalities and before the alarm died away, the magazines were open and the hydraulic pressure had gripped the turning gear of the big babies. The moment the ships were sighted the signal 250 was run aloft and a small gun fired from our forward bridge. This was an emergency signal and notified the rest of the fleet that the enemy was leaving the harbor. Now the captain was on the Bridge and full speed ahead was his first order as the ships swung toward the westward. The ships came out in the following order: The *Christobal Colon* [Cristobal Colon], *Vizc[a]ya*, *Merrea Tressa* [Infanta Maria Teresa] and *Oqundo* [Almirante Oquendo] torpedo boats *Pulton* and *Furor*. . . .

At 9:31 AM, the *Marie Tressa* was sighted and at 9:34, she opened up with her forward 11 inch gun at the same instant the forts on either side chimed in with guns and mortors but they were a side issue now and were hardly thought of. Nearer our leading ships steamed towards each other and as the Spanish flag ship swung to the westward, the *Oregon* opened with a 13 inch shell from her forward tunnel. We were nearest to the enemy but held our fire for close quarters, 3000 yds. 2000 yds, and 1000 yds. was called out from the range finders in the upper top and then is when we headed for the center of the enemy's fleet turning at the same time with a starboard helm so as to bring our ship on a broadsides to and in the same direction our main battery opened fire and our shells could be seen tearing the flag ship to pieces while her projectiles fell harmlessly around us: the smoke had surrounded all the ships by this time and the leaders were lost sight of for an instant but the *Vizcya* was seen next and the fire of our guns was directed on the pride of the Spanish Navy. The scene by this time became almost infernal for the ships were in close quarters and the roar of the big guns and the popping of the rapid fire and the shriek of the departing and arriving shells made conversation an impossibility. About this time, we were struck several times, one shell coming in through our forward berth deck smashing things up as it busted and riddled our starboard chain locker. Another imbedded itself in the cofferdam at the water line where it remains yet presumably unexploded. Our armor belt and quarter deck received several shells but the damage is hardly apparent. Soon the smoke was so dense that the fight went on in a dony-brook Fair fashion where as soon as you see a head, hit it for it was impossible to see what ship you were firing at. The *Iowa* forging ahead out of the smoke saw the *Vizcya* and *Colon* ahead but as two other ships of our fleet were with them, Cap Bob turned his attention to the other two for it seemed the *Marie Tressa* being disable in the first part of the battle had dropped to the rear with the *Oqunda* and now the cry from the top was heard repel torpedo attack on the starboard quarters. It seemed that the destroyers had lain back until the canopy of smoke enclosed the ships and they had darted forward on the *Iowa* to lance her while she was blind but luckily the smoke rose a little and then as the rapid fire guns turned on them, they were literally torn to pieces and to complete the work the *Gloucester* steamed straight for them and the destroyers were now the destroyed, riddled with shell and shrapnel with their boilers exploded and their crews shot, scalded or drowned. They ran along side of the beach but greater events were happening all this time for we now had the *Oqunda* and *Marie Tressa* on fire in several places with their torn sides and stem exposed and the smoke rising from a dozen places.

Seaman W. J. Murphy, USS *Iowa*, July 4, 1898

⟿⟾

Journal, West Indies Campaign

The first cheer went up from the parched throats of the crew. Being assured by this voluntary stranding of the enemy's two ships that they could be counted out of the affair, we next turned our attention to the *Vizcya* which was evidently trying to follow in the wake of the *Colon* but seeing she could not resist the storm of iron which fell around her, she imitated the *Oqunda* & *Tressa* and turned for the land. But the rain of shell never ceased for we were in a position now to rake her for and aft and as the *Iowa* drew in close to the shore line, the Flag of the *Vizcaya* could be seen coming down from her main mast. The ships company when they witnessed the first ship of the enemy strike her colors expended all their remaining energy in a wild cheer which must have grated harshly on the ears of the defeated survivors around the ill fated ship. Here ended the fight for the *Oregon*, *Brookline* and *Texas* were chasing the *Colon* and it could be seen that her capture was but a matter of time and distance.

Orders were now given for the boats to be lowered and as they commenced to drop into the water, the F.S. *New York* passed by to join in the pursuit of the fleeing survivor. Through the megaphone came the hail "*Iowa* there what casualties?" and when the answer came back "None," the cheer that arose from the *New York* told us that the crew had heard and appreciated. What next was now spoken towards the Admiral [Sampson] but the roar and cheer from both ships completely drowned the query for the *New York* with constantly increasing speed driving to the westward, the last sight of her being the blue flag of the Admiral at the Marine truck before she plowed into the smoke of the

Adm. William T. Sampson, c. 1898 (Special Collections and Archives Division, Nimitz Library, U.S. Naval Academy)

pursued; when the *New York* came along side, Captain Bob proposed
three cheers for the Admiral and it was now our company's turn to cheer
with bared head the Veteran of the War stood and listened to the cheer
the men he had led into battle and the hoarseness that prevailed next
day attest to the sincerity of those cheers but there was work ahead for

the boats could be seen returning from the burning ship and on coming alongside, the forms of men or parts of men could be made out beneath the throats stretchers were carried aft and as the mutilated forms were deposited on them, they were brought forward to the sick bay. Boat after boat arrived filled with wounded and mangled prisoners. But let us not recall the awful horrors of that afternoon. . . . Cap. Enlate of the *Vizcya* came aboard and was received with honors due his rank. Advancing towards Cap. Evans who was there to receive him, he unbuckled his sword and passionately kissing it, held it out towards our captain. Every eye was on the two central figures of what appeared to be a scene in a melodrama with bloody settings and every mind felt how hard it must be for a proud man to be thus humiliated. But such was not to be for no sooner did the victor see the offering than a hurried "No, No, Senor, a brave man always keeps his sword" as Enlate dazed as yet stood still for a moment, our captain raised his hand and a cheer loud and long burst from the assembled ships' company for they had realized what this action meant for it was a privilege and honor granted by one brave man to another. . . .

This is the most decisive naval battle of all times for the opposing fleets were by far the most destructive forces that have yet met in warfare. Dewy, Sampson and Evans, three names that will rank with the greatest of past ages and the battle of Manila and Santiago will live in the memory of men long after other victories will have ceased to be.

This is the true story written by Seaman W.J. Murphy on board the U.S.S. *Iowa* and hope it will prove interesting to those who care to read it.

Seaman W. J. Murphy, USS *Iowa*, July 7–15, 1898

Sampson Quotation

The Fleet under my command offers the nation as a Fourth of July present, the whole of Cervera's Fleet!

Message from Santiago, Cuba, July 4, 1898

West Indies Naval Campaign Medal (Sampson Medal), 1898

The Secretary of the Navy [is] hereby, authorized to cause to be struck bronze medals commemorative of the naval and other engagements in the waters of the West Indies and on the shores of Cuba during the War with Spain, and to distribute the same to the officers and men of the Navy and Marine Corps who participate in any of said engagements deemed by him of sufficient importance to deserve commemoration.

Burial Site

Arlington National Cemetery, Arlington, Virginia

From the English, History, and Government Department . . . I discovered, like so many had before me, that our collective pasts have a dominating effect on our collective futures. . . . I joked with my buddies about the folly of teaching of events which had happened centuries before, but deep down inside of me, I found that I was intensely interested in what the people before me had said and done, and how they had met and conquered life.

Lucky Bag, 1953

Sea Gate

Storm clouds roll out over the Chesapeake,
Tossing the ships at sea.
Only the stone steps of the Sea Gate
Separate me from the waves.

Reeve H. Meck, USNA 2009

Sea Gate (Randell Hunt "Doc" Prothro and Gustav F. "Gus" Swainson Jr.)

Between the *Maine* mast and Triton Light, a set of granite steps leads into the Chesapeake Bay. The Sea Gate provides a permanent landing for sail training craft and an entry point from the sea to the Academy. Christened with the waters of the twenty-two seas that USS *Triton* collected in her circumnavigation of the world and presented to the Academy in 1989 by the class of 1945, the Sea Gate is dedicated to "all those who left these shores to serve our country."

Along the riprap wall
That holds back the tide
And at night or dawn

In sleet or rain
Becomes a test of nerves
For mids who run,

Steps descend to the Chesapeake,
Gift of the class of '45,
For all who go in ships,

For fair winds and following seas.
And for all those returning
To these shores,

Triton Light flashes, green, alive,
a steady heartbeat,
Four-five, four-five.

Forrest Sherman Field

Sherman Field is where intramural soccer is played during the
fall sports season. I have played soccer for most of my life and
enjoy the sport immensely. When given the opportunity to
play for my company, I was quite excited. Playing soccer has
enhanced my life in two ways: First, it has allowed me to get
to known some of my fellow shipmates on a different level and
understand them better as individuals. Second, playing soccer has brought back memories of my life before the Academy
and gives me an opportunity to enjoy something that I liked to
do while I was a civilian as well. Just being on Sherman Field
brings these feelings out, and I think that I am able to express
myself differently in this environment. It is a very healthy part
of my life right now, and I am actually upset when we don't
have a game scheduled for every day of the week.

Anthony Atler, USNA 2004

Forrest Sherman Field (Randell Hunt "Doc" Prothro and Gustav F. "Gus" Swainson Jr.)

Forrest Sherman Field (across College Creek at Hospital Point) serves as the primary intramural field for midshipmen. Built on landfill in 1941, it also serves as the site of an obstacle course and endurance runs.

The field is named in honor of Adm. Forrest Percival Sherman (1896–1951), USNA 1918 (graduated 1917), chief of naval operations. Admiral Sherman first served in World War I, then earned his wings in Pensacola, serving on board the carrier *Lexington*. He became known as a naval aviator for his dive-bombing and fighter gunnery. During World War II he earned a Navy Cross for his role commanding USS *Wasp* (part of Adm. Frank Fletcher's carrier force) in the 1942 campaign to secure Guadalcanal in the Solomon Islands. Later, as deputy chief of staff under Adm. Chester W. Nimitz, Sherman earned a Distinguished Service Medal for his role in devising the Navy's brilliant island "leapfrog" tactics, planning the capture of the Gilberts, Marshalls, Marianas, Western Carolinas, Iwo Jima, and Okinawa. Appointed chief of naval operations in 1949, Admiral Sherman became known for his brilliant geopolitical mind as well as his naval tactical skill. While visiting Spain in 1951, he was instrumental in securing the use of Spanish bases for the defense of Europe. Following the conclusion of his mission Sherman died at age fifty-four in Naples, Italy, after suffering a series of heart attacks.

Sherman Quotation

Let's get some action.

Quotations about Sherman

Endowed with an ambition and a high sense of duty . . . hardworking and conscientious in the extreme . . . [h]e is our most convincing argument for the theory that "Brains is King." . . . Above all, Sherman knows his job; when he is given a thing to do he finds out all there is to be found about it, and the job is well done. "Let's get some action" is his motto, and he usually gets it.

Lucky Bag, 1918

Adm. Forrest P. Sherman (U.S. Naval Academy Photo Archive)

In addition to admiring this exceptional officer's enormous military contributions, I have a warm personal recollection about Admiral Sherman, despite the fact that I had never met him. When I was told as a plebe in 1950 that I had to have a coffee chit to drink coffee, in my naivete I decided to write directly to the CNO, Admiral Sherman, figuring that no upperclassman would deny a chit from him. Incredibly,

Admiral Sherman sent me a coffee chit on official CNO stationery and signed personally by him. In his gracious forwarding letter, Admiral Sherman said that "it is hoped that the enclosure (the coffee chit) will serve your purpose and will facilitate your relationships with the young gentlemen who are your messmates."

As I recall, when they saw the chit, some upperclassmen and officers were beside themselves either with awe or with consternation about a lowly plebe's gross ignorance of proper channels. In any event, I was edified by Admiral Sherman's kind consideration to an unknown "little guy."

Richard T. Boverie, USAF, USNA 1954,
USNA Alumni "Sea Stories"

⁓ঌ⃕⁓

Upon his death, at 54, the U.S. was only beginning to realize the full stature which Sherman had assumed. When Sherman took over the Navy, late in 1949, as the youngest Chief of Naval Operations in history, he found an embittered, bickering service, smoldering with animosity against its fellow services, the Administration, against Admiral Sherman himself. By his able advocacy of Navy views, by his quietly effective defense of Navy abilities, the new CNO quickly restored order and confidence. The newest member of the J.C.S. (replacing Admiral Denfeld, who was sacked in the unification row), he quickly proved himself its ablest member, a well-trained professional fighting man who also had a grip of world politics unmatched by any of his associates.

Time, July 30, 1951

⁓ঌ⃕⁓

He was able. He was a patriotic American. He was a fine gentleman. The country's loss is great, and so is mine.

President Harry S. Truman, response to Sherman's death,
reported in *Time*, July 30, 1951

Burial Site

Arlington National Cemetery, Arlington, Virginia

Stribling Walk

When walking Stribling, one is following in the footsteps of
some of the most famous and influential Americans of the past
and present. It is the path from anonymity to history.

Plebe

Stribling Walk, Macedonian gate (Randell Hunt "Doc" Prothro and Gustav F. "Gus" Swainson Jr.)

Stribling's Passion

Little do we know
> We tread on memories of the dead

Whose passion drew blood from his veins
> And colored the road a sacrificial red.

These bricks are here to guide
> Not just to work, school, or drill

But to be who we were created to be.

Tomás A. Grado, USNA 2007

Stribling Walk, which runs in a straight line from Tecumseh in front of Bancroft Hall to the Macedonian Monument facing Mahan Hall, is the main route for midshipmen from dorm to class. The walk is actually a pair of parallel brick paths separated by a strip of green lawn and bordered by towering oaks and maples and class benches.

> On Stribling Walk it's plain to see
> While looking up at every tree
> That fall is here, the summer's done
> The academic year begun
> The calm before the storm, some say
> That winter snow is on its way
> Soon will days be long and cold
> A time that makes the mind grow old
> But as for now the orange and red
> The only colors that fill my head

Christopher L. Powell, USNA 2008

Moffet Walk and Chambers Walk, named for the two "fathers of naval aviation" Adm. William A. Moffett (1896–1933) and Capt. Washington Irving Chambers (1856–1934), which run from Bancroft to the Macedonian Monument in opposing elliptical arcs, are off limits to plebes, who must stick to the straight paths through the central area of the Yard.

For almost two hundred years, the deep red brick of Stribling Walk has kept the secrets of midshipmen. If we take the time to listen, the echoes of the past will resound in our steps. The reflection in my low quarters illuminates the present and opens a window to my future. The clip-clop of my steps against the earth keeps cadence for my thoughts. As I pass the aging red oaks, their moss whispers my name. I am but a rolling stone in their existence. Every day, I walk this beaten path and I am reminded of those who have gone before me, who have shared this journey, who have lived this dream. The legacy left behind by those brave souls offers me hope to endure. As the first leaves fall, and the winds of autumn beckon change, I continue the walk of a lifetime.

Crystal J. Piraino, USNA 2008

Stribling Walk, command bench (Randell Hunt "Doc" Prothro and Gustav F. "Gus" Swainson Jr.)

As I walk from my classes, I turn onto the walk that is the heart of the Naval Academy. The view from this end of the walk is the great entrance to Bancroft rising between the yellow, orange, and red trees. Each step on the redbrick walk is a journey in the footsteps of many midshipmen before me. The clacking of my shoes on the hard brick sends me back to plebe summer when we marched down the walk every day. Our cadences sound off in my mind as we sing the words, "Cuz it won't be long, til I get on back home." A leaf falls and bounces off my shoulder. The turning of the leaves and the cadence in my head remind me of the short time it will be until I actually will go home. However, for now I must continue my slow march back to Bancroft, looming closer and closer as I near Tecumseh Court. Mighty Tecumseh himself casts a glance at this lowly plebe, perhaps just a quick check-up on one of his new warriors. Tecumseh's gaze fades as I enter Bancroft, the end of the journey along the walk known as Stribling.

Patrick Bookey, USNA 2003

Capt. Cornelius K. Stribling (1796–1880) was the third superintendent of the Naval Academy, serving from 1850 to 1853. He entered the Navy during the War of 1812 and, as a lieutenant in command of a sloop of war on the West India Station, captured one of the last pirate ships. Placed on the retired list in 1861, he was soon brought back to command the Philadelphia Navy Yard and then the East Gulf Blockading Squadron during the Civil War. During his tenure as superintendent of the Naval Academy, there were many changes: the name of the institution was officially changed from the Naval School to the U.S. Naval Academy; official class designations were also changed, from freshman to fourth class (or plebes), sophomore to third class (also known as youngsters), juniors to second class, and seniors to first class (or firsties); a training ship was brought in and the requirements of four years of schooling were changed to run consecutively, in contrast to the former method of two years of classroom training, three years of shipboard training, and a return to the classroom for two more years; Academy acreage increased by about 40 percent with landfill and the purchase of additional land; and an extensive construction program was begun, adding new dormitories, a recitation hall and chapel, and an observatory and gas works.

Cdr. Cornelius K. Stribling, c. 1852 (Special Collections and Archives Division, Nimitz Library, U.S. Naval Academy)

(With the gas works, the Academy became the first public institution in the New World to have central heat and central lighting.) Stribling also significantly strengthened discipline at the Academy, although the midshipmen still engaged in such pranks as loading the morning gun with bricks, sneaking off to town to drink, and setting pails of water atop doors to soak the duty officers. Stribling was later promoted to commodore, and he ended his career with service on the Lighthouse Board, a federal agency composed of naval officers, which was responsible for the oversight of lighthouses in the United States. He was promoted to rear admiral on the retired list.

Stribling Quotation

There was nothing connected with the Academy, which gave me so much anxiety, as the discipline of its students. So many boys just released from parental restraint, and a number of young men with the experience gained by associating . . . with older men; to be subjected to the same rules, was a problem of doubtful solution. The attempt was made, and that it succeeded at all, is to me a source of unceasing thankfulness.

Letter to Chevalier Thomas G. Ford, 1860

Burial Site

Oak Hill Cemetery, Georgetown, Washington, D.C.

A river in black passes over the crimson cobbles on its way to life, the life of classes and academia. The focal point of their attention, this river of uniformed midshipmen, rests solely upon the goal of seizing the challenges this day presents. The silent stones rest patiently, bearing the hard-soled black mirrors and their promising cargo on their way as the stones always do, and always have. Though the lattice of the brickwork has become smooth from the years of wear, duty stays the fatigue. The role of the walk plays out every morning, noon and night, as both the silent reminder of a rich and dutiful history, and as a gateway to success for the Naval Academy's future officers.

Jared M. Sutherland, USNA 2009

Submarine Memorials

Submarine Force Centennial Memorial (Randell Hunt "Doc" Prothro and Gustav F. "Gus" Swainson Jr.)

Depth Charge

Turbines spin faster
And the great beast yearns for depth.
Thunder strikes and each man
Holds his breath. Terror.
Creak and crick sounds, all too common.
"More splashes," reports the sonar man;
More boom baskets
Look for the kill.

Drowned explosion; the boat whirls
Power is gone; remain calm.
The ocean bellowing with anger
No longer hides the tin can.
Aft pipeline springs;
Water rushes: containment or death.
Fighting the unrelenting wave,
Brave men breathe water.
Compartment floods: fatal disaster.
Race to the ocean floor is no longer voluntary.
One hundred odd men, some young, some old.
Victims of the depth charge . . . story told.

Brian A. Quirk, USNA 2006

Submarine torpedo (Randell Hunt "Doc" Prothro and Gustav F. "Gus" Swainson Jr.)

Three memorials to "the silent service" stand in the Yard. The old-est, the Submarine Memorial, rests at Triton Point, honoring the fifty-two lost submarines "still on patrol" since World War II, and was donated in 1976 by the U.S. Submarine Veterans of World War II.

The newest submarine memorial and one of the newest monuments on the Yard, the Submarine Centennial Memorial, designed in 1999 by Paul D. Wegner (who also sculpted the bust of Rickover), commemorates a hundred years of submarine service, from 1900 to 2000. The bronze sculpture portrays a submarine cresting waves filled with figures of dol-phins and the faces of lost sailors. It sits on a marble base engraved with the motto of the submarine service —"from the depths, sea power"— and words of dedication to "those who serve beneath the seas and their families and support personnel."

> Submarine losses like the USS *Thresher* and USS *Scorpion* highlight the extreme risk and danger of serving on a submarine. Whether by equipment failure or faulty machinery, both of these submarines lost the ability to surface and communicate with their tenders. As they were sinking, I can only imagine what the crews onboard must have been thinking. With no chance of escape I know that they did not give up. I know that they stayed true to the service and to each other in the hope of rescue. They lived the ethos of ship, shipmate, self. This esprit de corps . . . motivates me each and every time I pass by the statue on the way to class. The monument is alive and the faces of those sailors speak to me.
>
> *Mark D. Knorr*, USNA 2010

A third memorial, the USS *Thresher* and USS *Scorpion* Memorial, is on display on the main floor of Nimitz Library. A tribute to the two U.S. nuclear fast-attack submarines lost at sea, the memorial consists of a polished glass sculptural "wall" of lightly tinted curved glass panels embossed with submarine warfare insignia, an outline of the *Thresher*, and from the Navy Hymn:

Eternal Father strong to save
Whose arm hath bound the restless wave
Protect them wheresoe'er they go
Whose arm doth reach the ocean floor

Live with our men beneath the sea
Traverse the depths protectively

Created by Eric S. Krag, the memorial in part honors the sculptor's father, Lt. Cdr. Robert Lee Krag (1928–63), USNA 1950, who perished with the rest of the crew and civilian technicians and observers when USS *Thresher* sank during deep-dive testing on April 10, 1963. After her remains were located on the sea floor, it was determined that she had sunk "due to a piping failure, subsequent loss of power and inability to blow ballast tanks rapidly enough to avoid sinking." Five years later, on May 21, 1968, USS *Scorpion* was reported lost after it failed to arrive at its scheduled stop in Norfolk, Virginia. Wreckage from the ship was later found, almost four hundred miles from the Azores, but the cause of its destruction is still uncertain. The memorial was donated by the class of 1950 as a reminder of the perils shared not only by the submarine community but by all members of the naval service.

When I first saw the *Thresher* memorial, I flashed back to my years as an enlisted instructor aboard the *Daniel Webster*, a moored submarine training ship. The story of the two unfortunate ships was well-known among submarine sailors. In our community, the loss of the *Thresher* and the *Scorpion* always served as a reminder of any submarine crew's potential fate once submerged. . . . The smooth sea glass faces of the memorial flowed from the base like frozen tears of loved ones left behind. The structure sang of the lost lives and the sharp pain felt by all who mourned. So striking was its symbolic message that I felt moisture forming at the corners of my eyes. . . . I stroked the smooth surface of the glacial formation. My hands immediately found the embossed words of the Navy Hymn. Softly, I began to recite them until choked by the grief of my shipmates' fate. As I turned to leave, the memorial's song continued where I could not: "Oh hear us when we cry to Thee, for those in peril on the sea."

Matthew O. Caylor, USNA 2004

Submarine Centennial close-up (Randell Hunt "Doc" Prothro and Gustav F. "Gus" Swainson Jr.)

Memorial Service for USS *Scorpion* Crew

For the ninety and nine whom we mourn today, there has been no deliverance from the deep. The separation of deployment has lengthened into the separation of death.

Rear Adm. James Kelly, June 6, 1968

In the deeps
Lost souls I keep
Those storm-tossed
Or of war's cost

Up above
Someone weeps
Here below
A quiet peace

All who pass
On hurrying feet
Pause and learn
What I can teach

Tecumseh

Tecumseh figurehead (U.S. Naval Academy Photographic Laboratory)

Stagnant, rigid, his painted body stands
Stained true blue and gold by adoring Navy fans.
The shining symbol of prosperity and luck
Will guide us on exams whenever we are stuck.
Tecumseh, overlooking scurrying squirrels,
A beacon of hope for midshipmen boys and girls,
Forever we turn to you, a constant in our lives.
In a world of changes your image survives.
Though we know you not, we know we need you so,
Master and keeper of the coveted 2.0.

Bayard N. Roberts, USNA 2010

The bronze bust that faces Bancroft Hall in front of T-Court is known as Tecumseh, "the god of 2.0," or passing grades. As midshipmen march by on their way to exams, they toss pennies into his quiver or present him with a left-handed salute for good luck. During football season he is decorated with war paint, and at other major events such as Ring Dance and Commissioning, he is also appropriately attired.

The sun dances over your bronze head.
You stand solid and firm, not willing to budge,
Decorated for war and scarred from pranks.
You are still the one we look to for hope,
You are Tecumseh, god of the 2.0.
We offer our pennies looking for your help
So we may pass our classes and graduate,
So we can reach the fleet,
Serve our country,
And represent all that USNA stands for,
To the best of our abilities.

Ryan C. Roeling, USNA 2007

Tecumseh is actually a reproduction of the wooden figurehead modeled to represent Tamanend, a Delaware Indian chief, from the ship-of-the-line *Delaware*, built in 1817–20. The original figurehead is the work of William Luke of Norfolk (1790–1839), who carved two Tamanend figureheads, the first a full nine-foot statue in 1921 and the second a replacement bust in 1836. Union forces sank *Delaware* in 1861 when they evacuated the Norfolk Navy Yard, but when the wreck was raised from the Elizabeth River in 1868, the wooden figurehead was removed and sent to the Naval Academy. The monument was nick-named variously "Powhatan," "Uncas," and "Old Sebree"—after Lt. Cdr. Uriel Sebree, head of the Seamanship Department from 1893 to 1896 (whose photographs bear remarkable resemblance to the sculpture). "Tecumseh" is the name that eventually stuck. From his earliest days on the Yard, Tecumseh has been revered as a patron of good luck. In 1929, when the weather threatened to deteriorate the wooden statue, the class of 1891 had the figurehead rendered in bronze. Thirty-five hundred pounds of metal from old ordnance material was melted down and cast, pieces of the wooden "heart" and "brains" from the original monument were sealed inside along with the original tomahawk, arrows, peace pipe, and memorabilia of the class of 1891, and the bronze monument was set on a new base carved by John Cross from a fifteen-ton block of green Vermont granite. The original Tecumseh now resides in the Armel-Leftwich Visitor Center.

Tamanend

Bronze Warrior

God of good luck,
god of the passing grade,

guardian of midshipmen
in formation
turning, swords gleaming,
on heels sharp, precise
as one body,
one rippling wave—

sometimes we recognize
you're not Tecumseh,
fierce Shawnee brave,

but Tamanend,
Delaware sachem who preferred
the art of negotiation
to the art of war.

Tamanend (c. 1628–c. 1698) was a great statesman who worked for peace between the whites and Indians. As chief of the Lape, or Delaware tribe, he welcomed William Penn to America in 1682 and negotiated the Treaty of Shackamaxon under the oaks in what is now Philadelphia, a scene made famous in a painting by Benjamin West. This treaty was important in persuading the Indians not to ally themselves with the French and Spanish against the British colonists.

On Pennsylvania

[I]n liberality [the natives] excel; nothing is too good for their friends. Give them a fine gun, coat, or other thing, it may pass twenty hands before it sticks. . . . Wealth circulateth like the blood, all parts partake. . . . Their government is by kings, which they call "Sachems" and those by succession, but always of the mother's side. . . .

Every king hath his council, and that consists of all the old and wise men of his nation, which perhaps is two hundred people. Nothing of moment is undertaken, be it war, peace, selling of land, or traffic, without advising with them, and which is more, with the young men too.

William Penn, 1683

Tamanend Quotation

We and the [whites] of his river have always had a free roadway to one another, and though sometimes a tree has fallen across the road, yet we have still removed it again and kept the path clean and we desire to continue the old friendship that has been between us and you.

Council Meeting, 1697

Tecumseh (c. 1773–1813)

Known to the native peoples as Tekamthi (Shooting Star) and to whites as "the red Napoleon" because of his dynamic leadership, Tecumseh was a Shawnee leader, the son of Pusksinway, who was killed in battle in 1774. Tecumseh fought with words and weapons to defend his native land. He became known for his brilliant military mind, his great leadership, and his rousing oratory. As whites began crossing the Alleghenies, Tecumseh traveled from the Great Lakes to the Gulf Coast to unite the various tribes into a single federation against encroachment. In 1812 the British enlisted his aid in their war against the States, appointing him a brigadier general. Under his leadership, the British soldiers at first won a number of victories. As governor of Indiana Territory, William Henry Harrison found Tecumseh a formidable leader.

Later, as an army officer sent by Congress to curtail the unrest in the Indian territories, General Harrison found Tecumseh to be a fierce but compassionate warrior, who after the defeat of the U.S. Army in a battle at Fort Meigs in Ohio in 1813, saved several hundred Kentucky captives from slaughter. By September 1813 the fighting had moved across the border, into the Lake Erie region in Ontario. On October 5 as the British retreated during the Battle of the Thames, Tecumseh was killed covering the retreat. British historians claim that Tecumseh's actions saved their troops—and saved Canada as a separate nation. With his death, Tecumseh became a legendary figure among both Canadians and Americans.

Tecumseh Quotations

The way, the only way to stop this evil [of war between reds and whites] is for the red men to unite in claiming a common and equal right in the land, as it was at first, and should be now—for it was never divided, but belongs to all. No tribe has the right to sell, even to each other, much less to strangers. . . . Sell a country! Why not sell the air, the great sea, as well as the earth? Did not the Great Spirit make them for all the use of his children?

Speech to Governor William Henry Harrison, 1810

Where today are the Pequot? Where are the Narragansett, the Mohican, the Pocanet, and other powerful tribes of our people? They have vanished before the avarice and oppression of the white man, as snow before the summer sun. . . . Will we let ourselves be destroyed in our turn, without making an effort worthy of our race? Shall we, without a struggle, give up our homes, our lands, bequeathed to us by the Great Spirit? The graves of our dead and everything that is dear and sacred to us? . . . I know you will say with me, Never! Never!

Council Meeting, Summer 1811

So live your life that the fear of death can never enter your heart.
Trouble no one about their religion; respect others in their view, and
Demand that they respect yours. Love your life, perfect your life,
Beautify all things in your life. Seek to make your life long and
Its purpose in the service of your people.

 Prepare a noble death song for the day when you go over
   the great divide.
 Always give a word or a sign of salute when meeting or
   passing a friend,
 Even a stranger, when in a lonely place. Show respect to all
   people and
 Bow to none. When you arise in the morning, give thanks for
   the food and
 For the joy of living. If you see no reason for giving thanks,
 The fault lies only in yourself. Abuse no one and nothing,
 For abuse turns the wise ones to fools and robs the spirit
   of its vision.

 When it comes your time to die, be not like those whose hearts
 Are filled with fear of death, so that when their time comes
 They weep and pray for a little more time to live their lives
   over again
 In a different way. Sing your death song and die like a hero
   going home.

Death song, c. 1813

Quotation about Tecumseh

[Tecumseh is] a bold, active, sensible man, daring in the extreme and capable of any undertaking.

[He was] one of those uncommon geniuses which spring up occasionally to produce revolutions and overturn the established order of things.

William Henry Harrison, Governor of Indiana Territory,
August 1811

Tecumseh Burial Site

Unknown; one legend situates his grave in the Ottawa reserve on Walpole Island in southwestern Ontario at the mouth of the St. Clair River, about thirty miles northeast of Detroit, Michigan.

Tecumseh Casting Ceremony

We have met today to witness the act of casting in enduring bronze the sculptured figure of this man who lived more than two hundred years ago, who may be truly called a Great American, and who, through his great virtues, so left the imprint of his character upon the History of America that those who have followed after him have been glad to do honor to his memory. . . .

[W]e have finally made the precious mold for our old Indian Chief and . . . I feel confident that we will have a TECUMSEH who, through his greater strength and resistance to the ravages of the passing years, will exert even greater powers than he did when he was made of wood.

Next Spring when we return TECUMSEH to his sacred precincts at the Naval Academy, he will go with the best wishes of the Naval Gun Factory where we have faithfully and tenderly made him into bronze, and we hope that he will shine in a new glory in keeping with those high principles which he exemplified when this nation was in its infancy.

Class of 1891 address, December 3, 1929

Presentation Speech

This statue in bronze resting on this solid block of Vermont granite will now defy the inroads of Time.

In presenting the statue of the Great Tamanend to the U.S. Naval Academy the Class of 1891 looks backward as well as forward.

BACKWARD, to the days when in the freedom of youth we enjoyed the good fellowship of our classmates and comrades, many of whom have passed from our midst but whose characters and deeds are still bright in our memory.

FORWARD, to all the years of the future when generations of young men of America will pass through this Academy, the great "melting pot" of the Navy, where minds are trained and characters are formed, for the service of our country.

Midshipmen of the present and the future, we ask you to bind to your hearts the Traditions of the Service and to emulate the courage and fortitude and patience of this great Indian Chief Tamanend, of the Delawares whose admirable traits of character are so well defined in the face of this statue. . . .

Officers and Midshipmen of the Naval Academy, we now place this symbol of our service traditions into your hands, with every confidence that the standards of this Institution will, in the future as in the past, be maintained in accordance with the best "Traditions of the Navy."

Vice Adm. Arthur L. Willard, USNA 1891, May 31, 1930

~≈~

To err is human; to forgive lies with the commandant.

"Tecumseh's Proverbs," *Lucky Bag*, 1897

~≈~

Cold and gray he stares forward
Into the heart of Memorial Hall
And on toward
The great spirit of his people
Burning bright in the sky,
Singing proudly of death
As their spirits fly by.

Mary E. Teague, USNA 2006

Tripoli Monument

Tripoli Monument (Randell Hunt "Doc" Prothro and Gustav F. "Gus" Swainson Jr.)

The Tripoli Monument stands as an eloquent memorial of brave patriotism and reckless devotion to lofty duty, and as a deathless mark of gratitude and loyal remembrance by surviving shipmates.

Capt. C. Q. Wright, 1922

From the Halls of Montezuma,
To the shores of Tripoli,
We fight our country's battles
In the air, on land, and sea

Marines' Hymn

A group of naval officers led by Commo. David Porter commissioned the Tripoli Monument, originally called the Naval Monument, in 1806 to honor six young naval officers killed in the Barbary War. An unknown sculptor carved the monument in highly allegorical style, of Carrera marble from the same quarry used by Michelangelo. The central or rostral column portrays the bows of captured enemy ships on one side and the sterns on the other, a design created by the Romans in about 260 BC to honor naval heroes. (This form was rediscovered in the eighteenth century and used on several monuments in England and at the Russian bourse in St. Petersburg.) Surrounding the column are four symbolic figures: the winged figure of Fame; the figure of History, recording the deeds of the young Americans in a book; Commerce, honoring the Navy's role in preserving free trade; and a female Native American figure with children at her feet, representing Columbia, or the New World, and symbolizing the young westward-expanding America. The names of the six naval officers who lost their lives—Decatur, Israel, Wadsworth, Dorsey, Somers, Caldwell—are recorded on the pedastal. Lt. James Decatur was killed aboard Gunboat No. 2 in action during the attack launched on August 3, 1804; Midn. Joseph Israel, Midn. Henry Wadsworth, and Midn. (trainee) John Dorsey were killed in the second gunboat attack on August 7, 1804; Master Commandant Richard Somers died when his ship, *Intrepid*, sent into Tripoli Harbor, prematurely exploded on September 4, 1804. The monument, first erected at the Navy Yard in Washington, D.C., in 1808, was then moved to the U.S. Capitol in 1830. In 1860 it was transported by the steamer *Anacostia* to the Naval Academy, and in 1907, with the completion of Sampson Hall, it was relocated to its present position in front of the Officer and Faculty Club. It is among the oldest military monuments in the nation.

The Barbary Wars, which took place between 1783 and 1815, were fought in part to keep the seas open for trade. In the late eighteenth century, the United States had been forced to pay tribute for the safe passage of merchant ships that sailed along the Barbary Coast, present-day Algeria, Tunisia, Morocco, and Libya (formerly known as Tripoli or Tripolitania, then part of the Ottoman Empire). The people of the United States rallied around the call to cease these payments—a popular saying at the time was "Millions for defense, but not one cent for tribute"—and in 1801, President Jefferson sent off a naval squadron to eliminate the need for tribute.

After a series of dramatic actions against the corsairs in 1804–6—including five bombardments of Tripoli, the boarding of the captured *Philadelphia* and its burning to prevent its use by the Tripolitans, the explosion of *Intrepid* in order to destroy the Tripolitan fleet, and the capture of pirate ships—Pasha Yusef Karamuli signed a treaty on June 10, 1810, to cease hostilities and waive all claims to future tribute.

However, while the United States was busy fighting the British in the War of 1812, the Barbary States once again began attacking American merchant ships in the Mediterranean. On March 2, 1815, after Congress declared war, President James Madison sent a squadron under Stephen Decatur to Tripoli. Decatur soon secured a treaty granting full shipping rights to the United States. By the 1830s France had colonized Algiers and Tunis, and Tripoli had reverted to control by the Ottoman Empire until it was taken over by Italy in 1911; Europeans remained in control of the former Barbary States until the mid-twentieth century, and the Barbary pashas' demands for tribute and ransom were no longer a problem.

Documents on Tripoli Actions

SIR You are hereby ordered to take command of the Prize Ketch which I have named the *Intrepid* and prepare her with all possible dispatch for a cruize of Thirty days with full allowance of Water, Provision &ca for Seventy five men. I shall send you five Midshipmen from the *Constitution* and you will take Seventy men including Officers from the *Enterprize* if that number can be found ready to volunteer their Services for boarding and burning the *Philadelphia* in the Harbor of Tripoli. If not, report to me and I will furnish you with men to compleat your compliment. It is expected you will be ready to sail tomorrow evening or some hours sooner if the Signal is made for that purpose. . . . After the Ship is well on fire, point two of the 18 Pdrs shotted down the Main Hatch and blow her bottom out—I enclose you a memorandum of the Articles, Arms, Ammunition, fire works &ca as necessary and which you are to take with you—Return to this Place as soon as Possible, and report to me your proceedings. On boarding the Frigate it is probable you will meet with Resistance, it will be well in order to prevent alarm to carry all by the Sword, May God prosper and Succeed you in this enterprize.

> *Capt. Edward Preble* to Lt. Stephen Decatur Jr.,
> commanding U.S. ketch *Intrepid*, January 13, 1804

⚓

I have the pleasure to announce to you intelligence of the Capture and destruction of the Tripoline Frigate of 40 Guns late the United States frigate *Philadelphia* by the U.S. Ketch *Intrepid* of 4 guns and 70 men commanded by Lieut Decatur of the *Enterprize* who volunteered his services on the occasion. It is to be regretted that she was so situated that it was impossible to have brought her out.

On the 3 Inst the Brig *Syren* Lt Stewart and Ketch *Intrepid* of 4 Guns commanded by Lieut Decatur with 70 volunteers from the Squadron and fitted for the purpose sailed for Tripoly with orders to burn the Frigate in that harbor : They this day returned having executed my orders much to my Satisfaction.

On the 16th Inst Lt Decatur entered the Harbor of Tripoly with the Ketch, laid her alongside the frigate, and in a gallant and officer like manner boarded and carried her against all opposition. After gaining complete possession, he proceeded to fire her with success, and left her in a blaze in which she continued until she was totally consumed : He had none killed and only one wounded : The Tripolitans lost about 20 men killed and we took one Prisoner. A Boat load made there escape : some ran below and perished in the flames, and some jumped overboard. She was moored close under the Batteries with a strong guard on board, and all her guns loaded : Two of their Corsairs full of men lay within half musket shot of her : A fire was kept up on the ketch by the Batteries Bashaws castle and Corsairs : not a musket or pistol was fired by our men:

Everything was settled by the sword—

The *Syren* anchored without the Harbor to cover the retreat of the Ketch, and sent her boats to assist, but unfortunately they did not arrive in season as the business was accomplished and the Ketch on her way out before the Boats met her : Had they got in sooner, it is probable some of the Tripolitan Cruizes would have shared the fate of the Frigate—

The Officers and seamen concerned in the execution of this Enterprize deserve the highest encomiums for their conduct.

Capt. Edward Preble, report on the *Philadelphia*'s capture,
February 16, 1804

Decatur Boarding the Tripolitan Gunboat, oil by Dennis Malone Carter (U.S. Naval Institute Photo Archive)

Fresh breezes from E b N. We are standing off shore 2 or 3 Miles from Tripoly with a signal out, for the Squadron to come within hail—We spoke them, & directed the Gun Boats & Bombards to be ready for immediate service—

. . . We made a short board off till 12 1/2 Noon when we tacked in for the Batteries, and made signal for the Gun boats & Bombards to cast off—Our Gun boats are in two divisions—The first is commanded by Capt Somers of the *Nautilus*, Lt Decatur & Lt Blake; The 2d division by Capt Decatur of the *Enterprize*, Lt. Tripp[e] & Lt. Bainbridge; The Bombards are commanded by Capt Dent of the Scourge & Lt. Robinson of the *Constitution* . . . At 1 1/4 PM made the Nautilus signal to make more sail, & a few minutes after made signal for the Bombards to take their stations, and for the Gun boats to advance Capt Decatur and Lieuts J. Decatur. Tripp & Bainbridge led in for the Eastern division of the Enemy's Gun boats—At 2 PM made signal to advance—We were now within gun shot of all the Enemys batteries and stood in within a mile of them before a shot was exchanged—At 2 3/4 Bombard No. 1 hove a shell—The enemy's batteries and Gun boats immediately commenced firing which we returned with our Larboard Guns. . . .

Although the *Constitution* was exposed to the fire of all the Enemys batteries & Gun boats for upwards of two hours, Nine shot only struck her—The Commodore had a very narrow escape—He was close to a gun disabled by one of the enemy's shot;—The shot broke & severely wounded one man—the Commodores cloathes were cut in several places by pieces of the shot—

Sailing Master Nathaniel Haraden, log book,
USS *Constitution*, August 4, 1804

❧

[August 3]: 1/2 past 2 general signal for Battle. The whole squadron advanc'd within point Blank shot of the Enemies Batteries & shipping, our Gun Boats in two divisions the 1st consisting of 3 Boats Commanded by Capt Somers the 2d of three Boats by Capt Decatur, at 3/4 past 2 the Action commenced on our side by throwing a shell into the Town, and in an Instant the whole Squadron were engaged.— . . . [A]t 3 observed our Gun Boats engaged in close action with the Enemies Boats, while a tremendous fire was kept up by this ship and the rest of the Squadron.

Capt Decatur with No. 4 Lt Trippe of No 6 & Lt Bainbridge of No. 5 & Lt James Decatur of No. 2 attacked the enemys Boats within Pistol shot. No. 1 Capt Somers fell to Leward but fetched up with the Enemys Rear of 5 Boats which he gallantly attacked disabled & drove in altho within pistol shot of the Batteries. No. 3 Lt Blake did not go into close Action, had he gone down to the assistance of Capt Somers it is probable they would have captured the Rear Boats. Capt Decatur Boarded and after a stout and obstinate resistance took possession of two of the Enemies Gun Boats, Lt Trip Boarded and carried a third. Lt James Decatur in the Act of Boarding to take possession of a fourth Boat was shot through the Head & Mortally wounded the officer next in command (Mn Brown) hauld off. . . . Three different times the Enemies Gun Boats rallied and attempted to surround ours. I as often made the signal to cover them, which was properly attended to by the Brigs & Schooners, and the fire from this ship not only had the desired effect on the enemies flotilla by keeping them in check and disabling them, but silenced one of their principal Batteries for some time, at 1/2 past 4 PM made the signal for the Bombs to retire from action out of Gun shot, and a few minutes after the general signal to Cease fireing and Tow out the Prizes & disabled Boats. Sent our Barge and Jolly Boat to assist in that duty. Tack'd ship & fired two Broadsides in stays which drove the Tripolines out of the Castle & brought down the Steeple of a Mosque, by this time the wind began to freshen from N E at 4 3/4 PM hauld off to take the Bombs in tow, at 5 PM Brought to, two miles from their Batteries, Recd Lt James Decatur on board from Gun Boat No. 2, he was shot through the Head (in Boarding a Tripoline Boat which had struck to him) he expired in a few moments after he was brought into the ship.— We lay to until 10 PM to receive the Prisoners on board captured in the Prizes, then made sail & stood off to the N E the wind Veering to the E S E.—we have all the surgeons of the squadron on board dressing the wounded.—

Capt. Edward Preble, journal, USS *Constitution*, August 4, 1804

───※───

Resolved by the Senate and House of Representatives of the United States of America in Congress assembled, That the thanks of Congress be, and the same are hereby presented to Commodore Edward Preble, and through him to the officers, petty officers, seamen and marines attached to the squadron under his command, for their gallantry and good conduct, displayed in the several attacks on the town, batteries and naval force of Tripoli, in the year one thousand eight hundred and four.

Resolved, That the President of the United States be also requested to communicate to the parents or other near relatives of Captain Richard Somers, lieutenants Henry Wadsworth, James Decatur, James R. Caldwell, Joseph Israel, and midshipman John Sword Dorsey, the deep regret which Congress feel for the loss of those gallant men, whose names ought to live in the recollection and affection of a grateful country, and whose conduct ought to be regarded as an example to future generations.

Congressional resolution honoring
Gold Medal recipient Commo. Edward Preble, March 3, 1805

~∾~

Tripoli

Midshipmen marching by
this eighteenth-century marble allegory—
    Angel of Fame, robed History,
    book in hand,
    a brave young America leading a child
    into the new land—

memorize the names of those who fell
in action off the shores of Tripoli—
    Somers, Caldwell, Dorsey,
    Decatur, Wadsworth, Israel—

and yearn to emulate that love of glory
that kept the oceans free.

Others of us, older, saddened
with the passing to another world
of ones who've just begun
their lives, are also stirred
enough sometimes to ask,
"Stone spirits,
teach us to be young."

Triton Light

Triton Light (Randell Hunt "Doc" Prothro and Gustav F. "Gus" Swainson Jr.)

Four flashes. Five. Four again. The rhythmic flash sequence of Triton Light illuminates the evening waters of the Severn River with a green glow not seen anywhere else. . . . Here, all is calm. Time comes to a standstill and one can focus on the meaning behind the mad rush of the day. Four flashes, five. Four again. It seems to call out to those who faced the peril of the sea and

did not return. It invites them back to their home: the Academy. Where else would be more appropriately suited for their
resting place? Triton Light is a tribute to all those who helped
make this Navy great. It represents the light that each one of
us has inside that can never be extinguished. Four flashes, five,
four again: so blinks that light in our souls and hearts.

Salvatore Pasquarelli, USNA 2003

Triton Light, a fully functional navigation light, is located along
the seawall at the Yard's far southeast corner, at the confluence of
Severn River and Spa Creek. Its official designation, Coast Guard
Chart #12283 GP Fl G (4-5) 30 sec 25 ft 8 M, signifies that its green
light, flashing in a four-five sequence, is visible at a maximum distance
of eight miles. The green light and its flash sequence honor its donors,
the "Look Alive" Class of 1945, who presented it in 1959 as an early
twenty-years-after graduation gift in order to secure a setting for it on the
new land reclaimed from the Severn River. The light's placement atop
a three-sided, nine-foot-high bronze open-work obelisk, with a water-
encased globe inside, is highly symbolic: the three sides of the stand
depict the three faiths of Navy sailors (God, country, and ship); the open
grating symbolizes the Navy's adaptability, its openness to change; the
rough, unpolished granite base represents the rigors of life at sea; and the
perpetual light itself stands for the overall purpose of the monument as
a beacon dedicated to the safe return "of all those who go down to the
sea in ships."

Triton Light is named after the mythological sea deity, son of Amphi-
trite and Poseidon, king of the Sea. Triton, who had the power to abate
storms, represents the spirit of the Sea. The light also pays homage to
the USS *Triton*, which completed the first underwater circumnavigation
of the world in 1960: the globe inside the obelisk holds water collected
from the twenty-two seas crossed in this voyage, presented by Capt.
Edward Beach Jr., USNA 1939.

A beacon calling those who can't call back
A light to guide home those who aren't coming home
A symbol of hope for those who have no hope
But as long as she stands so stands our memory
Of those who have no more memories

Ryan M. Shaughnessy, USNA 2006

᯽

Triton Light bonds together the past and future of the Navy with its dedication to the *Triton's* triumph and all those who proudly serve in the Navy. The monument, to me, represents the victory of high achievement, unity, and appreciation of those who have gone before us "down to the sea." I will always respect and honor those who have risked and given their lives in support of our county.

Jonathan D. Hagerman, USNA 2010

᯽

Dedication of Triton Light

A rainy and foggy day did not dampen the enthusiasm of loyal '45ers and friends who turned out for the ceremony in heartening numbers. The unveiling took place with just the proper amount of fouling up, and there wasn't an unimpressed soul in the crowd. Admiral Melson graciously accepted the Light, and it now stands as a landmark in what will soon be a beautiful landscaped park "where Severn joins the Bay."

Robert Baldwin, USNA 1945, January 1960

᯽

The sweat trickling down my body had already saturated my blue-rim shirt and mess shorts. We had blazed a path around Dewey and were approaching the corner of the seawall near Farragut Field. Suddenly the order "Platoon, halt!" echoed from behind. As my lungs burned for air, my focus shifted to the breathtaking sunset ahead. Our detailers told us to fall out and line up along the seawall. Standing in silence, I began to notice the smooth green flashes coming from Triton Light. Our detailers explained to us that we were straying from the path of good fourth-class midshipmen and that they were disappointed. They illustrated their point with examples of the platoon's poor performance in the aspect of rate knowledge and physical training.

Then Midshipman 1/C Taylor, our company administrative officer, rationalized the fact that the dangers we faced as plebes were similar to those faced by any ship that loses its way at sea. He instructed us to remain focused on our objectives in the same way that a ship must keep track of its position over its course of travel.

I gazed at the brilliant explosion of the multicolored sunset. However, the scope of his lesson shifted my attention to Triton's perpetual "4-5" message. I suddenly no longer saw it as just a visual aid for ships. Instead, I embraced it as a beacon of spiritual guidance. The rhythmic green flashes of light washed the pain and fatigue from me and I stood refreshed.

The order to fall in was given, and we each moved quickly to get into platoon formation. Just as we began our running stride again, I looked back to Triton Light. As long as it is there, I know I will never lose my way.

Matthew O. Caylor, USNA 2004

One night at the end of plebe summer, my squad leader walked us out to Triton Light. She told us that when she was a plebe her squad leader took her to the same spot to reflect upon the last six weeks of their lives. It had a profound effect on her so she thought that we deserved the same experience. We all gathered around the base of Triton Light looking out at the reflection of the full moon on the rippling water, and the atmosphere gave us a feeling of satisfaction that we had made it past the first milestone in plebe year. After we settled down, we started talking about our experiences during the summer and the improvements we had made. None of us could believe what we went through and some were amazed that we made it through the summer. All other squads in our platoon except ours ended the summer with fewer plebes than on Induction Day. We had made it through the summer with no casualties. At this point the next goal was to make it through the academic year.

Class of '45 crest (Randell Hunt "Doc" Prothro and
Gustav F. "Gus" Swainson Jr.)

Knowing that the year to come was going to be a long and arduous
one, we made a promise to ourselves and to each other that we were
not going to quit and we were going to meet at Triton Light at the end
of plebe year and at the end of our four years at the Naval Academy.
Whenever Academy life wears on me I can just remember that day and
think about the promise that I would not quit on my squad mates and
they would not quit on me.

Christopher D. Bernard, USNA 2004

Origin of the Class of 1945 Motto

There have been a number of stories about how the Class of 1945
adopted the phrase, LOOK ALIVE WITH '45 as its very own rallying cry
and Class Motto.

Nobody seems to know for sure just how this saying originated, but I think I have an explanation. . . . When we were midshipmen, the phrase "Look Alive" was in common use. First Classmen would say, "Look Alive in the Plebes" when we were marching onto the drill field or into the football stadium. So it was not unique. Only our adoption of "LOOK ALIVE WITH '45" took on the flavor of a unique saying, and the term became associated with our Class of 1945. With its unique rhythm and its pleasant rhyme, it just seemed to fit. How did it start? I think it started during plebe summer. . . .

One very hot afternoon we were marched down to the Cutter Sheds to learn Seamanship and be taught how to row a large, heavy boat called a Cutter that had served for many years as the liberty boat for ships of the "Old Navy." The Cutter also served as a lifeboat for many of the large ships; it had a gaff-rigged sail that could be hoisted on a stubby mast for emergency use in case of shipwreck. There were tales of survivors who sailed cutters across large stretches of the Pacific to safety.

A salty, grizzled old Chief Boatswain's Mate met us at the Cutter Sheds outboard of Luce Hall, just opposite the America's Dock, where the original yacht *America* was tied up for a number of years—long before we arrived at the Academy. The Chief was a character. He was dressed in CPO white uniform with blue service stripes all the way up to his left elbow. His voice was a powerful bellow, with a gravelly tone that was at once commanding and attention-getting. His job was to teach a bunch of land-lubber plebes how to row a cutter, and how to show some semblance of order in doing so. And he did it well. The Cutter Sheds were long, open buildings extending over the water of Santee Basin; and each one held four or five Cutters. They had no engines; their sails and spars were stowed on board for emergency use. They were hoisted up close under the roofs of the sheds for protection from the weather. We soon learned how to man the falls and lower away those heavy boats. When they reached the water, groups of plebes jumped in and manned the oars. Each cutter had a large rudder, to which was attached a long tiller, and 10 long, heavy oars, five on each side. With one plebe manning the tiller, and five on each side, each manning an oar, we proceeded to fumble our way out into the Severn River. Under the Chief's direction from one of the cutters, we all learned to "Toss Oars" and perform other esoteric maneuvers that we were told had a purpose and a traditional role in the Old Navy. We also learned that the

Battleships and Cruisers in ports around the world competed in "Cutter Races" with their well-trained enlisted crews to gain bragging rights and undoubtedly to win bets from other ships.

The Chief usually had three or four cutters under his supervision and his stentorian commands kept them all hard at work. Sometimes we would row up the Severn and put a boathook over to a piling of the old Severn River Bridge to rest in its shade, while the Chief had a smoke and told sea stories about some famous cutter races of the past. But when all boats were on the water and their plebe crews had been suitably trained to be able to row somewhat in unison, some would stray away from the lead boat—the one with the Chief aboard—and as the plebe rowers tired, they would slow down and coast along, sometimes resting on their oars. The Chief would awaken the surrounding waterfront with his thunderous call, "LOOK ALIVE OUT THERE, '45, LOOK ALIVE." And that, we knew, was his way of letting the slackers know that he saw them goofing off and would have no part of it. Repeated numerous times, the deep, strong, demanding calls of the Chief soon became, "LOOK ALIVE '45." And before long, we were saying it to our classmates as we marched or rowed or participated in various team activities. Thus we had our saying, and it has held its attraction for us over all the years that we have held together as a Class. We became the LOOK ALIVE class, and our LOOK ALIVE WITH '45 became our famous, and much admired, saying, well known to all USNA classes. Thanks, Chief. Even though we don't remember your name, we remember you and your lasting contribution to our class: LOOK ALIVE WITH '45.

M. *Dick Van Orden*, USNA 1945

❧

The same ocean that rinses
Small pebbles of sand
And ebbs at the beaches
Where green water meets land,
Holds the secrets of warriors
Who braved the blue deep
On a mission to establish
Our nation's own keep.
Their mission successful,

They've protected our shores;
Submariners thereafter
Follow those before.
To thank them we've erected
A light with their name.
In the cobblestone seawall
Where so many came
It glows there brightly
By night and by day
A beacon and reminder
Of the sacrifice they made.

Chelsea R. Brunoehler (née Gaughan),
USNA 2006

USNA Seal

Bows on, the ancient galley
Sails into action.
Torches flare,
A book stands open,
A hand at the ready
Grasps a trident.
The Academy seal:
From knowledge, sea power.

USNA Seal (Erik Ruden, Naval
Academy Athletic Association)

T he Academy seal was created by Park Benjamin Jr., USNA 1867, a midshipman author who helped organize the Naval Academy Alumni Association of New York in 1897. Benjamin described the coat of arms with "a hand grasping a trident, below which is a shield bearing an ancient galley coming into action, bows on, and below that an open book, indicative of education, and finally the motto, *Ex Scientia Tridens* (From knowledge, sea power)." Jacob W. Miller, one of Benjamin's classmates and a founder of the New York Naval Militia, facilitated the Navy Department's adoption of the crest in 1899.

> The seal that has the most meaning at the Academy is the bronze shield in front of the statue of Tecumseh. . . . Forged from the torpedo tubes of USS *Washington*. . . [it] is considered sacred ground and should not be tread upon.
>
> Plebe

USS *Maine* Foremast

Tall and white
Next to Triton Light
Stands the foremast.
Her other end at Arlington: a tribute to her past.
The longest ship in the Navy, she is
Just scenery for tourists looking at mids,
Standing where the Severn meets the bay,
Hardly noticed by anyone anyway.

Robert Chandler, USNA 2006

USS *Maine* foremast (Randell Hunt "Doc" Prothro and Gustav F. "Gus" Swainson Jr.)

The foremast of USS *Maine*, the ship that helped ignite the Spanish-American War, sits in Triton Park near Triton Light and the Class of 1945 Sea Gate. Known as "the longest ship in the Navy" because the mainmast sits almost fifty miles away in Arlington National Cemetery, it pays tribute to the U.S. goal of establishing hegemony over European powers in the Western Hemisphere.

In February 1898 the USS *Maine* was anchored in Havana Harbor as Spanish soldiers tried to quell an eruption of the ongoing Cuban independence movement against Spain when an explosion occurred on the ship, killing over 260 American sailors. The investigation, headed up by Rear Adm. William Sampson, determined that an underwater mine was the likely cause but asserted no blame. In America, however, newspapers blamed the Spanish, fanning the flames of an already high public hostility against Spain. "Gentlemen, remember the *Maine*," a toast overheard by a *New York Journal* reporter in a Broadway bar, gave rise to the nation's rallying cry, "Remember the *Maine* and to hell with Spain!" In April 1898 the United States declared war. Sampson, in command of the Blockade Squadron, quickly brought about the surrender of the Spanish fleet in Santiago Bay, Cuba, on July 3, 1898. A later investigation in 1911 of the causes of *Maine*'s destruction also threw blame on external causes, but an investigation by Admiral Rickover years later asserted that internal combustion of the powder stores caused the explosion.

On the Explosion of *Maine*

Sir, I have to inform you that the ship has blown up and is sinking.

Marine Pvt. William Anthony, orderly to Capt. Charles D. Sigsbee,
February 15, 1898

⁂

I was enclosing my letter [to my family] in its envelope when the explosion came. It was a bursting, rending, and crashing roar of immense volume, largely metallic in character. It was followed by heavy, ominous metallic sounds. There was a trembling and lurching motion of the vessel, a list to port. The electric lights went out. Then there was intense blackness and smoke. . . . The situation could not be mistaken. The *Maine* was blown up and sinking. For a moment the instinct of self-preservation took charge of me, but this was immediately dominated by the habit of command.

Capt. Charles D. Sigsbee, Naval Court of Inquiry testimony, February–March 1898

The whole starboard of the deck, with its sleeping berth, burst out and flew into space, as a crater of flame came through, carrying with it missiles and objects of all kinds, steel, wood, and human. [After the explosion] all was still except for the cries of the wounded, the groans of the dying, and the crackling of flame in the wreckage.

Lt. John J. Blandon, letter to wife, February 16, 1898

Victory Bells

The barbarians will come and invade if the Japanese lords and ministers fail to act rightly and do justice.

Translation of inscription on Perry Bell

Japanese (Perry) Bell (Randell Hunt "Doc" Prothro and Gustav F. "Gus" Swainson Jr.)

The two bells flanking the steps to Bancroft Hall, known as the Victory Bells, celebrate Navy athletic victories over Army. The *Enterprise* Bell is rung for the majority of triumphs over Army; for football victories, both bells are rung. The *Enterprise* Bell is rung from the moment the news reaches Bancroft until the team returns home. The Japanese (or Perry) Bell is rung by the team captain, the coach, the superintendent, and the commandant, and then by each team member.

Japanese Bell

The Japanese Bell, a replica of a six-hundred-year old Japanese tongue-less temple gong bell in wood frame, was a diplomatic gift from Sho-Tai, the regent of Okinawa and Ryukyu islands to Commo. Matthew C. Perry (1794–1858) in 1854. The bell, also known as the Perry Bell, commemorates Perry's 1853–54 voyage to Japan (later discussed). The original bell, cast in 1456, had been enthusiastically received by Commodore Perry, who first thought to place it at the Washington Monument, which was then under construction. When that idea was rejected, he decided to place it at the Naval Academy, an act carried out by his widow in 1858.

This original bell, initially mounted in a free-standing belfry along with a conventional western bell used for sounding time and alarms, was moved in the late nineteenth century to the central part of the Yard and hung in its own Oriental-style belfry. Following Navy's victory over Army in the 1900 football game, the team captain, Orie W. Fowler, USNA 1901, rang the victory score on the Japanese Bell, thus inaugurating a long tradition. The original belfry and bell were eventually moved to their current location in T-Court to the left of the main entrance to Bancroft Hall.

During World War II, despite calls for the removal of the Japanese Bell and the Japanese Monument, Academy authorities decided to leave both standing as "an ever-present reminder of the treachery of our enemies and of the job that lies before every Naval officer." On V-J day, August 15, 1945, the bell in its belfry was dragged to the center of Tecumseh Court and the midshipmen celebrated the war's end by beating the bell continually with two bowling pins, causing it to crack.

Because of concern that the crack would eventually give way to a break, a second bell, from USS *Enterprise*, was acquired.

In 1987 the governor of Okinawa requested the original bell's return because so much of Okinawa's cultural heritage had been destroyed in World War II. The Academy honored the request and delivered the bell to the Shuri Historical Museum in Okinawa. The Okinawans sent as a replacement an exact replica—minus the crack.

1854 Expedition to Japan

Commo. Matthew Calbraith Perry (1794–1858), sailor, diplomat, and naval reformer, served forty-two years in the Navy. His trip to Japan in 1854 opened the island nation to commerce with the West and secured protection for American whaling ships via the Treaty of Kanagawa (signed March 31, 1854). Perry's subsequent description of his voyage, *Narrative of the Expedition of an American Squadron to the China Seas and Japan*, kindled American interest in Japan.

> Steam engine and track
> Telegraph
> Audubon's Birds
> Colt's Revolver
> Telescope
> U.S. weights, measures and balances
> Box of Champagne
> Barrel Whiskey
>
>   Selected list of presents Perry gave to the emperor

～❧～

I have been endeavoring to create a little more interest in the expedition by a lecture on Japan, which I delivered through the Northern and Western States during the winter. I endeavored to give an idea of the character of the Japanese people, as contrasted with that of the Chinese, and the advantages which may accrue to us from the opening of the country; and disclosed nothing concerning the expedition which the Commodore had not authorized me to make public. . . . I am now engaged in preparing for the press my travels in Africa, and desire to give, in a later volume, my adventures in India, China, Loo-Choo and Japan. This, however, I cannot do until I receive my notes and journals which I gave up to Com. Perry according to the order of the Department, and I should like to know at what period I may be able to receive them. The Department will no doubt allow me the use of them as soon as they are received. . . . Is there any possibility of obtaining a copy of the Treaty for publication? The principal points have already been made public, and I suppose the Government will shortly give the whole of it to the world. Perhaps you are acquainted with the views of the State Department in this respect, and can tell me whether there will be any use in making application.

Baynard Taylor to Cdr. Henry A. Adams,
Captain of the Fleet, July 12, 1856

Enterprise Bell

The bronze *Enterprise* Bell, acquired in 1950, is the ship's bell from the aircraft carrier USS *Enterprise* (CV-6), the most decorated ship of World War II. *Enterprise*, also known as "The Big E" and "The Galloping Ghost," was involved in eighteen of the twenty major naval actions of the war, including the Doolittle Raid on Tokyo and the Battle of Midway in 1942 (see the Midway Memorial entry). Launched October 1936, she was commissioned May 1938 and had her shakedown cruise that summer. In January 1939, along with the carrier *Hornet*, she joined the carrier air group commanded by Rear Adm. William F. Halsey. *Enterprise* entered World War II on December 7, 1941, when her scout planes encountered Japanese squadrons attacking Pearl Harbor, and she remained in operation in the war until May 14, 1945, when she was heavily damaged by a kamikaze suicide mission. All told, *Enterprise* accounted for 911 enemy planes downed, 71 ships sunk, and 192 more ships damaged or destroyed during the war. The *Dictionary of American Naval Fighting Ships* lists twenty battle stars given *Enterprise*; "Battle Streamers of the U.S. Navy" lists fifty-two, covering both the Pacific theater and the European–African–Middle Eastern theater.

Enterprise and Task Force 16 Actions in World War II

Battle Order Number One

1. The ENTERPRISE is now operating under war conditions.

2. At any time, day or night, we must be ready for instant action.

3. Hostile submarines may be encountered.

4. The importance of every officer and man being specially alert and vigilant while on watch at his battle station must be fully realized by all hands.

5. The failure of one man to carry out his assigned task promptly, particularly the lookouts, those manning the batteries, and all those on watch on the deck, might result in great loss of life and even loss of the ship.

6. The Captain is confident all hands will prove equal to any emergency that may develop.

7. It is part of the tradition of our Navy that, when put to the test, all hands keep cool, keep their heads, and FIGHT.

8. Steady nerves and stout hearts are needed now.

Capt. C. G. D. Murray, order approved by
Vice Adm. W. F. Halsey, Commander Aircraft,
Battle Force Pacific, November 28, 1941

～∘～

This force is bound for Tokyo.

Vice Admiral Halsey to Task Force 16, April 13, 1942

Doolittle Raid, April 18, 1942

The Doolittle Raid, led by Army Air Corps Lt. Col. James "Jimmy" Doolittle, was a secret bombing mission against Tokyo launched from the deck of the carrier *Hornet* by Task Force 16, flagship USS *Enterprise*. The mission was designed to put America on the offensive in the war against Japan. It was especially dangerous because the large planes could not

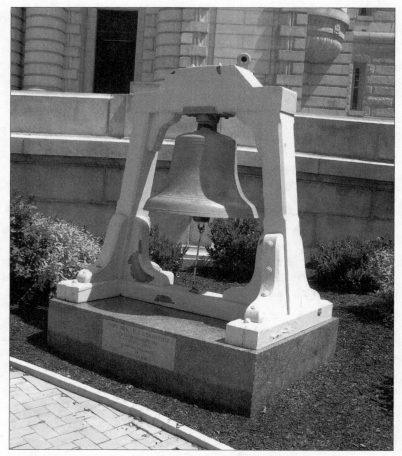

Enterprise Bell (Randell Hunt "Doc" Prothro and Gustav F. "Gus" Swainson Jr.)

return to the carrier, but instead would have to try to land in Chinese-controlled territory. Furthermore, because Imperial Japanese forces detected the carrier 150 miles earlier than anticipated, the planes had to launch earlier, with too little fuel to make it to safe territory. Most of the planes were shot down over water or Japanese territory, and the airmen who were not killed immediately were captured by the Japanese. A few were rescued by Chinese, but were soon retrieved by the Japanese.

In retaliation for the bombing, which killed tens of thousands of Japanese civilians in addition to destroying military targets, the Japanese military executed the captured pilots; they also killed tens of thousands of Chinese in retaliation for the assistance the Chinese provided the American pilots.

> The necessity for launching the Army planes at 0820 on the 18th about 650 miles east of Tokyo was regrettable. The plan was to close to the 500 mile circle and there launch one plane to attack at dusk and thus provide a target for the remaining planes which would strike about two hours later. This plan was evolved by Lieutenant Colonel Doolittle, in command of the Army flight, and was designed to inflict the greatest damage with the least risk. The remote location of the desired terminus for the flight was also a factor influencing the selection of this plan of attack. However, contacts with enemy surface vessels early in the morning compromised the secrecy of the operation, and after the third contact, at 0744, the decision was made to launch. Japanese radio traffic was intercepted indicating that the presence of the raiding force was reported. The prime consideration then was the launching of the Army planes before the arrival of Japanese bombers.

> *Admiral Halsey*, Commander, Task Force 16,
> report of action of April 18, 1942

At 1232 (VW) April 8, 1942 this vessel stood out of Pearl Harbor in company with Task Force Sixteen, consisting of ENTERPRISE (Flagship), NORTHAMPTON, SALT LAKE CITY, BALCH, BENHAM, FANNING, ELLET and SABINE, under command of Vice-Admiral W. F. Halsey, Jr., U.S.N., Commander Carriers, Pacific Fleet, for operations not disclosed at this time. . . .

On April 18, the day it was planned to reach the 500 mile circle from Tokyo at about 1600, ENTERPRISE launched the usual dawn search flight and combat patrol. These were maintained continuously throughout the day. The contacts and action, indicated on the track chart by capital letters, were reported by pilots of these flights. . . .

At 0310 radar disclosed two enemy surface craft bearing 255°T., distance 21,000 yards, and at 0312 a light was seen approximately on that bearing. Ship went to General Quarters, set Material Condition Affirm and energized the degaussing gear. Course of the Force was changed to 350°T., and at 0341 the two enemy vessels went off the screen bearing

201°T., distance 27,000 yards. Our presence was apparently unnoticed by the enemy and a westerly course was resumed at 0415.

At 0508 fighter patrol and search flight were launched. At 0715 one search plane returned and, by message drop, reported sighting an enemy patrol vessel in Latitude 36° 04' North and Longitude 153° 10' East at 0558 and that he believed he had been seen. Later developments indicate that this vessel made the original contact report.

At 0744 an enemy patrol vessel was sighted bearing 221°T., distance approximately 10,000 yards. There was no doubt now that our force had been detected and almost certainly had been reported. NASHVILLE was ordered to sink the patrol vessel by gunfire as the carriers turned into the wind (320°T., 26 knots); HORNET to launch Army B-25's for attack and ENTERPRISE to relieve patrols. The first Army bomber was launched at 0820 approximately 650 miles from Tokyo, and the last one was off at 0921.

At 0927 the Force commenced retirement on course 090°T., speed 25 knots.

Capt. George D. Murray, USS *Enterprise*,
report on ship's actions during Doolittle Raid,
April 23, 1942

Enterprise Commendations

The carrier that fought the most through the entire war.

Dedicatory plaque, *Enterprise* Elevator Tower,
Navy-Marine Corps Memorial Stadium

❧

For consistently outstanding performance and distinguished achievement during repeated action against enemy Japanese forces in the Pacific war area, December 7, 1941, to November 15, 1942. Participating in nearly every major carrier engagement in the first year of the war, the Enterprise and her air group, exclusive of far-flung destruction of hostile shore installations throughout the battle area, did sink or damage on her own a total of 35 Japanese vessels and shoot down a total of 185 Japanese aircraft. Her aggressive spirit and superb combat efficiency are fitting tribute to the officers and men who so gallantly established her as an ahead bulwark in the defense of the American nation.

Presidential Unit Citation, USS *Enterprise*, May 27, 1943
(first Presidential Unit Citation awarded a carrier)

～❧～

Task Force 16 Honors

[I]t gives me great pleasure to welcome the members of Task Force 16 to the Pentagon and to this ceremony honoring their outstanding contribution to winning the World War we fought some 50 years ago. The events [of that war] are etched into our consciousness, but our commitment to peace requires that we retell the story of those brave men so that we never forget how free men rise to defend liberty when challenged. We do so today by honoring the men of Task Force 16 and the story of one of the greatest truly joint operations of all times.

Honorable Bernard D. Rostker, Assistant Secretary of the Navy,
Pentagon ceremony, May 15, 1995

Vietnam War Memorial

Under blue Annapolis skies
I dream of rivers red with fire

Long ago and far away,
Young men dying for their brothers.

Standing where they started from,
I toss my thoughts upon the Severn:

For our newest sons and daughters,
hopes for courage, prayers for peace.

Vietnam War Memorial (Randell Hunt "Doc" Prothro and Gustav F. "Gus" Swainson Jr.)

This freestanding polished pink granite cenotaph sits on the edge of College Creek across from Alumni Hall in honor of the 118 Naval Academy graduates who were killed in action or listed as missing in the Vietnam War. Donated in 1975 by the Naval Academy Alumni Association, it first sat in the cemetery before being moved to its present location. A number of memorials at the Academy honor men who served in the Vietnam War, including the Armel-Leftwich Visitor Center and a diorama in Memorial Hall depicting a dramatic bridge-traversing action by Marine Col. John W. Ripley, USNA 1962. The museum collection includes a number of items, such as a pair of dice molded from bread dough and ashes, used by American prisoners of war in Vietnam, as well as items related to the secret communication code developed by Vice Adm. James B. Stockdale, USNA 1947, the highest ranking POW in Vietnam. During the war years, a placard in Bancroft Hall announced the names of the graduates recently killed. (For more on USNA graduates who fought in the Vietnam War, see the Armel-Leftwich Visitor Center entry; and the Other Selected Monuments entry).

In grateful remembrance of Naval Academy graduates killed or missing in action in the Vietnam Conflict.

Monument dedication

❧

On the Prisoner of War Experience in Vietnam

I never lost faith in the end of the story. I never doubted not only that I would get out, but also that I would prevail in the end and turn the experience into the defining event of my life, which, in retrospect, I would not trade. . . . You must never confuse faith that you will prevail in the end—which you can never afford to lose—with the discipline to confront the most brutal facts of your current reality, whatever they might be.

I thought plebe year turned out to be one of the most helpful nudges I'd had in a lifetime of preparation for military challenges, particularly those of prison. At the Naval Academy the system had provided for physical hazing of plebes, and I had profited from it in prison.

The test of character is not "hanging in" when you expect light at the end of the tunnel, but performance of duty, and persistence of example when you know no light is coming.

In order to do something you must be something.

Adm. James B. Stockdale

Ward Hall

Ward Hall (Randell Hunt "Doc" Prothro and Gustav F. "Gus" Swainson Jr.)

ow home to the Information Technology Center, when it was built in 1941 Ward Hall first housed the Department of Ordnance and Gunnery, which became the Weapons Department in 1959. In the 1970s Weapons moved first to Melville Hall, then to Maury Hall, and Ward Hall, among other uses, came to house the computer labs.

Ward Hall was named in honor of Cdr. James Harmon Ward (1806–61), the first commandant of midshipmen (a position then called executive officer), first line officer to serve as an instructor, and first naval officer killed in action during the Civil War. As a shipboard midshipman, Ward had served in the Mediterranean, off Africa, and in the West Indies. His interest in education led him to become a driving force in establishing the Naval School in 1845. He also composed steam-engineering texts useful both for students and the general public. During the Mexican War, Ward commanded the frigate *Cumberland* (the flagship of Commo. Matthew Perry), and during the Civil War, the Potomac Flotilla. In June 1861, while aiming the bow gun of his flagship, USS *Thomas Freeborn*, at confederate troops at Mathias Point, Virginia, he was mortally wounded. The Potomac Flotilla (or, as originally proposed by Ward, "the flying flotilla") was designed to defend areas south of the Union capital against the Confederate navy. Composed of three steamships—*Freeborn*, *Freelance*, and *Alliance*—and three coast survey ships, the flotilla eventually routed the Confederate navy from the Potomac and continued to provide invaluable service in dealing with smugglers and with land forces on the Virginia shore of the river, which occasionally sniped at Union ships. After Gen. Ulysses S. Grant's move south in 1864, the Potomac Flotilla moved into the Rappahannock River to help destroy mines—a service also performed by a Maryland African-American regiment, the Thirty-sixth U.S. Colored Infantry.

Presidential Proclamation

Whereas, The laws of the United States have been for some time past and now are opposed, and the execution thereof obstructed, in the States of South Carolina, Georgia, Alabama, Florida, Mississippi, Louisiana, and Texas, by combinations too powerful to be suppressed by the ordinary course of judicial proceedings, or by the powers vested in the Marshals by law :

Now, therefore, I, ABRAHAM LINCOLN, President of the United States, in virtue of the power in me vested by the Constitution and the laws, have thought fit to call forth, and hereby do call forth, the Militia of the several States of the Union, to the aggregate number of 75,000, in order to suppress said combinations, and to cause the laws to be duly executed. The details for this object will be immediately communicated to the State authorities through the War Department.

I appeal to all loyal citizens to favor, facilitate, and aid this effort to maintain the honor, the integrity, and the existence of our National Union and the perpetuity of popular government, and to redress wrongs already long enough endured.

I deem it proper to say that the first service assigned to the force hereby called forth will probably be to repossess the forts, places, and property which have been seized from the Union . . . an efficient blockade of the ports of those states (Virginia and North Carolina) will therefore be established.

President Abraham Lincoln, April 19, 1861

～୧୨～

Potomac Flotilla Farewell

Officers and men of the Potomac Flotilla: The war for the preservation of American liberty being at an end, the Potomac flotilla, which took its rise with it and grew with its growth, until it had become a fleet rather than a flotilla, this day happily ceases to exist.

In taking leave of those with whom I have been so long associated, my heart is filled with varied emotions—with sorrow at parting, gladness that our beloved country no longer has need of us, and pride—just pride—that when I reflect upon the past and remember the taking up of the torpedoes from the Rappahannock, with the destruction or capture of the whole rebel force engaged in placing them there, thereby making Fredericksburgh a secure base of supplies for Gen. Grant's vast army—the burning of the schooners at Mattox Creek, under the severe musketry of the enemy, and the almost daily expeditions up the creeks and through the swamps of the northern neck of Virginia, all requiring skill and nerve, I can truly say: "The Potomac Flotilla has not been unmindful of the traditional honor and glory of the navy."

Your services, however eclipsed by the daring deeds of your more fortunate comrades in arms on other stations, have, equally with theirs, contributed to the suppression of the rebellion; and in discipline, in drill, in unity of action—in all the requirements, in short, of an organized force—I have not, in the course of a naval experience of twenty-eight years, served in a squadron which excelled the one which it has been my good fortune to command for the last nineteen months.

Cdr. James Harmon Ward, 1853–60 (Special Collections and Archives , Nimitz Library, U.S. Naval Academy)

To those who are about to return to civil life I would say: render the same cheerful obedience to the civil law that you have rendered to the naval laws, cast your votes as good citizens, regularly and quietly, at the polls: so keeping your hearts "with malice toward none, with charity for all," that after each Presidential election, whether it be with or against you, you may be enabled to respond heartily to your old naval toast, "The President of the United States, God bless him." And now may God be with you all. Farewell.

Cdr. Foxhall Parker, July 31, 1865

Ward Quotation

The author's present purpose is, to strip from the subject of steam the veil of mystery which hides it from popular view. . . . Passengers on ocean-steamers, suffering from ennui and impatience, may find in these pages pleasant relief. By engaging attention, they will beguile the time and thus shorten a passage. . . . Abstraction is a happy faculty; and the employment which induces it, next to religion the best solace. Obviously at sea, no other occupation is so useful or appropriate as a study of the grand and powerful motor which hurries one over the waves. . . . Such an opportunity . . . for acquiring this useful knowledge, without detriment to other pursuits, ought not to be neglected.

> *Steam for the Million: A Popular Treatise on Steam,*
> *and Its Application to the Useful Arts,*
> *Especially to Navigation,* 1860

Burial Site

Old North Cemetery, Hartford, Connecticut

Worden Field

Shiny plastic shoes glisten in the spring sunshine,
   Eyes forward,
Feet dancing to the rhythm, left-right-left,
Parade rest, at-ten-Hut!
A performance to remember.
Fix bay-o-nets!
The air is filled with drumbeats.

Plebe, USNA 2006

Worden Field (Randell Hunt "Doc" Prothro and Gustav F. "Gus" Swainson Jr.)

Worden Field, a large grassy field bordered by Decatur Road, the Officer and Faculty Club parking lot, and the officers' quarters on Upshur and Rodgers roads, is the official Academy parade ground. Parades have been held here since the early 1900s, when Worden Field also served as the home field for Navy football, baseball, and lacrosse.

Marching By

The drums resound, a martial sound
    Beats forth across the Bay;
The trumpets crash, the cymbals clash,
    The band begins to play.

The column nears, the roadway clears,
    The stripers give command;
The trumpets blare, the startled air
    Gives way before the band.

Long lines of blue swing into view,
    The gang is underway;
The steady beat of a thousand feet
    Rings out across the Bay.

The steady beat of a thousand feet
    Goes swinging slowly by;
And banners bold of blue and gold
    Stand out against the sky.

The Log, 1924

One morning we had a practice parade on Worden Field, a place where all midshipmen have stood, a place of history and tradition. We drilled . . . following commands . . . "Present arms!" [when] a yellow ladybug landed on the muzzle of my rifle. Suddenly the scene—the green grass, the dew, and the early morning shadows—seemed so peaceful, much like the happy, carefree life I used to live. . . . My thoughts were not on what the menu was for lunch or how many days there were until Navy beats Army in football. Even though I was still literally in this military setting,

Rear Adm. John L. Worden, 1865–80 (U.S. Naval Institute Photo Archive)

this ladybug, so peaceful against the greenery . . . let me remember what it's like to stop for a second and look around. . . . [At] "Order arms!" I snapped my hand to my rifle to bring it down and the moment of peace . . . was lost, gone with one snap.

Katherine A. Adler, USNA 2009

The parade ground is named for Rear Adm. John L. Worden (1818–97), commander of the ironclad USS *Monitor* in the historic battle with CSS *Virginia*. Worden, wounded in the battle, recovered and went on to direct the construction of ironclads for the rest of the war. From 1869 to 1874, he served as superintendent of midshipmen. It is appropriate that the "New Naval Academy" parade field was named in 1912 for this superintendent who loved parades.

Monitor-Merrimack Documents

(Editor's note: USS *Merrimack* was the name of the steam frigate commissioned in Boston in 1856 and decommissioned in Norfolk in 1860. Federal forces burned and sank her when Virginia seceded in 1861, but the Confederates retrieved and renamed her, converting her into the ironclad CSS *Virginia*. The converted ship is sometimes still referred to as the *Merrimack* (although some of the documents below misspell the name), but the *Merrimack* should not be confused with USS *Merrimac*, also in service 1861–65.)

I received your letter of the 11th instant yesterday and thank you for the feeling which prompted you to name me for the command of the Ericsson battery. I went immediately to see her, and, after a hasty examination of her, am induced to believe that she may prove a success. At all events, I am quite willing to be an agent in testing her capabilities, and will readily devote whatever of capacity and energy I have to that object.

Lieutenant Worden, letter to Commo. Joseph Smith,
Chief, Bureau of Yards and Docks, January 13, 1862

SIR: I have the honor to report that I have this day reported for duty for the command of the U.S. ironclad steamer built by Captain Ericsson.

Lieutenant Worden, telegram to Assistant Secretary of the Navy
Gustavus V. Fox, January 16, 1862

~~❧~~

I congratulate you and trust she will be a success. Hurry her for sea, as the Merrimack is nearly ready at Norfolk and we wish to send her here.

Assistant Secretary of the Navy Fox to
Lieutenant Worden, January 30, 1862

~~❧~~

A better [crew] no naval commander ever had the honor to command.

Lieutenant Worden, USS *Monitor*, March 1862

~~❧~~

My Dear Wife & Children,

I have but a few minutes to spare just to say that I am safe. We have had an engagement with the *Merrimac* continuing for three hours & have driven her off, we think in a sinking condition. We have three men disabled, among them & the worst is our noble Captain who has lost his sight, I hope only temporarily. The first opportunity I get you shall have full details & my own experience. With my best & kindest love to you all.

William F. Keeler, Acting Paymaster, USS *Monitor*,
to his family, March 9, 1862

~~❧~~

Worden lost no time in bringing [the *Monitor*] to test. Getting his ship under way, he steered direct for the enemy's vessels, in order meet and engage them as far as possible from the *Minnesota*. As he approached, the wooden vessels quickly turned and left. Our captain . . . made straight for the *Merrimac*, which had already commenced firing; and when he came within short range, he changed his course so as to come alongside of her, stopped the engine, and gave the order, "Commence firing!" . . . The *Merrimac* was quick to reply, returning a rattling broadside (for she had ten guns to our two), and the battle fairly began. The turrets and other parts of the ship were heavily struck, but the shots did not penetrate; the tower was intact, and it continued to revolve. A look of confidence passed over the men's faces, and we believed the *Merrimac* would not repeat the work she had accomplished the day before.

Once the *Merrimac* tried to ram us; but Worden avoided the direct impact by the skillful use of the helm, and she struck a glancing blow, which did no damage. At the instant of collision I planted a solid 180-pound shot fair and square upon the forward part of her casemate . . . but the charge, being limited to fifteen pounds, in accordance with peremptory orders to that effect from the Navy Department, the shot rebounded without doing any more damage than possibly to start some of the beams of her armor-backing.

Soon after noon a shell from the enemy's gun, the muzzle not ten yards distant, struck the forward side of the pilot-house directly in the sight-hole, or slit, and exploded, cracking the second iron log and partly lifting the top, leaving an opening.

Worden was standing immediately behind this spot, and received in his face the force of the blow, which partly stunned him, and, filling his eyes with powder, utterly blinded him. . . . The flood of light rushing through the top of the pilot-house, now partly open, caused Worden, blind as he was, to believe that the pilot-house was seriously injured, if not destroyed; he therefore gave orders to put the helm to starboard and "sheer off." Thus the *Monitor* retired temporarily from the action, in order to ascertain the extent of the injuries she had received. At the same time Worden sent for me. . . . I went forward at once, and found him standing at the foot of the ladder leading to the pilothouse.

He was a ghastly sight, with his eyes closed and the blood apparently rushing from every pore in the upper part of his face. He told me that he was seriously wounded, and directed me to take command. . . . I found that the iron log was fractured and the top partly open; but the steering gear was still intact, and the pilot-house was not totally destroyed, as had been feared. In the confusion of the moment resulting from so serious an injury to the commanding officer, the *Monitor* had been moving without direction. During this time the *Merrimac*, which was leaking badly, had started in the direction of the Elizabeth River; and, on taking my station in the pilot-house and turning the vessel's head in the direction of the *Merrimac*, I saw that she was already in retreat. A few shots were fired at the retiring vessel, and she continued on to Norfolk. . . . The fight was over.

Lt. Samuel Dana Greene, Executive Officer, USS *Monitor*,
battle report, March 1862

SIR: I have the honor to report to your Department the casualties that occurred on board this vessel during her action with the rebel steamer *Merrimac* on Sunday, March 9.

The engagement began at 8:30 AM, but no injury was experienced by either officers or crew until 10 o'clock [when two sailors suffered concussions when the turret was struck by a shot from *Merrimack*].

These were the only accidents that occurred until a percussion shell near the close of the action exploded against the lookout chink of the pilot house and resulted in severe injury of the eyes of Lieutenant Commanding John L. Worden, who was stationed there during the engagement. I made an examination and succeeded in removing from the corneal conjunctiva some minute scales of iron and a small quantity of paint forced by the exploding shell from the bars composing the pilot house. He also, in a small degree, suffered from concussion, but this complication required no treatment. My further treatment of Captain Worden consisted entirely in making cold applications to his eyes, which was continued until, at the solicitations of his friends, Assistant Secretary of the Navy Fox, and Lieutenant Wise, U.S. Navy, he was removed from the *Monitor* to be taken to Washington. I am pleased to report that on the morning following the engagement the injured parties remaining on board were ready and reported for duty.

Daniel C. Logue, acting assistant surgeon,
report of casualties aboard USS *Monitor*,
March 11, 1862

To our Dear and Honered CAPTAIN

DEAR SIR These few lines is from your own Crew of the *Monitor* with there Kindest Love to you there Honered Captain Hoping to God that they will have the pleasure of Welcoming you Back to us again Soon for we are all Ready able and willing to meet Death or any thing else only gives us Back our own Captain again Dear Captain we have got your Pilot house fixed and all Ready for you when you get well again and we all Sincerely hope that soon we will have the pleasure of welcoming you Back to it again (for since you left us we have had no pleasure on Board of the *Monitor* we once was happy on Board of our little *Monitor* But since we Lost you we have Lost our all that was Dear to us Still) we are Waiting very Patiently to engage our Antagonist if we could only get a chance to do so the last time she came out we all thought we would have the Pleasure of Sinking her But we all got Disapointed for we did not fire one Shot and the Norfolk papers Says we are Coward in the *Monitor* and all we want is a chance to Shew them where it lies with you for our Captain we can teach them who is cowards But there is a great Deal that we would like to write to you But we think you will soon be with us again yourself But we all join in with our Kindest Love to you hoping that God will Restore you to us again and hopping that your Sufferings is at an end now and we are all so glad to hear that your eye Sight will be Spaired to you again, we would wish to write more to you if we have your Permission to do so But at Present we all conclude By tendering to you our Kindest Love and affection to our Dear and Honered Captain.

> We Remain untill Death your Affectionate Crew
> THE MONITOR BOYS

Letter to Lieutenant Worden, April 24, 1862

~❧~

Resolved by the Senate and House of Representatives of the United States of America in Congress assembled, That the thanks of Congress and of the American people are due and are hereby tendered to Lieutenant J. L. Worden, of the United States Navy, and to the officers and men of the ironclad gunboat *Monitor*, under his command, for the skill and gallantry exhibited by them in the late remarkable battle between the *Monitor* and the rebel ironclad steamer *Merrimack*.

Congressional Resolution, July 11, 1862

~ᴇϙ~

Dear Wife

You should feel very proud to think your Husband is not a Coward at home, but is fighting for a country for his Wife and Children. And at the same time be thankful that I am not in some of these old Wooden tubs.

They are fixing the *Monitor* up much bettor than she was before. They will make a perfect little Pallace of her. The workmen work nights and Sundays. I can hear them hammering away as I am writing. They have named her Guns Worden and Ericsson, and have the names engraved on them in very large lettors, and also have engraved every shot mark where it come from, so People do not have to ask so many Questions.

George S. Geer, Fireman 1/C, USS *Monitor*, November 1862

Worden Quotation

At the beginning of the Academic year in 1879 I determined to take the most stringent measures with my power to suppress the cowardly and cruel practice of "hazing" which I find to prevail here [at the Naval Academy], and issued an warning order upon the subject. In spite of that warning and of my friendly advise to many of the students, I found that it was being carried on under circumstances of great cruelty, I at once instituted an investigation by a Board of Officers, and 13 of the cadets were convicted of having committed gross inhumanities upon members of the jr class, and were recommended to be dismissed.

Letter to E. J. Horton, May 3, 1874

Burial Site

Pawling Cemetery, Pawling, New York

The picture of Worden Field during the formal parade definitely gives the onlookers a pleasant view. From a distance drill looks like one solid team working simultaneously, but . . . it is all a great show. Here I stand in the center of my company amidst the upper class. The second class to my right is chewing his gum and blowing bubbles, while the youngster to the left of me has his cover on so crooked it is a wonder that it even stays on. A first and a second class behind me are playing some sort of celebrity name game, while the youngsters in front are trying to remove each others' bayonets. As the midshipman gets older he finds better and more subtle ways to goof around during drill, all the while deceiving the onlooking crowd.

Charles Dawson, USNA 2002

Drill

We march out onto the field
The sun beats mercilessly on our back
There is Gunny
Monotonous sound of everyone in step
Column-left
We miss our mark yet again
"Get it back!"
Our timing off, we
Do it again
Will it stop?
Port-arms—order-arms
Finally, pass and review
I drill

Plebe, USNA 2006

Zimmerman Bandstand

Zimmerman Bandstand, practice parade (Randell Hunt "Doc" Prothro and Gustav F. "Gus" Swainson Jr.)

[The Class of 1907 is] eager to have a piece of music that would be inspiring, one with a swing to it so it could be used as a football marching song, and one that would live forever.

Midn. Alfred Hart Miles, Brigade Commander, USNA 1907,
to Bandmaster Charles Zimmerman, 1906

The Zimmerman Bandstand, which was erected in 1922 on Chapel Walk across Blake Road from the Chapel, offers not only an official site for a band but also an inviting location both for meeting with friends and for obtaining a heightened perspective on the Yard. It replaced the "old bandstand," which appears in the first edition of Hart's picture book of the Academy (1890) and may date back to 1889 when the "Star-spangled Banner" was given sanction for official use by the Navy. USNA Museum curator Jim Cheevers notes that a bandstand is said to have been built to commemorate the original manuscript of the "Star-spangled Banner," which was held in the nearby Nicholson House, home of Judge Joseph H. Nicholson, brother-in-law of Francis Scott Key, who authored our national anthem. Key had begun scribbling the poem on the back of an envelope while aboard a ship during the bombardment of Fort McHenry in Baltimore in 1814. He finished the poem in a hotel in Baltimore, then gave it to his brother-in-law. Nicholson suggested it be set to the music of "To Anacreon of Heaven," a popular British drinking song, and had it published. Within days it was reprinted in local newspapers and became very popular. The song became the official U.S. national anthem in 1931.

> Friday—An excited formation in the armory; a few instructions back of new quarters; then we are on our way to the Chapel. Here we are prayed over by the Chaplain, preached patriotism by a member of the Board of Visitors. Then we are marched out for the presentation of diplomas. We form in front of the [old] band stand, and the graduates—happy fellows— march to the front and centre, and take their positions facing the Secretary of the Navy and the Superintendent, who deal out those cherished sheepskins. As the last diploma leaves the Secretary's hand, every man's head becomes a trifle more erect, and his eyes a little brighter.
>
> *Lucky Bag*, 1897

The Naval Academy Band is one of the oldest professional musical organizations in the country, officially founded on November 22, 1852, but essentially in existence since the founding of the Academy in 1845, when a drummer and fifer began the almost-daily ritual of signaling reveille, tattoo, morning roll call, assembly, meals, morning and evening

Charles A. Zimmerman (U.S. Naval Institute Photo Archive)

studies, and sick call. The initial steps for the establishment of a true band occurred when the Board of Examiners suggested to Commo. Cornelius Stribling, superintendent from 1851 to 1853, that "a more rigid observance of those Military forms and ceremonies, which are so essential in the order and discipline of the Navy," needed to be provided for the midshipmen. In November 1852 the secretary of the Navy, who found "the want of Music at the Naval Academy" dramatically "evident," followed up on the board's suggestion with an order to the chief of the Bureau of Ordnance and Hydrography (immediately above the Academy in the Navy hierarchy) to organize "a Band to consist of not less than twelve instruments to be directed by a leader or Master." On May 17, 1853, Midn. Edwin O. Dooley dutifully recorded the following note in the Officer of the Day journal: "At 7:30 the barque 'UNION' came to anchor in the harbor, having aboard a 'Band for the Academy.'"

These days, the Academy Drum and Bugle Corps plays at Noon Meal Formation, and the band performs public concerts in the Yard, at the Annapolis city dock in the summer, and during Commissioning Week, when the strains of "Anchors Aweigh" drift almost daily across the Yard.

The bandstand is named for Charles A. Zimmerman (1862–1916), who was the USNA bandmaster for thirty-four years. He also served as Chapel organist and choir director. After the USNA theatrical troupe, the Masqueraders, was founded in 1907, their early productions were all original musicals written and composed by midshipmen with help from Bandmaster Zimmerman. Almost yearly from 1887 until his death, "Zimmy," as he was known by the midshipmen, composed a march for each graduating class. His most famous song, "Anchors Aweigh" (a phrase meaning that the anchors are hoisted), was composed in 1906. It was recently discovered that it was first performed on February 12, 1906, at the Farewell Ball for the Class of 1906, as a two-step dance dedicated to the Class of 1907. It was one of the "never-to-be-excelled waltzes and two-steps of Mr. Zimmerman's Academy Band," as remembered in the 1907 Lucky Bag. "Anchors Aweigh" was probably first played publicly at the 1906 Army-Navy game, which Navy then won for the first time in many years.

Midshipmen know ["Anchors Aweigh"] by heart, and thousands of sailors take pride in hearing it played. . . . I was part of the march-on during December 2, 2006, that commemorated the original performance of the 1906 Army-Navy game and another Navy victory on the football field.

Adam M. Meyer, USNA 2010

Quotation about Zimmerman

The Class of 1915 take this opportunity to express to Professor Charles A. Zimmerman their sincere thanks for the readiness with which he has granted to them, during the life at the Academy, any favor within his power. He has trained them in the Glee Club, in the Choir, and in the Masqueraders; and if it were not for him, these institutions would never have attained their present high standards. . . . His Band is recognized by everybody as being one of the leading military bands in the country.

Lucky Bag, 1915

Burial Site

USNA Cemetery

Epitaph

For 34 years leader of the Naval Academy band.

⚜

"The bandstand!" Grandma crooned. She put her arm around my waist and mine around hers, and standing side by side at the railing of the Zimmerman Bandstand, facing the water, she told me the story of her first kiss with my grandfather, Class of 1938. The man I barely remembered—he had died when I was seven—had been a destroyer commander at the age of twenty-seven, a Bronze Star and Navy Cross recipient, and father of three sons raised in true Navy fashion, who learned random rates like "table salt" and "why didn't you say 'sir'?"— and that nothing in life is more important than honor, courage, and commitment. Because of poor eyesight, my father had not been able to go to the Academy, but when I was accepted, I think he felt he had finally lived up to his father. My grandmother, however, did not feel the same way; in fact, when she heard I was applying to the Academy, she told Dad that Grandpa would be rolling in his grave to hear that his granddaughter might be a midshipman at his Naval Academy; after all, the military was for brave, honest, and hardworking men.

But last year, she finally came to visit me at the Academy. And after that moment in the bandstand, she has begun to talk with me about Academy life, the parades and rushing back for TAPS, about being a mid's girlfriend. Now whenever she talks to my dad, she always asks about the Academy. After a recent conversation, when he told her about my upcoming Ring Dance, I received a package. Racing down Stribling, about to be late for my fifth period class, I quickly opened it and stopped dead in my tracks. It was Grandma's miniature, the ring Eleanor Roosevelt had christened, the ring that was dipped in water from the Seven Seas on the same ribbon as Granddad's class ring, the ring she wore her whole life next to her wedding ring. And with it was a note, just a scribble in her familiar handwriting: "Love, Grandmom and Granddad." The bell rang and I hurried the rest of the way down Stribling, closing the cool, gold metal in my hand as I ran past the bandstand.

Fiona F. McFarland, USNA 2008

❦

"Anchors Aweigh"

Stand Navy down the field
Sails set to the sky
We'll never change our course
So Army you steer shy-y-y-y
Roll up the score, Navy
Anchors Aweigh
Sail Navy down the field
And sink the Army, sink the Army grey!

Get under way, Navy
Decks cleared for the fray
We'll hoist true Navy Blue
So Army down your grey-y-y-y

Full speed ahead, Navy
Army heave to
Furl Black and Grey and Gold
And hoist the Navy, hoist the Navy Blue!

Blue of the Seven Seas
Gold of God's great sun
Let these our colors be
Till all of time be done-n-n-ne
By Severn shore we learn
Navy's stern call
Faith, courage, service true
With honor over, honor over all.

Original lyrics for verses 1 and 2 by
Midn. Alfred Hart Miles, 1906;
verse 3 by Midn. Royal Lovell, 1926

Other Selected Memorials

Class of 1942 Memorial Park (Randell Hunt "Doc" Prothro and Gustav F. "Gus" Swainson Jr.)

Class of 1942 Memorial Park

Navy Blue and Gold

Four years together by the bay
Where Severn joins the tide,
Then by the Service called away,
We've scattered far and wide;
But still when two or three shall meet,
And old tales be retold,
From low to highest in the Fleet

Will pledge the Blue and Gold

This small park with its large Vermont marble globe and benches, a gift of the Class of 1942, is situated on the north side of Alumni Hall overlooking College Creek and the cemetery beyond on Hospital Point. The park is also, in the words from "Navy Blue and Gold" engraved on the base of the globe, a memorial to the class's "four years together by the bay." In his class history, "'42 at Sixty," Jerry (Gerald E.) Miller, USNA 1942, describes his class as a unified team, "a collection of solid individuals who came to the Academy with an intense desire to be career naval officers." He adds that the class was "serious during the days at the Academy and served as good examples to junior classes, becoming known after their departure as 'the Pearl Harbor Class.'" This class, the first of the World War II-era classes to graduate on an accelerated schedule, graduated on December 19, 1941, just days after the December 7 attack on Pearl Harbor.

> An officer of the line in the United States Navy is not, as are officers in most military organizations throughout the world, a trained specialist. It is not sufficient that he be merely a trained engineer, a crack gunner, a radio and communications expert, a competent navigator and seaman, a talented diplomat, or an able executive—instead he must combine all of these qualifications. He may at any time be ordered to duty in one, several, or all of these capacities.
>
> *Lucky Bag*, 1945

❧

The world turns—
But in this memorial spot
Overlooking creek
And cemetery hill
Stands still—

Four years together by the bay
Where Severn joins the tide—

The mind drifts wide
Until a mower slicing

Grass draws reveries
Of what's been done
What's yet to do
Back to present life.

Class of 1943 Compass Rose Plaza (Randell Hunt "Doc" Prothro and Gustav F. "Gus" Swainson Jr.)

Class of 1943 Compass Rose Plaza

The last few boats drift in as a breeze straightens the colorful flags and wind socks. The view from the granite bench eases your mind, tricking you, if only for a short while, into thinking you have nothing to do but sit and gaze. . . . At night when the town lights are multiplied by the

water's reflection, the light at the plaza, mounted on a wrought-iron
pole, flashes with class pride: four blinks, three blinks, four, three.

J. Adam Pegues, USNA 2003

This brick and granite plaza—a granite compass oriented toward the
magnetic north and integrated into a brick patio, along with a naviga-
tional light flashing four-three—is a gift of the Class of 1943 (which had
graduated a full year early to serve in World War II). It is one of several gifts from different classes along this curving, shoreline walk near
the Visitor Center and Ricketts Hall. Compass Rose Plaza was dedicated
in June 1995 to the accompaniment of the Academy's Drum and Bugle
Corps, an invocation from the chaplain, and an acceptance speech from
Superintendent Adm. Charles Larson.

Halyards clank, pennants flutter,
A breeze kicks up
From where the river
Opens to the bay.

The petals of the compass rose
Can tell
From which direction
You have come

And the bench
Can offer
Room to dream
Of where in ten or twenty
Or fifty years you'll be.

Vice Adm. William P. Lawrence Statue

Lawrence and Stockdale

The two stand strong and tall,
Men of iron will, now bronze composure
Gazing down upon those who pass by,
Young but longing to live up to their honor

Kevin C. O'Malley, USNA 2009

A statue of Adm. William P. Lawrence, created by Lawrence M. Ludtke of Houston, Texas, donated by H. Ross Perot, USNA 1953, and dedicated in October 2008, stands in front of Wesley Brown Field House, facing a similar statue of Vice Adm. James Stockdale in front of Luce Hall. The two were prisoners of war and senior officers together in the Vietnam War.

William Porter Lawrence (1930–2005), USNA 1951, became a test pilot after earning his wings in 1952. After his Phantom jet was shot down in 1957 in North Vietnam, he was held as a POW in Hanoi until 1973. In prison, he and Stockdale developed a wall-tap code used to communicate in isolation. He also kept his mind active by writing stories and poetry in his head. ("Sir Walter Scott had genius," he wrote in his memoir, *Tennessee Patriot* (2006), "But I got time.") His poem, "Oh Tennessee, My Tennessee," was adopted as the state poem in 1973.

Admiral Lawrence served as superintendent at the Academy from 1978 to 1981, when his daughter was a midshipman. (Wendy Lawrence, USNA 1981, went on to become an astronaut.) Lawrence was awarded a number of service decorations and, in 2000, received the Alumni Association's Distinguished Graduate Award.

Lawrence Quotations

One of our most familiar and reassuring phrases, passed on liberally throughout imprisonment, was G-B-U. God Bless You. It helped.

❧

[As a POW] I learned what it feels like for one human to be totally subjugated to the will of another, and it was a terrifying experience.

❧

The pain, solitude, oppressive heat, and loneliness took their toll on me. I forced myself to continue playing my mind games, creating poetry,

Vice Adm. William P. Lawrence Statue, 2008 (Randell Hunt "Doc" Prothro and Gustav F. "Gus" Swainson Jr.)

building houses, remembering names and faces from my earlier years, and so forth. . . . There's no doubt my Naval Academy training helped me live up to my responsibilities as a senior officer.

Quotations about Lawrence

We had the unique privilege of serving in the company of heroes. We observed a thousand acts of courage and compassion and love. And perhaps the one who epitomized that the most and was the very best of us was Billy Lawrence. . . . And when times were tough and we came back beaten down, we could always count on Billy to lead us and to restore our faith, our competence, and our ability to go one more round with our captors.

Senator John McCain, endorsement for *Tennessee Patriot*, 2006

Admiral Bill Lawrence is one of the Navy's finest heroes. As a prisoner of war in North Vietnam he exhibited supreme courage and perseverance, raising the spirits and hopes of fellow prisoners while enduring the terrible brutality of his captors. Throughout his life he always put other people first and was a role model and example of a great military leader to all who knew him and served with him.

Ross Perot, endorsement for *Tennessee Patriot*, 2006

Oh Tennesee, My Tennessee

Oh Tennessee, My Tennessee
What love and pride I feel for thee
You proud ole state, the Volunteer,
Your proud traditions I hold dear

And o'er the world as I may roam
No place exceeds my boyhood home

And oh how much I long to see
My native land, my Tennessee

Vice Adm. James B. Stockdale Statue

Like you in life the stoic statue stands,
Holding its pose against the snow and rain,
As you your honor kept through stormy life,
The countless lives you kept from despair.
To you we lift our eyes, salute your likeness,
The example that you set for us forever.

Benjamin M. Gallo, USNA 2009

A ten-foot tall statue of Adm. James B. Stockdale stands on a five-foot-tall base in front of Luce Hall, home of the Stockdale Center for Ethical Leadership, and faces the Lawrence statue in front of Brown Field House. The sculptor, Lawrence M. Ludtke, was a prominent portrait and figurative sculptor whose work is held by major institutions across the country, including the Pentagon, CIA Headquarters, Texas A & M University, the Air Force Academy, and Gettysburg National Battlefield Park. Ludtke based his sculpture on a 1963 photograph of Stockdale striding across a flight deck. One of many symbolic touches in the sculpture is the mathematical symbol of infinity on the flight helmet, an expression of the pilot's boundless spirit. Donated by H. Ross Perot, USNA 1953, the statue was dedicated October 31, 2008. Admiral Stockdale (1923–2005), USNA 1947, was a fighter pilot, author, statesman, and scholar, and the highest ranking prisoner of war in Vietnam. He was shot down in 1965 on a flying mission and held for over seven and a half years in a prison camp in Hanoi. As the leader in the prison, Stockdale established a set of rules governing behavior and developed a wall-tap code to communicate with fellow captives. For his bravery and leadership he was awarded the Congressional Medal of Honor. His four years in solitary confinement and repeated torture left him with a life-long limp but undaunted spirit. Admiral Stockdale credits the teachings of Epictetus,

Vice Adm. James B. Stockdale Statue, 2008 (Randell Hunt "Doc" Prothro and Gustav F. "Gus" Swainson Jr.)

Sir Winston Churchill, and other thinkers and writers with helping him endure his imprisonment.

While waiting for her husband to return home, Stockdale's wife Sybil fought ceaselessly for her husband's release and for the humane treatment of American prisoners of war. Their separate wartime experiences are chronicled in the book they wrote together, *In Love and War* (1984). Retired in 1979, Stockdale went on to become a fellow at the Hoover Institute at Stanford University and the vice presidential candidate on Ross Perot's independent ticket in the 1992 presidential campaign.

Stockdale Statue Inscriptions

Never give in; never give in; never, never, never give in. . . . Never yield to force; never yield to the apparently overwhelming might of the enemy.

Sir Winston Churchill

❧

Lameness is an impediment to the leg but not to the will.

Epictetus

Stockdale Quotation

What attributes serve you well in the extortion environment? We learned there, above all else, that the best defense is to keep your conscience clean.

"The World of Epictetus," 1993

Quotations about Stockdale

From the fertile plains of Illinois came this self-confident, rugged little guy with the practical mind, who combined his "know how" with his "know when" to become a leader in the brigade.

Lucky Bag, 1947

For conspicuous gallantry and intrepidity at the risk of his life above and beyond the call of duty while senior naval officer in the Prisoner of War camps of North Vietnam. Recognized by his captors as the leader in the Prisoners' of War resistance to interrogation and in their refusal to participate in propaganda exploitation, Rear Adm. Stockdale was singled out for interrogation and attendant torture after he was detected in a covert communications attempt. Sensing the start of another purge, and aware that his earlier efforts at self-disfiguration to dissuade his captors from exploiting him for propaganda purposes had resulted in cruel and agonizing punishment, Rear Adm. Stockdale resolved to make himself a symbol of resistance regardless of personal sacrifice. He deliberately inflicted a near-mortal wound to his person in order to convince his captors of his willingness to give up his life rather than capitulate. He was subsequently discovered and revived by the North Vietnamese who, convinced of his indomitable spirit, abated in their employment of excessive harassment and torture toward all of the Prisoners of War. By his heroic action, at great peril to himself, he earned the everlasting gratitude of his fellow prisoners and of his country. Rear Adm. Stockdale's valiant leadership and extraordinary courage in a hostile environment sustain and enhance the finest traditions of the U.S. Naval Service.

Congressional Medal of Honor Citation

Make no mistake. . . the magnificent young men and women who wear the cloth of our nation. . . in Iraq, Afghanistan and around the world. . . have been shaped by the example and legacy of Americans like Admiral Jim Stockdale. . . .[His] courage and life stand as timeless examples of the power of faith and the strength of the human spirit.

Gordon England, former Secretary of Defense, July 5, 2005

His moral compass was always sure, his passions always in service to noble ideals, and his character always his greatest, most precious asset.

Secretary of the Navy Donald C. Whiter, statue dedication,
October 31, 2008

❧

Displayed in stone for all to see
So motivating, his first two names of three
James Bond, aviator, not fictional spy
Absorbing our eyes' focus whenever we walk by

Michael A. Bell, USNA 2009

list of midshipmen authors

Jason M. Abel, 2004 . . . . Fitch Bridge, Porter Road
Katherine A. Adler, 2009 . . . . Worden Field
Erin E. Arthur, 2009 . . . . Ingram Field
Anthony Atler, 2004. . . . . Fitch Bridge, Sherman Field

Ryan G. Beall, 2008. . . . . Mahan Hall
Michael A. Bell, 2009 . . . . Stockdale Statue
Serge J. Bermudez, 2006 . . . . Halsey Field House
Christopher D. Bernard, 2004. . . . . Herndon Monument, Triton Light
Patrick Bookey, 2003. . . . . Stribling Walk
Patrick J. Bray, 2007 . . . . Dahlgren Hall
Jordan P. Bradford, 2009 . . . . Administration Building
Chelsea R. Brunoehler . . . . Triton Light
   (née Gaughan), 2006
Michael A. Byrd, 2010 . . . . Michelson Hall

Matthew O. Caylor, 2004 . . . . Submarine Memorials, Triton Light
Robert Chandler, 2006 . . . . USS *Maine* Foremast
Matthew E. Charles, 2007. . . . . Michelson Hall
Russell G. Cude, 2009. . . . . Cemetery

Matthew E. Danielson, 2010. . . . . Macedonian Monument
Sandeep Dasgupta, 2003 . . . . Dahlgren Hall

Charles Dawson, 2002 . . . . Alumni Hall, Halsey Field House, Mahan Hall, Preble Hall, Worden Field

Nelson B. Diggs, 2007 . . . . Lejeune Hall
Aaron D. Dixon, 2010 . . . . *Jeannette* Monument
Darby C. Driscoll, 2009 . . . . Nimitz Library

Trevor J. Felter, 2002 . . . . Administration Building, Gate 3
Matthew C. Forman, 2009 . . . . Bancroft Hall
Tyler W. Forrest, 2002 . . . . Alumni Hall, Robert Crown Sailing Center, Farragut Field, Lejeune Hall
Nathaniel T. Frazier, 2010 . . . . Ricketts Hall

Philip Galindo, 2006 . . . . *Jeannette* Monument
Benjamin M. Gallo, 2009 . . . . Sampson Hall, Stockdale Statue
Isaiah D. Gammache, 2006 . . . . Macdonough Hall
Tomás A. Grado, 2007 . . . . Stribling Walk

Jonathan D. Hagerman, 2010 . . . . Triton Light
Alexander D. Hagness, 2007 . . . . Rickover Hall
Benjamin R. Hawbaker, 2003 . . . . Robert Crown Sailing Center

Keith R. Jackson, 2007 . . . . Nimitz Library
Ernest T. Jaramillo-Hanes, 2006 . . . . . . Robert Crown Sailing Center
David O. Jones, 2010 . . . . Macdonough Hall, Michelson Hall

Stephen P. Kelly, 2006 . . . . Rickover Hall
Travis E. King, 2008 . . . . King Hall
Kenton P. Knop, 2006 . . . . Dewey Field
Mark D. Knorr, 2010 . . . . Submarine Memorials
Lt. Matthew B. Krauz, 2001 . . . . Levy Center and Jewish Chapel

David R. Lawrence, 2006 . . . . Rickover Hall

Jeffrey Lenar, 2010. . . . . Cemetery, Ricketts Hall

Andrew L. Lewis, 2009 . . . . Luce Hall

Joshua J. Lostetter, 2003 . . . . Memorial Hall

Jamison L. Lupo, 2006. . . . . Mitscher Hall

Joseph H. Manaloto, 2007. . . . . Moreell Monument

Ryan C. McDonough, 2009 . . . . Memorial Hall

Fiona F. McFarland, 2008 . . . . Zimmerman Bandstand

Reeve H. Meck, 2009 . . . . Sea Gate

Adam M. Meyer, 2010. . . . . Zimmerman Bandstand

Evan J. Miller, 2006. . . . . Dahlgren Hall

Ryan P. Murtha, 2010 . . . . Chauvenet Hall

Courtney E. Natter, 2008 . . . . Bancroft Hall

Brandi N. Olson, 2004 . . . . King Hall

Kevin C. O'Malley, 2009. . . . . Lawrence Statue

Salvatore Pasquarelli, 2003 . . . . Triton Light

J. Adam Pegues, 2003 . . . . Mexican War Monument,
Compass Rose Plaza

Richard M. Pescatore, 2009 . . . . Cemetery

David A. Pilko, 2006. . . . . Mahan Hall

Crystal J. Piraino, 2008 . . . . Stribling Walk

Steven Podmore, 2005 . . . . Macdonough Hall

Christopher L. Powell, 2008 . . . . Stribling Walk

Brian A. Quirk, 2006. . . . . Submarine Memorials

Bayard N. Roberts, 2010 . . . . Halsey Field House, Tecumseh

Ryan C. Roeling, 2007 . . . . Tecumseh

Evan S. Rutherford, 2010 . . . . Hubbard Hall

bibliography

General historical information about the Naval Academy was taken mostly from "vertical files" (identified below as VF) in the Archives and Special Collections Division of Nimitz Library at the Naval Academy; the 2006 edition of *Reef Points*, the Naval Academy "plebe Bible"; the Naval Academy website; Jack Sweetman's *The U.S. Naval Academy: An Illustrated History* (Naval Institute Press, 1995); and Taylor Baldwin Kiland and Jamie Howren's *A Walk in the Yard* (Naval Institute Press, 2007). General information about naval figures and events was gathered mainly from the Naval Historical Center website, with additional information from Sweetman, *Reef Points*, and the Naval Academy website. Midshipmen contributions are in the author's files, English Department files, or Special Collections files, or they were published in *Lucky Bag* and *Labyrinth*; unattributed poems are the author's original work.

Unpublished Material

James Cheevers, Chief Curator, Naval Academy Museum, interviews and correspondence, 2003–8, author's files.

Correspondence and personal reminiscences by or about naval figures and events from online government sources, state historical societies, veterans' groups, and other organizations; and from information submitted to the author by family members, now in author's files.

Brochures and dedication speeches related to monuments and memorials, in the Buildings and Grounds VF. Information also from the dedicatory plaques associated with individual buildings and memorials.

Burial information, from headstones at the Naval Academy Cemetery and Naval Academy website; the Arlington National Cemetery website; and Find-a-Grave website (see website addresses below).

OFFICIAL RECORDS

Architectural plans, midshipmen records, and official correspondence related to the Naval Academy, housed in Archives and Special Collections, Nimitz Library.

Official records of the U.S. Navy and Marine Corps, maintained at the Naval Historical Center, Washington Navy Yard, Washington, D.C., including battle reports, award citations, and other documents, many available online (see websites below).

Official records printed by the Government Printing Office and other printers, many available online (see "Books and Articles" and websites below).

Resolutions of the U.S. Congress available online from various government websites.

BOOKS AND ARTICLES

Anonymous. "The False Muster of Tecumseh." *Trident*, March 1946: 13. Tecumseh VF.

Baldridge, H. A. "Naval Academy Museum—the First 100 Years." U.S. Naval Institute *Proceedings* 71, no. 9 (September 1945).

Bancroft, George. *The History of the United States of America from the Discovery of the Continent*. Abridged and edited by Russell B. Nye. Chicago: University of Chicago Press, 1966.

"Battle of Midway: 4–7 June 1942, Online Action Reports." June 28, 1942. World War II Action Reports. Modern Military Branch, National Archives, College Park, MD. www.history.navy.mil/docs/wwii/mid1.htm.

Beach, Edward L., Sr., and Edward L. Beach Jr. *From Annapolis to Scapa Flow: The Autobiography of Edward L. Beach Sr.* Annapolis, Md.: Naval Institute Press, 2003.

Benjamin, Park. *The United States Naval Academy, Being the Yarn of the American Midshipman*. New York: G. P. Putman's Sons, 1900.

"Bombardment of Tripoli, 1804." *Naval Documents Related to the United States War with the Barbary Powers*. http://www.history.navy.mil/docs/war1812/const3.htm.

Brown, Wesley A., U.S.N. "The First Negro Graduate of Annapolis Tells His Story." *Saturday Evening Post*, [c. June 1949]: 26–27; 111–113. Reprinted in Jack Sweetman. *The U.S. Naval Academy: An Illustrated History*, 2nd ed. Revised by Thomas J. Cutler. Annapolis: Naval Institute Press, 1995, 207–208.

Carter, Jimmy. *Why Not the Best?* Nashville: Broadman Press, 1975.

Corbin, Diana Fontaine Maury. *A Life of Matthew Fontaine Maury*. London: Sampson, Low, Marston, Searle, & Rivington, Ltd., 1883.

Cox, Tommy. "Run Silent Run Deep," song lyrics. EDCO Records, 2002 (printed by permission of author).

Crane, John, and James F. Kieley. *The United States Naval Academy: The First 100 Years*. New York: Wittlesey House/McGraw-Hill, 1945.

Cushman, H. B. *History of the Choctaw, Chickasaw and Natchez Indians*. Greenville, Tex.: Headlight Printing House, 1899.

Dahlgren, John A. *Ordnance Instructions for the United States Navy: Relating to the Preparation of Vessels of War for Battle*. 2nd ed. Washington, D.C.: G. W. Bowman, 1860.

Dalton, John H. "Alfred Thayer Mahan: Where There's a USS There's an HMS." Trafalgar Night Dinner, Marine Barracks, Washington, D.C. October 15, 1988. www.navy.mil/navydata/people/secnav/dalton/speeches/traf1015.txt.

De Long, George W. *The Voyage of the Jeannette: The Ship and Ice Journals of George W. De Long, Lieutenant-Commander U.S.N., and Commander of the Polar Expedition of 1879–1881*. Edited by Emma De Long. Boston: Houghton, Mifflin, 1883.

De Weese, Wade. "The United States Naval Academy Museum." Preble Hall VF.

Dewey, George. *Autobiography of George Dewey, Admiral of the Navy*. New York: Scribner, 1913. Reprint, Annapolis: Naval Institute Press, 1987.

"The Engagement in Hampton Roads." Report of Acting Assistant Surgeon. www.navyandmarine.org/ondeck/1862hamptonroads_usn.htm.

Erikson, Mark St. John. "Iron Fist: Ironclad Virginia Shows Its Mettle Against Ill-Matched Wooden Ship." *Daily Press*, January 1, 1998.

Farragut, Loyall. *The Life of David Glasgow Farragut, First Admiral of the United States Navy, Embodying His Journal and Letters*. New York: D. Appleton and Company, 1879.

Gay, George. "Recollections of Lieutenant George Gay, Sole Survivor of Torpedo Squadron Eight (VT-8)." Adapted from Ensign George Gay, Interview Box 11, World War II Interviews, Operational Archives, Naval Historical Center. www.history.navy.mil/faqs/faq81-81c.htm.

Halsey, William F., and J. Bryan III. *Admiral Halsey's Story*. New York: Wittlesey House, 1947.

Harber, Giles B. *Report of Lieutenant Giles B. Harber of His Search for the Missing People of the Jeannette Expedition, Etc.* USNA Special Collections, Annapolis, Md.

Hearn, Chester G. *Admiral David Glasgow Farragut: The Civil War Years.* Annapolis, Md.: Naval Institute Press, 1988.

Holland, Jeffrey. "Saluting Tecumseh." *Annapolitan,* October 1986.

Irving, Washington. *Washington Irving to Henry Breevort.* New York: G. P. Putnam's Sons/Knickerbocker Press, 1918.

Jones, John Paul. *The Life and Correspondence of John Paul Jones.* Edited by Janette Taylor. Boston: N. B. Parsons, 1855.

Kiland, Taylor Baldwin, and Jamie Howren. *A Walk in the Yard: A Self-Guided Tour of the U.S. Naval Academy.* Annapolis, Md.: Naval Institute Press, 2007.

King, Ernest. "Education of Naval Officers." Lecture, Naval Postgraduate School, May 16, 1925. King VF.

———. "Establishment of the Combat Intelligence Division of Fleet Headquarters, 1 July 1943." Halsey VF.

———. "Our Navy at War: A Report to the Secretary of the Navy." March 1944. King VF.

———. *Third Report to the Secretary of the Navy.* Halsey VF.

King, Ernest, and Walter Muir Whitehall. *Fleet Admiral King: A Naval Record.* New York: Norton, 1952.

Labyrinth. Annapolis, Md.: U.S. Naval Academy, 1923 to present.

LaValley, Gary A. "Bancroft/Buchanan." *The Record,* 1998. Naval Academy Archives, Annapolis.

Leahy, William D. *I Was There: The Personal Story of the Chief of Staff to Presidents Roosevelt and Truman.* New York: Whittlesey House, 1950.

Leech, Samuel. *Thirty Years from Home, Or A Voice from the Main Deck: Being the Experience of Samuel Leech.* Boston: C. Tappan, 1844.

Leftwich, William G., III. "Remembering the Man Behind the Trophy." *Shipmate,* November 1993, 17–18.

Lejeune, John A. *The Reminiscences of a Marine.* Philadelphia: Dorrance & Co., 1930.

Lucky Bag. Annapolis, Md.: U.S. Naval Academy, 1894 to present.

Mahan, Alfred Thayer. *The Interest of America in Sea Power, Present and Future.* Boston: Little, Brown, 1918.

———. "President's Address." *Annual Report of the American Historical Association,* 1902. www.historians.org/info/AHA_History/atmahan.htm.

Marian, Professor H. "John Paul Jones' Last Cruise." John Paul Jones VF.

Mason, John T. *A Cluster of Interviews on Fleet Admiral Nimitz.* Annapolis, Md.: Naval Institute Press, 1969.

Maury, Matthew Fontaine. *The Physical Geography of the Sea, and Its Meteorology*. 8th ed. New York: Harper & Brothers, 1861. Reprint, with an introduction by John Leighly, Cambridge, MA: Belknap Press, 1963.

Melville, George W. *Report of George W. Melville, Chief Engineer, U.S.N., in Connection with the Jeannette Expedition*. Washington, D.C.: GPO, 1882.

Morgan, William James, ed. *Naval Documents of the American Revolution*. Vol. 6. Washington, D.C.: Naval History Division, 1972.

Morris, W. Maury. "Commodore Matthew Fontaine Maury, 'America's Most Decorated Man,' 'Pathfinder of the Seas.'" www.geocities.com/commanderscvcamp1722/Commodore_Matthew_Fontaine_Maury.html (accessed July 25, 2007).

Murphy, W. J. "Battle of Santiago," July 4, 1898. Naval Historical Center Manuscripts. http://www.history.navy.mil/library/manuscript/santiagobattle.htm.

Official Records of the Union and Confederate Navies in the War of the Rebellion. Series 1, Volume 5: *Operations on the Potomac and Rappahanock Rivers: Atlantic Blockading Squadron*. Washington, D.C.: GPO, 1897.

O'Meara, Henry. "Ode to Our Naval Heroes." *Ballads of America*. Copy, David Dixon Porter VF.

Peterson, Gordon I. "The Pen and the Sword." *Sea Power*. Navy League Archives. www.navyleague.org/seapower/pen_and_the_sword.htm.

Pickett, Russ. "One of Delaware's Heroes: Thomas McDonough." http://www.russpickett.com/history/mcdobio.htm.

Pinkowski, Edward. "Admiral of the Air." Wartime Press. http://wartimepress.com/images/Our%20Navy/Articles/Admiral%20of%20the%20Air.htm.

Porter, David Dixon. *Memoir of Commodore David Porter, of the United States Navy*. Albany: J. Munsell, 1875.

Preble, Edward. Journal, USS *Constitution*. www.history.navy.mil/docs/war1812/const3.htm.

Ramsey, H. Ashton. "The Story of the *Merrimac*'s Engagement with the *Monitor*, and the Events that Preceded and Followed the Fight, Told by a Survivor." *Harper's Weekly*, Febrary 10, 1912, 11-12. www.cssvirginia.org.

Reef Points: The Annual Handbook of the Brigade of Midshipmen. Annapolis, Md.: Naval Institute Press, 2006.

Ross, Donald Gunn, III. "The Era of the Clipper Ships." www.eraoftheclipperships.com/page14web.html.

Rules for the Regulations of the Navy. 1802. www.history.navy.mil/faqs/faq59-5.htm.

Sheehan, Jack. *Class of '47: Annapolis—America's Best.* Las Vegas: Stephens Press, 2005.

Sherwood, John. "Rambler: Among the Stones of Strawberry Hill." *Annapolitan*, April 1991.

Soley, James Russell. "Address of J. R. Soley, Assistant Secretary of the Navy, at the Unveiling of the Jeannette Monument, October 31, 1890, United States Naval Academy." Privately printed bound booklet, Special Collections, Nimitz Library, Annapolis, Md..

Statutes of the United States of America Passed at the Third Session of the Fifty-Fifth Congress, 1898–1899, and Recent Conventions, Treaties, Executive Proclamations, and Concurrent Resolutions of the Two Houses of Congress. Washington, D.C.: GPO, 1899: 995. Reprint of Dewey resolution, Naval Historical Center. http://www.history.navy.mil/bios/dewey_george. htm#act.

Still, William N. "Porter . . . Is the Best Man." *Civil War Times*, May 1977.

Sugden, John. *Tecumseh: A Life.* New York: Holt, 1997.

Sweetman, Jack. *The U.S. Naval Academy: An Illustrated History.* 2nd ed. Revised by Thomas J. Cutler. Annapolis, Md.: Naval Institute Press, 1995.

Thatcher, Benjamin B. *Indian Biography: Or, an Historical Account of Those Individuals Who Have Been Distinguished among the North American Natives as Orators, Warriors, Statesmen and Other Remarkable Characters.* New York: J. & J. Harper, 1832.

Thompson, Rick. "Remembrance Service Commemorates 65th Anniversary of Midway Victory." *Tester*, June 14, 2007. http://www.dcmilitary.com/ stories/061407/tester_27959.shtml (accessed July 27, 2007).

Thorn, Martha. "SEAL, Academy Grad, 'Shaped to Do Something Extraordinary.'" *Trident*, 2005.

Thulesius, Olav. "USS *Monitor*: The Crew Took Great Pride in Serving on the Famous Ship." *Civil War Times*, December 2004. http://www.historynet. com/air_sea/ships_boats/3035496.html.

USNA Class of 1945. *Fifty Years After.* Lewiston, Minn.: Herff Jones Photography, 1994.

Ward, Thomas. *Steam for the Million.* New York: D. Van Nostrand, 1864.

Wilson, Elizabeth, "'A Gallanter Fellow Never Stepped a Quarter Deck': The Story of Stephen Decatur." 2004. http://www.foundersofamerica.org/ decatur.html.

Wright, C. Q. "The Tripoli Monument Stands." *U.S. Naval Institute Proceedings* 48, no. 11 (November 1922): 96.

OTHER INTERNET SOURCES

About Buddhism: http://buddhism.about.com

American Historical Association: www.historians.org

American Presidency Project: www.presidency.ucsb.edu

Arlington Cemetery: www.arlingtoncemetery.net

Civil War Home: www.civilwarhome.com

Congressional Gold Medal: www.congressionalgoldmedal.com

CSS Virginia Organization: www.cssvirginia.org

CV6 Organization: www.cv6.org

Daily Press: www.dailypress.com

DC Military: dcmilitary.com

Decatur House: www.decaturhouse.org

Digital History: www.digitalhistory.uh.edu

Famous Americans: www.famousamericans.net

Find a Grave: http://findagrave.com

Google Books: http://books.google.com

Historic Lakes: www.historiclakes.org

History Net: www.historynet.com

Home of Heroes: www.homeofheroes.com

Indigenous People: www.indigenouspeople.net

Mariner: www.mariner.org

Military Quotes: www.military-quotes.com

National Endowment for the Humanities (NEH) Online: www.h-net.org

Navy and Marine Organization: www.navyandmarine.org

Navy Historical Center: www.history.navy.mil

Navy League: www.navyleague.org

New York Sun: www.nysun.com

Nobel Prize Organization: http://nobelprize.org

Office of the Clerk, U.S. House of Representatives: http://clerk.house.gov

PBS Online: www.pbs.org

Spanish-American War Centennial: www.spanamwar.com

Submarine Sailor: www.submarinesailor.com

Time Magazine Online: www.time.com/time/magazine

U.S. Coast Guard Academy: www.cga.edu

U.S. Marine Corps: www.usmc.mil

U.S. Naval Academy: www.usna.edu

U.S. Naval Academy Cemetery: www.usna.edu/cemetery

U.S. Naval Academy Class of 1947: www.annapolisclassof47.com

U.S. Naval Academy Parents Organization: www.usna-parents.org

USS *West Virginia*: www.usswestvirginia.org

Washington Post: www.washingtonpost.com

Washington University Chancellor: http://chancellorsroom.wustl.edu

White House History: www.whitehousehistory.org

World of Quotes: www.worldofquotes.com

index

Professor Nancy Prothro Arbuthnot has taught in the English Department at the Naval Academy since 1981. The daughter of a career naval officer, she was born in Jacksonville, Florida, and grew up on naval bases in California and in military communities in northern Virginia. She earned her BA and MA at the University of Maryland, and her PhD at the University of Virginia. Her publications include *An American Artist in World War II: Jason Schoener at Eniwetok Atoll*; *Mexico Shining* (English versions of Nahuatl poems); *From Where the Wind Blows* (English versions of Vietnamese poems by Le Pham Le); and *Wild Washington: Animal Sculpture A to Z*, co-authored with Cathy Abramson. With her father, she coauthored "Looking Alive with Doc, '45," published in *Shipmate*. She is married with three children and lives in Washington, D.C.

Capt. Randell Hunt "Doc" Prothro, USNA 1945, graduated with orders to USS *Hornet* in the Pacific. After the war he attended the Navy Photographic School and flight school. He became a carrier pilot serving in both the Pacific and the Atlantic and as a test and evaluation pilot for Navy air warfare programs. After retiring from the Navy, he had a second career in the civilian world and a third career as a volunteer at Walter Reed Army Medical Center. Captain Prothro's awards include the Navy Commendation Medal, the Red Cross Clara Barton Award, and the Department of the Army Commander's Award for Public Service. He is married with seven children and proud to have a part in his daughter's book about his alma mater.

Capt. Gustav F. "Gus" Swainson, USNA 1945, spent two years at MIT prior to his years at the Academy. He served on a destroyer in World War II, then attended the Navy Postgraduate School, followed by two more years at MIT, from which he earned a master's degree in engineering. Captain Swainson also served at the New York Naval Shipyard and the Naval War College. His photography and his motto, *Illegetimus non carborundum*, have kept him looking alive. He makes his home in New York but returns often to Annapolis to visit friends.